Praise for
50 Prosperity Classics

"Anyone interested in achieving an understanding of true prosperity and demonstrating a higher level of fulfillment should read this book... 50 Prosperity Classics is a treasure chest of golden nuggets to use in realizing a life more abundant."

John Randolph Price, author of *The 40 Day Prosperity Plan* and *The Abundance Book*

"Everything you could ever want to know about both the nuts and bolts of personal finance and metaphysical abundance is included in this comprehensive volume. Tom's insightful commentaries show that it is more than possible to be well off financially and live with a good conscience. With this knowledge at your fingertips, you will be inspired to live a more abundant and prosperous life."

Andrea Molloy, author of *Success – The Ultimate Guide to Success at Work* and *Redesign Your Life*

"A terrific compendium of the best ever books written on the sources of prosperity, from famous classics to off-beat unknowns, distilled to the point of joyous clarity."

Richard Koch, author of *The 80/20 Principle*

50 Prosperity Classics

ATTRACT IT, CREATE IT, MANAGE IT, SHARE IT

Wisdom from the best books on

wealth creation and abundance

Tom Butler-Bowdon

NICHOLAS BREALEY PUBLISHING

LONDON • BOSTON

First published by
Nicholas Brealey Publishing in 2008
Reprinted 2008, 2010

3–5 Spafield Street
Clerkenwell, London
EC1R 4QB, UK
Tel: +44 (0)20 7239 0360
Fax: +44 (0)20 7239 0370

20 Park Plaza, Suite 1115A
Boston
MA 02116, USA
Tel: (888) BREALEY
Fax: (617) 523 3708

www.nicholasbrealey.com
www.butler-bowdon.com

ISBN: 978-1-85788-504-0

British Library Cataloguing in Publication Data
A catalogue record for this book is available from the British Library.

Printed in India by Gopsons Papers Ltd., Noida

For Cherry

James Allen
Robert G. Allen
David Bach
P. T. Barnum
Genevieve Behrend
John C. Bogle
Richard Branson
Warren Buffett
Rhonda Byrne
Andrew Carnegie
William D. Danko
Felix Dennis
Joe Dominguez
Peter Drucker
T. Harv Eker
Gary W. Eldred
Chuck Feeney
Charles Fillmore
Joel T. Fleishman
Milton Friedman
Thomas Friedman
Bill Gates
Michael E. Gerber
Benjamin Graham
Mark Victor Hansen
Paul Hawken
Esther Hicks
Jerry Hicks
Napoleon Hill
Conrad Hilton
Joe Karbo
Guy Kawasaki
Robert Kiyosaki
Amory B. Lovins
L. Hunter Lovins
Peter Lynch
Andrew McLean
Jerrold Mundis
William Nickerson
Suze Orman
Duane Packer
Paul Zane Pilzer
Catherine Ponder
Dave Ramsey
John Randolph Price
Ayn Rand
Vicki Robin
Anita Roddick
Sanaya Roman
Howard Schultz
Marsha Sinetar
Adam Smith
Thomas J. Stanley
Donald Trump
Lynne Twist
Max Weber
Muhammad Yunus

Contents

Introduction

In the pages of this book you will find the secrets to prosperity. All you have to do is to act on them, making them your own.

The *Oxford English Dictionary* defines wealth as "an instance or kind of prosperity"; that is, it is contained within the larger concept of prosperity. But whereas wealth is simply the possession of money or assets, or the process of getting more and keeping more for ourselves, prosperity is the state of "flourishing, thriving or succeeding." In short, wealth is about money but prosperity is about life, taking in the wider ideas of good fortune, abundance, and wellbeing.

John Wesley, the great religious reformer, told people to "Make all you can, save all you can, give all you can." Andrew Carnegie, perhaps history's most famous philanthropist and the founder of thousands of free libraries, noted, "No man becomes rich unless he enriches others." More recently, the authors of *The One Minute Millionaire* provided a similar creed for the enlightened person:

I make millions
I save millions
I invest millions
I give millions away.

50 Prosperity Classics celebrates the act of wealth creation, but it also recognizes the joy of giving. Prosperity is best appreciated as a circle in which money is first attracted and created, then managed well and shared to good effect. It is often said that money can't buy happiness, and this book does not try to suggest otherwise. However, it is also true that the abilities to attract, create, manage, and share wealth are important to living a contented life, and many of us seek to be better off financially not to amass money for its own sake, but to be in control of our time and spend it in meaningful ways.

The idea of prosperity suggests that we are *stewards* of wealth who create it from existing resources and eventually give it back in some form. There is no real satisfaction to be gained by the thoughtless plunder of natural resources just to make profits, or by being a mindless consumer. However, wealth that is created in a way that involves the least possible harm to people and the planet is certainly part of the circle of prosperity. For this reason, this book covers titles that celebrate sustainable wealth, including Hawken's *Natural Capitalism*, The Body Shop founder Anita Roddick's autobiography

Business as Unusual, and *Your Money or Your Life*, a seminal "simpler living" guide. While many would argue that it is the fantastic growth in wealth over the last century that has caused our environmental problems, it is also true that without continued prosperity we will lack the resources to research and invest in new energy sources, for instance, or repair what has been damaged.

For some, there is still a stigma attached to the pursuit of wealth. However, if you understand wealth creation as part of the larger concept of prosperity, nothing should hold you back. You have a duty to yourself and the world to maximize resources, use your imagination, and work hard to bring new, valuable things into being. In taking this larger view, you may find that it is possible both to be well off financially and to live with a good conscience.

What's inside

50 Prosperity Classics covers many of the great writings on wealth and abundance. Titles on the attraction of wealth clearly constitute a whole genre on their own, and a selection of them is covered here. The business biographies try to inspire or reinspire the entrepreneur in you, and the titles on personal finance aim to provide a vital, practical education in how to manage and grow what you have. Wealth creation does not happen in a societal vacuum, therefore also highlighted are some of the landmark titles and most thought-provoking reads in economics and political economy. The book also highlights a handful of inspiring titles on how to give wealth away intelligently, to those who will do most with it.

There is a natural divide between books relating to "prosperity consciousness," or the inner or psychological aspects of creating wealth, and more worldly titles on the nuts and bolts of personal finance, entrepreneurship, and economics. *50 Prosperity Classics* aims to bridge this divide. If you are naturally drawn to the philosophical aspects of prosperity, you will learn much from the commentaries on investing, finance, and economics. If you are well read in these more practical areas, you may have your eyes or heart opened by the more metaphysical classics of abundance. Your ultimate aim should be to integrate both, so that you become a master of the inner *and* the outer game of wealth.

The titles in the book can be organized according to its four elements: attracting, creating, managing, and sharing wealth. Though it is divided into 50 chapters, the book is designed to be like a conversation that introduces you to a myriad of ideas and strategies. Some will profit you more than others, and at different times in your life. Read whatever fascinates you most now.

ATTRACT IT
Mastering the inner game of wealth and abundance

James Allen *The Path of Prosperity* (1905)
Genevieve Behrend *Your Invisible Power* (1921)
Rhonda Byrne *The Secret* (2006)
T. Harv Eker *Secrets of the Millionaire Mind* (2005)
Charles Fillmore *Prosperity* (1936)
Esther Hicks & Jerry Hicks *Ask and It Is Given* (2004)
Napoleon Hill *The Master-Key to Riches* (1965)
Catherine Ponder *Open Your Mind to Prosperity* (1971)
John Randolph Price *The Abundance Book* (1987)
Sanaya Roman & Duane Packer *Creating Money* (1988)
Marsha Sinetar *Do What You Love, the Money Will Follow* (1987)
Max Weber *The Protestant Ethic and the Spirit of Capitalism* (1904–5)

We tend to think of wealth as involving the ability to shape the world around us to profitable ends, yet wealth really begins in the mind, with your ideas, vision, beliefs, and character. You attract or repel wealth according to what you think and believe about yourself, therefore it's never a waste of time to work on your own development. Aristotle said "The hardest victory is the victory over self," but it is a victory that enables you to win in all other aspects of life.

James Allen's *The Path of Prosperity* underscores this concept, noting that a disciplined mind and a focus on serving others are basic to the achievement of any prosperity. Napoleon Hill comments in *The Master-Key to Riches* that definiteness of purpose and a desire to "go the extra mile" are essential to creating value and, by extension, wealth. Max Weber's famous essay *The Protestant Ethic and the Spirit of Capitalism* argues that the early Protestant merchants were able to attract fortunes as a direct result of their intense preoccupation with the personal virtues of honesty and frugality.

Books on achieving "prosperity consciousness" now have a high profile thanks to the success of contemporary titles such as *The Secret*, but this genre has a heritage going back almost a century. Charles Fillmore's book *Prosperity*, for instance, and the writings of Genevieve Behrend introduced readers to the metaphysical basis of prosperity, noting that feelings of lack simply indicate a separation from the "source" (God or the universe), a lack that can easily be remedied through prayer, affirmation, or visualization. Later in the twentieth century, writers such as Catherine Ponder kept these ideas alive, before the books of Esther and Jerry Hicks and Rhonda Byrne created an explosion of new interest in the idea that our emotional state of being can act as a magnet that "attracts" wealth.

In *Secrets of the Millionaire Mind*, Harv Eker demonstrates the primary importance of this "inner game" by showing how each of has a mental "financial blueprint" that either allows money to flow to us or stops it. You can change the blueprint, but the first step is to become a person open to opportunities rather than focused on complaints.

In her 1980s bestseller *Do What You Love, the Money Will Follow*, Marsha Sinetar asserts that the key to an abundant life is simply doing work you love. Not only does this lead to excellence in what you produce, which tends to attract more rewards, but aligning your life with your deepest values and talents creates a well of sustainable happiness.

All the above titles have a common thread: Prosperity begins with prosperous thoughts, which in turn set up an emotional state that can only attract good into your life.

CREATE IT
Secrets of the wealth creator

Robert G. Allen *Multiple Streams of Income* (2000)
P. T. Barnum *The Art of Money Getting* (1880)
Richard Branson *Losing My Virginity* (2002)
Felix Dennis *How to Get Rich* (2006)
Peter Drucker *Innovation and Entrepreneurship* (1985)
Bill Gates (by James Wallace & Jim Erickson) *Hard Drive* (1992)
Michael E. Gerber *The E-Myth Revisited* (1995)
Conrad Hilton *Be My Guest* (1957)
Joe Karbo *The Lazy Man's Way to Riches* (1973)
Guy Kawasaki *The Art of the Start* (2004)
Paul Zane Pilzer *God Wants You to Be Rich* (1995)
Anita Roddick *Business as Unusual* (2000)
Howard Schultz *Pour Your Heart into It* (1997)
Donald Trump *The Art of the Deal* (1987)

Once the psychological aspects of prosperity are understood, we can turn to the actual business of creating wealth. Conventional wisdom suggests that there is no substitute for learning as we go, yet the smart wealth creator will want to "stand on the shoulders of giants," absorbing the rich wisdom stored in business biographies.

P. T. Barnum is often described as the "world's greatest showman," but in his 1880 success manual he advises surprisingly simple ingredients for achieving prosperity: good health, personal character, the right vocation, and the right location to practice it in. Conrad Hilton, who built a rundown hostelry in a mining town into a global hotel chain, was told by his parents that prayer and work were the basic elements of success in life, but his own experience added a third element: the need to dream and think big. When times are tough, as they were for him during the Depression, a powerful vision may be the only thing you have to pull you along. For Bill Gates such a big vision was instrumental in building the world's largest private fortune. No one really anticipated the personal computing boom, but his dream of a computer on everyone's desk, running software that was "easy enough for his mother to use," ensured that Microsoft was ready to seize any opportunity that came its way. And though he attributes much of his success to being a master deal maker, Donald Trump has also risen to the top of his field through his ability to think big.

The autobiographies of Richard Branson, Felix Dennis, Anita Roddick, and Howard Schultz show that passion is the basis for building great companies (such as Virgin, The Body Shop, and Starbucks), and that an individual's wish to stay true to their conscience is often a hugely underestimated basis for creating wealth. Though in time they may become part of the establishment, initially it is the mavericks and outsiders who create surprising, outstanding value. This fact is emphasized by management legend Peter Drucker, who notes that entrepreneurs provide new value not simply by doing things better, but doing them *differently*. All businesses begin small, but Michael Gerber's book *The E-Myth Revisited* is a vital reminder to be far-sighted and avoid getting bogged down by day-to-day management. You become an entrepreneur not in order to "buy yourself a job," but to create powerful systems that deliver satisfaction to people.

Milton Friedman *Capitalism and Freedom* (1962)
Thomas Friedman *The World Is Flat* (2005)
Ayn Rand *Capitalism* (1966)
Adam Smith *The Wealth of Nations* (1778)

No wealth can be created without a supportive economic framework, and Adam Smith's famous *The Wealth of Nations* amply demonstrates that a society in which everyone is free to pursue their own economic interests is most likely to deliver prosperity to the greatest number. Smith's modern heir, Milton Friedman, shows that while government intentions are often good, free markets are a better guarantee of personal liberties. In her turn, Ayn Rand provides a convincing case that capitalism is the only moral system of economic organization, because at its center lies an insistence on personal freedom. Wealth on its own may be obtained by rogue states or corrupt individuals, but prosperity (understood as peace of mind based on material abundance) naturally rests on the assumption of such freedom. More recently, Thomas Friedman has provided a compelling argument that technology is creating a "flat" world that allows millions more people to compete in the global marketplace. Governments cannot stop this shift; they can assist it by making sure that their citizens are well educated and well connected.

MANAGE IT
Strategies of personal finance and investing

David Bach *The Automatic Millionaire* (2003)
John C. Bogle *The Little Book of Common Sense Investing* (2007)
Warren Buffett (edited by Lawrence Cunningham) *The Essays of Warren Buffett* (1997)
Joe Dominguez & Vicki Robin *Your Money or Your Life* (1992)
Benjamin Graham *The Intelligent Investor* (1949)
Robert Kiyosaki *Cashflow Quadrant* (1998)
Peter Lynch *One Up on Wall Street* (1989)
Andrew McLean & Gary Eldred *Investing in Real Estate* (2005)
Jerrold Mundis *How to Get Out of Debt, Stay Out of Debt, and Live Prosperously* (1988)
William Nickerson *How I Turned $1,000 into Three Million in Real Estate—in My Spare Time* (1969)
Suze Orman *Women and Money* (2007)
Dave Ramsey *Financial Peace Revisited* (2003)
Thomas J. Stanley & William D. Danko *The Millionaire Next Door* (1996)

It's wonderful to make money, but even better to be able to keep it. Whether you have a windfall to invest or are a regular wage earner socking away a little each month, the titles in this category show you how to make the most of what you have.

David Bach reveals how the habit of "paying yourself first" can make a person of modest means into a millionaire, thanks to the power of compound interest over decades, while Stanley and Danko's *The Millionaire Next Door* provides a remarkable portrait of the "quiet wealthy" who get that way by living within their means and investing their savings.

What is the best form of investment? Apart from your own business, if you have one, the best returns seem to come from either stocks or real estate. Regarding the stock market, legendary investors Warren Buffett, Benjamin Graham, and Peter Lynch all stress the difference between long-term investing in companies and market speculation for short-term gain. The small investor may be best off putting their money into an index fund that simply buys a piece of every listed company in a market, which ensures that they have a stake in their country's business growth. Property investment can also be a surprisingly easy route to wealth, particularly if the investor takes the long view rather than looking for quick returns. William Nickerson wrote the original real-estate "bible" in this vein, and McLean and Eldred provide a contemporary, comprehensive recipe for attaining riches from property.

In an era of record levels of consumer debt, however, many of us need to jump the first hurdle of becoming solvent. There is a wealth of excellent titles in this area, with Jerrold Mundis's manual on becoming debt free still perhaps the best. As a former bankrupt, Dave Ramsey's advice on the pernicious effect of debt on families, and how to regain prosperity, is also valuable. At a more holistic level, Dominguez and Robin's *Your Money or Your Life* challenges readers to embrace old ideas of simpler living and frugality, showing that controlling your finances is key to a fulfilled life.

SHARE IT
The flow of wealth and giving something back

Andrew Carnegie *The Gospel of Wealth* (1889)
Chuck Feeney (by Conor O'Clery) *The Billionaire Who Wasn't* (2007)
Joel T. Fleishman *The Foundation* (2007)
Paul Hawken, Amory B. Lovins, & L. Hunter Lovins *Natural Capitalism* (2000)
Lynne Twist *The Soul of Money* (2003)
Muhammad Yunus *Banker to the Poor* (1999)

Prosperity is not simply the making and managing of wealth, but also its circulation. If we have been fortunate enough to generate it, as a citizen of the earth and a member of humanity we have an obligation to use our money to heal or inspire. As Lynne Twist argues in *The Soul of Money*, based on her work as a global fundraiser, not only the recipients but the givers are healed by active philanthropy. Hoarding money only stops the flow and tends to corrupt the possessor or their descendants.

Andrew Carnegie believed that a person who dies rich "dies disgraced," and in his huge charitable endowments provided the model for modern giving by rich individuals. Joel Fleishman's masterly work on foundations reveals the massive amounts of private money now being set aside to help address the world's ills, much of it from entrepreneurs who wish to bring the passion and focus on results that allowed them to succeed in business to addressing social problems and opening up opportunity. A living embodiment of this attitude is Chuck Feeney, a duty-free goods retailer who, inspired by Andrew Carnegie, renounced his massive wealth to spend it on worthwhile projects around the world.

If prosperity means anything, it must include the "poorest of the poor." Muhammad Yunus won a Nobel Prize for his creation of a bank that provides very small loans to women who dream of becoming economically self-reliant. His fascinating book relates that ultimately it is not charity but simple things we take for granted, like access to finance and ownership of property, that are the bases of wealth and wellbeing.

We also cannot continue generating wealth at the expense of our planet, and Hawken's *Natural Capitalism* stresses that genuine prosperity means taking as much care of our natural capital as we do of our financial capital.

Final word

Before you begin reading the commentaries, please note some practical points:

- At the back of the book is a section called Prosperity Principles, which distills some key points from the 50 classic titles. You may find it a useful recap.
- Also at the end is a list of 50 More Classics, which may provide you with ideas for further reading.
- Some themes recur through a number of titles. Take this as a sign that the ideas they address have proven themselves over time. Other books in the list may appear to contradict each other. Only you can judge which approaches or strategies are likely to work best for you.
- Many of the 50 titles have American authors. The United States has always placed great emphasis on monetary wealth and gloried in the entrepreneur, and as a consequence has produced much of the best writing in these areas. The link between spirituality and wealth is partly a legacy of the US's Puritan roots, which continues today through its copious writings on the mental and metaphysical aspects of abundance. In truth, though, the themes are universal and will have the same impact wherever you live.
- Quite a few books were written after the year 2000. While insufficient time may have passed for them to be considered "landmark," they stand out for the quality of their ideas or information that is likely to be valued for years to come.
- Some commentaries do not have separate biographical boxes, since they contain a reasonable amount of biographical material within the text itself.
- A number of the books are now in the public domain, meaning that in many parts of the world their copyright has expired. See the Credits section at the back of the book for details on how to access these titles for free.

In addition...

- Readers of this book can receive a bonus. I will be delighted to send you a free extra book commentary if you simply email me at tom@butler-bowdon.com. The book in question is a personal favorite that has sold millions of copies, and—as long as you keep an open mind—provides a secret means of unlocking your potential and bringing you real prosperity.
- You are also invited to visit www.Butler-Bowdon.com. Here you will find further prosperity resources, plus a wealth of free material on the key writings and ideas relating to personal success.
- The idea for this book emerged from an earlier one, *50 Success Classics*, which explored many of the great writings in personal achievement and motivation and some financial classics. Take a look there for commentaries on titles such as Benjamin Franklin's *The Way to Wealth*, George S. Clason's *The Richest Man in Babylon*, Napoleon Hill's *Think and Grow Rich*, and Wallace Wattles'

The Science of Getting Rich. Also included are stories of some famous wealth creators, including Andrew Carnegie, John Paul Getty, Michael Dell, and Sam Walton.

When reading the stories of financial or business success in these pages, you may begin to think that the same can't happen to you. It can. This book aims to remind you that others experienced similar fears and doubts, and yet broke through them. Life constantly tests us to believe that we live in an abundant universe, and if we do believe then remarkable things can happen.

In times of doubt, think of the acorn. An ancient symbol of abundance, this seed of the mighty oak begins growing only when its tree reaches maturity. Prosperity always involves an element of *time*. Nothing great is achieved overnight, and all things begin small.

1905

The Path of Prosperity

"Rectify your heart, and you will rectify your life. Lust, hatred, anger, vanity, pride, covetousness, self-indulgence, self-seeking, obstinacy—all these are poverty and weakness; whereas love, purity, gentleness, meekness, compassion, generosity, self-forgetfulness, and self-renunciation—all these are wealth and power."

"Whatever your position in life may be, before you can hope to enter into any measure of success, usefulness, and power, you must learn how to focus your thought-forces by cultivating calmness and repose."

"You say you are chained by circumstances; you cry out for better opportunities, for a wider scope, for improved physical conditions, and perhaps you inwardly curse the fate that binds you hand and foot. It is for you that I write; it is to you that I speak... I know this pathway looks barren at its commencement... but if you undertake to walk it... you will be astonished at the magical changes which will be brought about in your outward life."

In a nutshell

You will only become truly prosperous when you have disciplined your mind. Paradoxically, wealth (and happiness) comes most easily to those who forget themselves in their service to others.

In a similar vein

Genevieve Behrend *Your Invisible Power* (p 34)
Rhonda Byrne *The Secret* (p 58)
Charles Fillmore *Prosperity* (p 98)
Catherine Ponder *Open Your Mind to Prosperity* (p 218)
Max Weber *The Protestant Ethic and the Spirit of Capitalism* (p 282)

CHAPTER 1

James Allen

Where is the path to prosperity? Can you find it through stocks, bonds, or real estate, or perhaps in ownership of a company? These are tangible expressions of wealth, but they say nothing about who has gained them or how. In fact, prosperity is created by individuals, and therefore those individuals need particular personal qualities. In *The Path of Prosperity*, James Allen argues that prosperity is *always* personal, resting squarely on the degree to which you have refined and bettered yourself. Though it is possible for anyone to get wealthy, to be happily prosperous suggests that you have peace of mind in addition to monetary riches.

Allen is most famous as the author of *As a Man Thinketh* (see commentary in *50 Self-Help Classics*), which beautifully expresses the idea that you create your world through your thoughts. *The Path of Prosperity* goes deeper into the link between your mindset and material abundance, and is one of the more spiritual prosperity titles. Allen himself was a pious, modest man who died relatively young, and his writings are suffused with a sense of peace and wellbeing.

This book is a superb beginning for anyone's journey of abundance, since it goes to the heart of what prosperity is all about: having a good heart, and becoming a person who is truly valuable to your fellow human beings.

Follow the path to light

The book's first chapter is, surprisingly, on "evil." Allen defines evil not as some cosmic force outside you, but simply as "ignorance of the true nature and relation of things." The universe is filled with light, he explains, and your experience of "night" on earth is really just an illusion. In the same way, when you have a dark night of sorrow, pain, or misfortune, you must realize that it is temporary and illusory, and that your true nature is light filled ("the dark shadow that covers you is cast by none and nothing but yourself"). Your dark emotions have no fundamental reality, and the light of truth is waiting to burst into your life if you allow it.

Whatever your difficulties and pains, they have come fully as a result of your previous thoughts and actions. These problems are a gift: When you accept that you have attracted them, and then choose to endure them, you have learned the basic law of life, and become free to be a careful molder of your own circumstances. You have learned how to turn evil or setbacks into good. Such knowledge is worth more than any fortune, and yet it is also essential to the creation of real prosperity. Control your thoughts and your emotions, and you become master of your destiny.

Have the power to choose

In his chapter "The world a reflex of mental states," Allen recalls the Buddha's statement: "All that we are is the result of what we have thought. It is founded on our thoughts; it is made up of our thoughts."

If you are happy, it is because you are thinking happy thoughts. If you are miserable, it is thanks to your despondent thoughts. In one of the nice verses that supplement the book's prose, Allen writes:

Do you wish for kindness? Be kind.
Do you ask for truth? Be true.
What you give of yourself you find;
Your world is a reflex of you.

Of course, he notes, we can be affected by external events, but we will be swayed by them only to the extent of our understanding of the power of thought. He gives the example of two men he knew who both, when young, lost their hard-won savings. The first fell into deep despondency and regret, while the other told himself that "worry won't bring it back, but hard work will." Throwing himself into his work with great vigor, he was quickly able to eclipse his former worth. The other man continued to mourn his loss and his bad luck, which duly snowballed into even worse circumstances. To one the loss was a blessing, to the other a curse. Allen observes:

If circumstances had the power to bless or harm, they would bless and harm all men alike, but the fact that the same circumstances will be alike good and bad to different souls proves that the good or bad is not in the circumstance, but only in the mind of him that encounters it.

This is not just metaphysical theory. In his psychological classic *Learned Optimism*, Martin Seligman notes that people with a "positive explanatory style" quickly get over setbacks and prosper. Crucially, optimism—which is essentially choosing to think in a certain way despite current reality—can be *learned* and often makes all the difference to a person's career success or failure.

To progress, fill your current position

In the chapter "The way out of undesirable conditions," Allen expounds further on the workings of universal law. Cease to be a complainer, he says, because the more you complain the tighter the chains that bind you become. The route to a better life is not through complaining but through finding ways to deliver service and provide love. If you're not totally pleased with your current circumstances, the secret to your release is to *make the best of what you have now*. You can't move on to something better without having fulfilled what is expected of you in the current position.

If you are living in poor or cramped accommodations, keep your space spotlessly clean and make it as charming as possible; only such an effort will attract the house that you deserve. If you are suffering under a terrible boss, absorb the negative comments and see the situation as an opportunity to practice patience and self-control. In time it is *you* who will become strong, mentally and spiritually. "Shake off the delusion that you are being injured or oppressed by another," Allen tells the reader, "you are only really injured by what is within you. There is no practice more degrading, debasing, and soul-destroying than that of self-pity."

Master the self and gain everything

Allen himself would spend the first hour of each day at a quiet spot looking down onto the sea. He saw this time not as a luxury but a necessity:

If you would walk firmly and securely, and would accomplish any achievement, you must learn to rise above and control all such disturbing and retarding vibrations. You must daily practice the habit of putting your mind at rest, "going into the silence," as it is commonly called. This is a method of replacing a troubled thought with one of peace, a thought of weakness with one of strength.

In our busy world it can be hard to believe that strength comes from silence, yet many people note that their most valuable ideas and their most loving acts are born in moments of stillness. In addition to lifting anxiety, we gain illumination, arrive at correct judgments, and our "scattered thought-forces are reunited," bringing us back to the right course of action. Our worries are mostly illusory, the result of either ignorance or lack of faith. In collecting our thoughts, we can avoid being enslaved by our changing moods and the need to control other people. Allen writes:

Give up that narrow cramped self that seeks to render all things subservient to its own petty interests, and you will enter into the company of the angels, into the very heart and essence of universal Love.

He goes on to say:

There is absolutely no other way to true power and abiding peace, but by self-control, self-government, self-purification. To be at the mercy of your disposition is to be impotent, unhappy, and of little real use in the world.

The paradox of real prosperity is that it comes to those who forget about themselves in providing service to others. As they become highly valued, they are showered not only with money but with love.

Anyone can gain wealth if they try hard enough, but prosperity and peace of mind only arrive at the door of people who have first mastered themselves. You can pursue wealth directly, but it is wiser to perfect yourself in the provision of service. Even in the midst of riches you will remain virtuous, seeing yourself less as an owner than as a steward of divine abundance. Allen affirms:

The way to true riches is to enrich the soul by the acquisition of virtue. Outside of real heart-virtue there is neither prosperity nor power, but only the appearances of these.

Final comments

It is fitting that Allen's book is the first among the 50 presented here, as it takes us to the very foundation of wealth and success—personal character.

Aristotle said "The hardest victory is the victory over self," but it is a victory that enables you to win in all other aspects of life. The early Protestant merchants created fortunes because they had gold-plated reputations for honesty. The trust bestowed on them was the result of constant refinement of personal attributes that they believed were required of them by God. Yet you do not need religious faith to understand that the greater your moral depth and courage, the more you stand out from your peers. Money alone can make you financially rich, but to be both rich and happy you must be able to live easily with yourself. No work on refining your virtues (honesty, diligence, sympathy, and so on) is ever a waste, either in a spiritual or a material sense. The more abundant such qualities, the more easily riches are attracted to you, compared to people who only chase short-term gain.

In its emphasis on the power of the mind to create circumstances and with its metaphysical underpinnings, *The Path of Prosperity* was a forerunner of books such as *The Secret*, and has been an important influence in the self-development field. At only 30 pages it is a little treasure.

James Allen

Allen was born in Leicester, England, in 1864. At 15 he was forced to leave school and work in factories when his father, who had left for the United States to find work with the intention of then bringing his family over, was robbed and murdered.

Allen was employed with several British manufacturing firms until 1902, when he began to write full time. Moving to the coastal town of Ilfracombe in Devon, Allen settled down to a quiet life of reading, writing, gardening, and meditation. In a decade he wrote 19 books, The Path of Prosperity *being the second. Others include* From Poverty to Power, Byways of Blessedness, The Life Triumphant, *and* Eight Pillars of Prosperity. *Allen died in 1912.*

More information can be found in John Woodcock's James Allen and Lily L. Allen: An Illustrated Biography *(Ilfracombe: JLW, 2003).*

2000

Multiple Streams of Income

"Every dollar bill is a money seed. Just as a tiny acorn contains the power to grow into a mighty oak tree, each dollar bill has the power to grow into a mighty money tree."

"Prosperous people have always known... If one stream dries up, they have many more to tap into for support. So-called ordinary people are much more vulnerable. If they lose one of their streams, it wipes them out... In the future, you will need a portfolio of income streams—not one or two, but many streams from completely different and diversified sources—so that if one stream empties, you'll barely notice. You'll be stable. You will have time to adjust. You will be safe."

In a nutshell

The prosperous do not depend on only once source of income, but grow orchards of "money trees."

In a similar vein

CHAPTER 2

Robert G. Allen

In the 1950s, Robert Allen notes, most families could survive on one income. These days, most families need two. In the future, we will need multiple streams of income to be truly prosperous. People think that having a good job means security, but if something happens to that job, prosperity can turn to poverty with amazing speed. Widening your income sources provides peace of mind, because you know that if one stream dries up you not only have others but have the time to find more.

Allen is famous for his "nothing down" and "creative financing" real-estate books, so you would expect *Multiple Streams of Income* to focus on only the flashier, high-growth ways to wealth. The surprise is that the first part covers conservative investment strategies such as having a "survival account" containing three months' emergency cash, making sure that 10 percent of your income is always channeled into investments, and, if you go into the stock market, sticking mainly to index funds. Allen is also big on the power of compound interest (Baron de Rothschild described it as "the eighth wonder of the world"), noting that in the span of a normal lifetime a mere $1 a day, or $30 a month, will grow into $1 million. Allen admits to having "lost everything" twice over, so it is perhaps unsurprising that he was drawn back to these financial fundamentals.

Most readers will be looking to make money at a faster rate than over a lifetime, however, and this is where *Multiple Streams of Income* gets interesting. Allen identifies three "money mountains"—investing, real estate, and marketing—from which the average person should, with just a little knowledge and effort, be able to obtain at least 10 streams of income that keep flowing in, in the process creating freedom from a single employer. There are too many ideas in the book to cover each "mountain" properly, but the following points should give you a taste of the contents.

First stop the leaks

For the concept of multiple streams of income to work for you, Allen explains, you must "stop the leaks." One leak is taxes. Wealthy people are not afraid to spend money on getting the best tax advice available.

The other major leak is spending. Prosperous people do things differently when they spend, things that only take a few minutes but reflect their mastery of money:

- They make sure that most of their purchases are planned. Generally, the longer the timeframe before a purchase, the less you will pay (as oil magnate J. P. Getty put it, "I buy my straw hats in the fall").
- They ask for and get discounts ("never pay retail").
- They always get receipts, check them, and then once they get home put the receipts into a categorized file.
- They balance their accounts on a regular basis.

Allen notes that some people are great at finding bargains, but then do nothing constructive with the money they save. Prosperous people are both good at finding bargains and invest what they save—they love "saving" in both senses.

The main difference between the rich and the poor is this: Poor people see money simply as cash in their hands, to be used as soon as they get it. Rich people, in contrast, understand money primarily as seeds to be planted that will grow into "money trees."

Gain residual income

Allen asks, "How many times do you get paid for every hour you work?" Most people get paid only once for every hour they put in; this is what earning a salary is all about, and it applies even if you are in a highly paid position like a doctor. You are paid to be in a certain place at a certain time, doing certain things, so however much you earn doing it you are on a sort of treadmill. Allen remarks, "Working for someone else, unless you own a piece of the profits, is not security. It's just the illusion of security."

The secret of the wealthy lies not so much in the amount of money they earn, but in the fact that they earn it in a different way. With "residual" income, you work hard once and that effort generates a flow of income for years afterwards, often for the rest of your life. Allen puts it another way: "Poverty is when large efforts produce small results. Wealth is when small efforts produce large results."

His own example is writing *Nothing Down*, a real-estate manual that he wrote "on spec" in 1980. He spent over 1,000 hours on the book and had zero return for two years. "Teenagers working at McDonald's earned more money than I did," he notes. "But I wasn't looking for a salary. I wanted a royalty." The book eventually became a bestseller and Allen is still earning tens of thousands of dollars a year—from a product he created almost three decades ago.

Software designers, artists, inventors, and film actors can all earn royalties for things they did or produced once. Investors can have streams of income without end (through dividends, interest, or appreciation) as a result of making one wise investment. Real-estate owners get a continual flow of cash from paid-out properties. Many others get a "piece of the action"—marketing consultants, business partners, insurance agents—in place of, or in addition to, normal paid work. Thanks to streams of residual or passive income that come in even while they sleep, such people's time is freed up to design, create, or source even more streams of income.

Win big in real estate

People engage in a huge array of money-making schemes, Allen notes, when the simplest and most powerful is right in front of them: property. He calls real estate "the poor person's millionaire maker," because with little or no money (he includes a whole section on "nothing down" financing) you can become quite wealthy within a few years, using the power of leverage and assuming modest rates of appreciation.

The example he gives is buying a property today for $150,000, putting $10,000 down as a deposit. If it appreciates at a rate of 5 percent, the property will be worth $244,000 in ten years. By that time, your mortgage will only be $131,000, which means that your equity minus outstanding loans will be over $130,000. This equals a return of over 20 percent a year on the original $10,000 investment. How many people get a 20 percent return from the stock market, Allen asks, over such a long period? Warren Buffett perhaps, but he is one in a million.

With only modest property appreciation, the average home owner makes money while they sleep. It's a pity, Allen suggests, that they don't buy more properties and multiply the effect.

However, even if the property market is not appreciating, you can still do very well with real estate using a little knowledge and creativity. Allen elaborates on a potentially lucrative way to earn great returns: buying out or taking over the mortgages of people who can't keep up the payments on them or have a desperate need to sell. This is not about taking advantage, more that you are solving a problem for them that ensures they avoid bankruptcy or foreclosure, while also making a good profit for yourself. Hundreds of thousands of properties go into foreclosure every year. You only need to find one where you can solve a problem that delivers you a bargain property, and this can set you up for life.

Even if you don't get into real-estate investing, remember this fact: The average net worth of renters is about 30 times less that of home owners. Getting your own home is an important first step on the road to wealth.

Be an information king

Allen's unattractive term for establishing streams of income from the creation or sale of information products is "infopreneuring." The beauty of information products (books, CDs, newsletters, and so on) is that they are inexpensive to produce, alter, and inventory, have a high markup, have copyright protection, plus you enjoy the prestige and satisfaction associated with being the creator of ideas and intellectual capital.

Allen notes that most experts haven't a clue how to package or sell their knowledge, yet if it were made accessible there would probably be a market for it. The key to success is the internet, which thanks to the magic of search engines can bring your particular expertise to thousands of people. Package that expertise into an inexpensive e-book that nevertheless has a high markup, and you can bring in a lot of money in a short space of time. But to find the "hungry fish" of users and buyers, you first need to learn about creating "irresistible bait."

Most infopreneurship involves a new slant on an old product. Don't be afraid to pursue niches that seem small but could be very lucrative. Thousands of books had been written on real estate before Allen's, for instance, but no one had written one on buying with "nothing down." He tapped into an unknown need for information. Focus on the basic human needs of money, self-esteem, health, God, relationships, and beauty, and you can't go far wrong.

Marketing: Crack the code

Packaging and title can make all the difference to selling a product. Allen mentions an entrepreneur who had condensed hundreds of classic books into only two pages each, and put them together as a volume called *Compact Classics*. But no one bought it. The same content was repackaged into *The Great American Bathroom Book* (perfect reading for the "little room") and it brought in millions of dollars. He had "cracked the code" for getting the greatest return from his product.

Sometimes changing just one word, or adding a word, will make all the difference to your ability to sell something. Allen mentions Joe Karbo's book *The Lazy Man's Way to Riches*, which Karbo originally tried to sell via an expensive, large newspaper ad including the line "How to make $50,000 a year the lazy way." Only a trickle of orders came in. Next time he changed the figure to $20,000, a small difference that brought him a fortune. What was the difference? People could not see themselves making an extra $50,000 a year, but they could imagine making an extra $20,000. Through a little experimentation Karbo had matched irresistible bait to the hungry fish. (Incidentally, it was a great product in the first place; see the commentary on this book on p 168.)

At a deeper level, never forget that the purpose of building a business is to create long-term customers, who over a 10–15-year period will be worth a lot of money to you. Therefore, the "most important function you must perform as an infopreneur is to constantly maintain and update your database." You can sell a range of products to your database of loyal customers; they don't even need to be your own products. If they trust you, people will buy what you recommend.

Final comments

Is Allen's idea of multiple streams of income from investments and intellectual capital an impossible dream? Not only is it possible, he argues, it is the way of the future. Only 100 years ago most people were still small-time entrepreneurs who earned their money from a range of sources. Only with the move from farms to factories and offices did we become dependent on single, large organizations for our money. But with more and more people choosing to rely on their ingenuity as creators, innovators, and investors, what we now think of as normal may end up being a historical anomaly. When so many other sources beckon, it is the idea of receiving all your income from one source (your employer) that will seem risky and strange.

Allen has been criticized for being a marketing genius while not actually providing anything of real value. Although you may disagree with some of his techniques and ideas, the basic idea of multiple streams of income is a valuable one. Many readers will not be interested in some of the more involved strategies Allen discusses, including buying tax lien certificates, network marketing, licensing, and selling options on shares that you own, but these will at least get you thinking about extra sources of income. Be warned that the chapter on income streams from the internet is now out of date (even in the latest edition).

Robert G. Allen

Raised in small-town Alberta, Canada in the 1950s by religious parents, as a young man Allen spent two years doing missionary work for his church in Tahiti. In 1974 he obtained an MBA from Brigham Young University in Utah, but on graduating was unable to gain the corporate job he wanted. Having enjoyed William Nickerson's How I Turned $1,000 into $1 million in Real Estate—in My Spare Time, *Allen apprenticed himself to a wealthy real-estate developer and became a property investor himself. He shared his success secrets with a few friends, who did well. Allen then put an ad in a local newspaper offering to teach people "how to buy real estate with little or no money down." It was an instant success, and he licensed his ideas to a seminar company and received millions in royalties. In 1985 he launched his own training company to promote his ideas, and he continues to run seminars and write.*

Allen's books include Nothing Down: How to Buy Real Estate with Little or No Money Down *(1980),* Creating Wealth *(1983),* Nothing Down for the 2000s *(2004), and* Multiple Streams of Internet Income *(2005). He is co-author of* The One Minute Millionaire *with Mark Victor Hansen* *(see p 140).*

2003

The Automatic Millionaire

"In order to become an Automatic Millionaire, you've got to accept the idea that regardless of the size of your salary, you probably already earn enough money to become rich. I can't stress enough the importance of believing this—not just with your mind but with your heart as well. It's an 'Aha!' moment that can truly change your life financially."

"Please trust me on this. Nothing will help you achieve wealth until you decide to Pay Yourself First. Nothing. You can read every book, listen to every tape program, order every motivational product, subscribe to every newsletter there is, and none of it will get you anywhere if you let the government and everyone else have first crack at your salary before you get to it. The foundation of wealth building is Pay Yourself First."

In a nutshell

There is no easier or surer way of attaining wealth than through the habit of paying yourself first through automatic deductions.

In a similar vein

Suze Orman *Women and Money* (p 208)
Dave Ramsey *Financial Peace Revisited* (p 228)

CHAPTER 3

David Bach

Before he wrote *The Automatic Millionaire*, David Bach was already an adviser, popular speaker, and media guest on financial matters. But whatever he talked about, people still kept asking him: What is the secret to getting rich?

The "secret" had been crystallized for Bach several years before, when a manager at a utility plant and his wife came to see him for advice. They seemed like an average working couple, with an average wage, two grown kids, and no pretensions.

Bach was all ready to help out this couple, the McIntyres, but in the end it was *he* who got the education. When he looked over their financial statements, it quickly became clear they were not average. They owned their home outright, owned another one that gave them a stream of income, had large pension funds, sat on a small mountain of cash and bonds, and enjoyed three cars and a boat. Total net worth: well over $1 million.

The McIntyres revealed their secret: Taking their parents' advice, since they got married in their early 20s they had automatically saved 10 percent of whatever they earned. As they had always done this, they never really noticed that the money wasn't there. Even though they had never earned more than modest wages, they could now retire early and without any money worries. The couple claimed, "If we can do it, anyone can."

Bach's secret to wealth, as he admits in the first few pages, is not what most people expect. It will not "transform your financial situation overnight," he warns. You can become a millionaire, but over the course of a normal working life, following "the tortoise's approach to wealth, not the hare's."

Understand the latte factor

The secret to becoming wealthy is not, as most people think, working out how to make a lot more money. Everyone thinks that a new job or a raise will open up new vistas of life enjoyment and power—until they get the new job or pay increase. They then realize that the more you earn, the more you spend, and they're still living from one pay check to the next, caught in an endless cycle of work–spend–work. This is an "unwinnable race." In such a state, wealth remains just a pipe dream.

One such person was Kim, a 23 year old who came to one of Bach's personal finance courses. After Bach had been talking about the effect of saving a few dollars a day over time, she complained that his ideas were "not realistic" for someone living on a normal wage. When Bach asked about her daily habits, it transpired that she was spending $5 on a double nonfat latte and a muffin before she even got to work each morning, then another $5 or $6 on a juice and energy drink before she had even had lunch.

We all like our treats, Bach notes, but consider if Kim had put only $5 of this money into a pension scheme that was invested in the stock market. It would amount to $150 a month. Assuming a return of 10 percent a year (the stock market average over the last century), what would Kim's "latte money" be worth at age 65, the normal retirement age? $1.2 million—and if her employer matched her contributions, it would be more like $1.75 million. After seeing Kim's reaction when she realized that her daily takeout coffees were costing her millions of dollars, Bach's famous "latte factor" was born. As *People* magazine later put it, "A latte spurned is a fortune earned."

Pay yourself first

Bach counts the ways you can get rich: marry into money, inherit money, win it, sue someone, budget for it. All of them have problems, and particularly budgeting, which he says "goes against human nature." Some people are sticklers for detailed spending plans, but most are not.

The only way to get rich easily is to "pay yourself first," automatically putting aside at least 10 percent of your income into savings, a pension scheme, or investments. Most people are aware of the concept, Bach notes, but few really appreciate how it works, and fewer again actually live it.

Once upon a time, people did not have tax automatically deducted from their pay, but had to stump up for it at the end of the financial year. But governments soon learned that people were not very good at budgeting, so they made sure they got paid first through automatic deductions. Governments know about human nature and base their revenue systems around it. To get rich you must follow their lead; that is, pay yourself first (before you pay your bills, mortgage, school fees, whatever) and make the payment automatic.

Who do you work for? Bach notes that most people save no more than 5 percent of their gross income. Based on an average working day, this comes to only 22 minutes a day working for yourself and your retirement. To "finish rich," you need to start contributing at least 10 percent of your income to a pension scheme that allows you to avoid paying tax. Taking this simple step will mean you end up with more money than 9 in 10 people.

If you're dead broke, you can begin by paying yourself only 3 or 4 percent of what you earn. To make sure it didn't hurt, when Bach had nothing in his 20s he started off putting aside only 1 percent. What matters most is the habit; as you earn more you can increase what you put aside. If you own your own home, for instance, you may be able to pay yourself 20 percent of your gross income. What you must think about, like Kim, is the large amount of money you will lose (for most people in most circumstances, over $1 million) if you *don't* pay yourself first.

Bach notes that some people don't want to hear this secret to getting wealthy. They are more attracted to larger, one-off gains or get-rich-quick schemes, but the foundation of all wealth is having savings and adding to them regularly.

"Automation plus compound interest equals serious wealth"

Bach has a chart he likes to present in his seminars, "The time value of money," which tracks how much a few thousand dollars would be worth at retirement age if invested while young. Most people's reaction to it is: "I wish I had seen this earlier." The chart gives the example of two young people, and the salient point is this: The first person, though he invested only $15,000 before he was 19, would end up with more money than his friend who put in $24,000, but only did so between the ages of 19 and 26. The later you start, even though you put more money in, the longer it takes to get the astonishing effect of compounding.

Yet there is still hope for the rest of us who start later. Over a period of 30 years, $3,000 invested a year ($90,000 in total), if compounded at a 10 percent return, will still come to a handsome $1,324,000. Given how much longer people are living, this means that you could start saving properly at 40, and by 70 (when many people are retiring now) you could still be a millionaire.

What about my debts?

Lots of people look rich, Bach notes, but then you find out they are living on a mountain of credit card debt. It is impossible to become a millionaire by keeping your credit card balances high, making the minimum repayments, because with the extortionate interest rates the banks charge it could take you 30 years to pay them off. Bach himself racked up $10,000 of credit card debt on consumables just while he was in college. He stopped abusing credit cards only when he made sure that they were not in his pocket when he went shopping.

If you have credit card debt, the logical thing would seem to be to pay it all off first before you began "paying yourself first." In fact, you will be more motivated if you start saving at the same time as paying off your credit cards. Bach recommends putting half your "pay yourself first" money and applying it toward your monthly credit card debt to pay it off more quickly, and meanwhile begin saving with the other half. He calls this strategy "bury the past and jump to the future."

Have a cushion

A whole chapter in *The Automatic Millionaire* is devoted to the need to set aside a "rainy day" fund that will cover all your living expenses for at least three months if you lose your income or encounter the unexpected. The fund could be enough to cover a whole year or more, but the main criterion is how much you feel you need behind you to get a good night's sleep. You can still, of course, earn good interest on the fund.

The record levels of bankruptcies and home repossessions, Bach notes, is partly because people no longer make sure they have such a cushion in place. Our parents and grandparents routinely created such a fund, but we live under the illusion that life is one long easy financial ride—until something happens. His grandma would tell him, "David, when the going gets tough, the tough have cash." Cash is king for all sorts of reasons, and the combination of a rainy-day fund plus long-term investments should lighten any heart.

Pay it off early

If you really want to be a millionaire, Bach says, you need do just three things:

> *(1) decide to Pay Yourself First 10 per cent of what you earn, (2) Make it Automatic, and (3) buy a home and pay it off early.*

He offers various secrets for paying off your home loan much more quickly than the normal 25 or 30 years, thus saving yourself a fortune in interest. One way is to pay an extra 10 percent on top of your normal monthly repayment. If, for instance, your monthly repayment is $1,834, you pay the bank $2,017 instead (not a great difference). This will end up shaving off around $129,000 over the life of your mortgage.

Tithe automatically

Bach notes that we think that money will make us feel good, but in fact it is having meaning in your life that makes you feel good. Tithing, or giving away 10 percent of what you earn, is common to many cultures. You can make it more or less than 10 percent, but the main thing is to feel joy in giving. Doing so reminds you that you are a person who can give, and who is blessed with the ability to make more. It is your way of saying thanks to the universe.

However, as with paying yourself, make your tithing automatic. Make sure that the organization you are giving money to is officially a charity and you will also get tax benefits on what you contribute.

Final comments

The Automatic Millionaire shows that there is another way out of the rat race other than creating wealth through your own business. You can stay in your job and amass wealth slowly through automatic saving, the effect of compounding over time, and tax rules that benefit "those who help themselves." Indeed, what Bach learned from his exemplary couple the McIntyres is: "how much you earn has almost no bearing on whether or not you can and will build wealth." With a sufficient degree of diversification in your investments (even if you put all your money into one diversified fund), the regularity and long timescale of the Bach way mean that nasty surprises in the stock or real-estate markets affect you less. Your attainment of wealth becomes an inevitability, not just a hope.

The concepts in *The Automatic Millionaire* may not be exciting (as Bach notes, "Managing your money should be boring") and are certainly not original—any reader of George Clason's classic *The Richest Man in Babylon* will be familiar with the concept of paying yourself first—but they make up for it in terms of clarity and certainty. Though Bach had written books before, this one was his breakthrough work, selling a million copies. *Smart Couples Finish Rich* and *Smart Women Finish Rich* may be "better" books from a critical point of view, but *The Automatic Millionaire* is powerful because it is so simple.

David Bach

Before becoming a high-profile personal finance guru, Bach was a senior vice-president at financial services firm Morgan Stanley and ran the Bach Group, which invested money for wealthy individuals.

His company FinishRich media presents "Finish Rich" seminars across America, he is a keynote speaker for corporate events, and he has appeared as a guest money coach on many US television shows, including Oprah.

Other books, of which there are five million copies in print, include Smart Women Finish Rich *(1999),* Smart Couples Finish Rich *(2001),* Start Late, Finish Rich *(2005), and* The Automatic Millionaire Homeowner *(2006).*

1880

The Art of Money Getting

"The foundation of success in life is good health: that is the substratum of fortune; it is also the basis of happiness. A person cannot accumulate a fortune very well when he is sick."

"We are all, no doubt, born for a wise purpose. There is as much diversity in our brains as in our countenances. Some are born natural mechanics, while some have great aversion to machinery... Unless a man enters upon the vocation intended for him by nature, and best suited to his peculiar genius, he cannot succeed."

"The possession of a perfect knowledge of your business is an absolute necessity in order to insure success."

In a nutshell

There are no shortcuts to wealth, aside from right vocation, good character, and perseverance—and don't forget to advertise.

In a similar vein

Mark Victor Hansen & Robert G. Allen *The One Minute Millionaire* (p 140)
Marsha Sinetar *Do What You Love, the Money Will Follow* (p 254)
Donald Trump *The Art of the Deal* (p 272)

CHAPTER 4

P. T. Barnum

P. T. Barnum was possibly the greatest showman who ever lived, famous for his circuses and museums of "curiosities." He is also considered a master of promotion whose ideas are still studied by marketers today.

Barnum's autobiography tells his colorful story, but it is *The Art of Money Getting or Golden Rules of Making Money* that offers a recipe book for prosperity. Consistent with a great marketer, the title is a slight exaggeration of the content. There are, in fact, no detailed ideas or techniques for getting rich. Instead, the author provides 20 rules for personal success and the development of good character that, indirectly, will make a person's financial rise almost inevitable.

Health and wealth

Barnum draws attention to something that is obvious on the face of it, yet is so often overlooked: You need to have good health in order to be successful. The pursuit of riches requires physical and mental gusto. If you are successful and wish to remain so, you ignore the laws of health at your peril.

Barnum himself once smoked ten to fifteen cigars a day and in the book goes on the offensive against the "filthy weed" tobacco. However, he reserves his greatest attack for alcohol:

> *To make money, requires a clear brain. A man has got to see that two and two make four; he must lay all his plans with reflection and forethought, and closely examine all the details and the ins and outs of business... if the brain is muddled, and his judgment warped by intoxicating drinks, it is impossible for him to carry on business successfully. How many good opportunities have passed, never to return, while a man was sipping a 'social glass,' with his friend!*

Recalling the phrase "wine is a mocker," Barnum notes the way alcohol initially flatters the drinker into feeling omnipotent, then drains them of vital energy. There is also the sheer amount of time wasted when they could be building a business.

Choose the right career in the right location

Barnum notes that in a country like the United States, which has "more land than people," anyone who properly applies themselves can make money. There is room for good people in any vocation—but you have to make sure you choose the right one.

In emphasizing the importance of choosing a career that you love, Barnum was perhaps ahead of his time. He goes as far as saying that selecting a vocation on the basis that it was "congenial to [your] tastes" was the surest way to success for a young person. We are all born for some purpose, he opines, and the extraordinary differences between us suggest that people were made to do some things and not others.

Yet Barnum explains that it is not enough just to do the work you love. You must be careful *where* you do it:

> *You might conduct a hotel like clock-work, and provide satisfactorily for five hundred guests every day; yet, if you should locate your house in a small village where there is no railroad communication or public travel, the location would be your ruin.*

He refers to a man he met running a museum of curiosities in London. The man was good at what he did, but was not attracting much custom. Barnum suggested he move to the United States where his show would find more enthusiastic audiences. The man duly did, working first for two years in Barnum's New York Museum and then establishing his own "traveling show business." Some years later, Barnum reported, the man was rich, "simply because he selected the right vocation and also secured the proper location."

Persistence

Sheer persistence is often the difference between someone who succeeds and someone who fails. We all experience the "horrors" or the "blues," as Barnum phrases it, but you must be determined to shake them off and keep your eyes on your goals. "How many," he wonders, "have almost reached the goal of their ambition, but, losing faith in themselves, have relaxed their energies, and the golden prize has been lost forever."

Don't waste your time waiting for something to "turn up." People who do this, Barnum notes, often "turn up" in a poorhouse or a jail. When you see an opportunity, seize it and do the work needed to make it succeed. Remember the words of Solomon in the Bible: "He becometh poor that dealeth with a slack hand; but the hand of the diligent maketh rich."

It is a cliché to say that whatever is worth doing at all is worth doing well, but Barnum observes that many a man acquires a fortune by doing his business thoroughly, while his neighbor remains poor for life, because he only half does it.

Stick to your business, master your field

Many people scatter their powers, Barnum notes, when dedication to a single task would have seen them succeed: "A constant hammering on one nail will generally drive it home at last." When you are focused on one thing only, you will soon see ways in which it can be improved and made more valuable. While it is tempting to have "many irons in the fire," a lot of fortunes have passed people by because they cast themselves too wide and not deeply enough. Barnum quotes a maxim from the founding member of the famous Rothschild banking family: "Be both cautious and bold." At first glance a paradox, this simply means being very careful in the making of your plans, but once you have made them do not hold back on their execution.

No one succeeds, Barnum asserts, without knowing their field inside out. His reflection on his nineteenth-century countrymen could be applied to people in any time and place:

As a nation, Americans are too superficial—they are striving to get rich quickly, and do not generally do their business as substantially and thoroughly as they should, but whoever excels all others in his own line, if his habits are good and his integrity undoubted, cannot fail to secure abundant patronage, and the wealth that naturally follows.

Learn your own lessons

Even in Barnum's time most successful businesspeople were self-made, and the same is true today. He warned not to depend too much on other people's capital, particularly inheritances. If anything, this "easy money" will hold you back.

It may be convenient to be given or to borrow a load of money to start a business, but as Barnum notes, "Money is good for nothing unless you know the value of it by experience." The tycoon John Jacob Astor commented that it was more difficult for him to make his first thousand dollars than it was to accrue all his succeeding millions. But the lessons learned in creating the initial capital—self-denial, industry, perseverance, and patience—were priceless.

Barnum recalls what the proverbial old Quaker farmer said to his son, "Never get trusted [i.e. lent money]; but if thee gets trusted for anything, let it be for 'manure,' because that will help thee pay it back again." Going into debt to buy land or raw materials is one thing, but beware of any kind of debt incurred for food, drink or clothing. Money, Barnum notes, is a great servant but a terrible master.

If it's good, tell people about it

You would expect the greatest showman of his time to give advice about promoting your wares, but his advice really applies to anyone in business:

When you get an article which you know is going to please your customers, and that when they have tried it, they will feel they have got their money's worth, then let the fact be known that you have got it. Be careful to advertise it in some shape or other because it is evident that if a man has ever so good an article for sale, and nobody knows it, it will bring him no return.

In short, if you have produced something good, make sure that the world knows about it.

Read a good newspaper

A person who does not read newspapers, Barnum says, is "cut off from his species." Even in Barnum's time there were rapid daily advances in terms of technologies and changes to industries, and that is all the more so now. To succeed in any field you have to know what is happening.

Final comments

Though the examples given are typical of the pen of a nineteenth-century American, with glowing mentions of the rich and famous of his day, *The Art of Money Getting* is remarkably relevant for anyone wanting to make the most of their talents and chances in life today.

Contrary to the image of Barnum as an over-the-top impresario, this book is actually a solid success manual. Some of the points may seem obvious, but it does not hurt to be reminded of them, especially the idea that personal virtue is the foundation of wealth. Without honesty and reputation, fortunes can disappear overnight; with these things, an enterprise or a service can create prosperity for all involved. Barnum himself saw both setbacks and triumphs in his career, but he never actually uttered the remark famously attributed to him, "There's a sucker born every minute" (it was a competitor). If this really had been his attitude, according to his own rules he would not have become so well established or so wealthy. It should not be a surprise that the Rothschilds are mentioned twice in the book, a family who built a fortune not on taking advantage but on trust.

The Art of Money Getting is short because it was essentially a speech Barnum often gave on the public speaking circuit. It is in the public domain and can be downloaded free from the internet.

P.T. Barnum

Phineas Taylor Barnum was born in Bethel, Connecticut, in 1810, the oldest of five children. His father ran an inn and a store. Barnum displayed early business sense, and by the age of 12 had done well from selling lottery tickets. However, his father died when Barnum was 15, and for the next few years he had to try his hand at a range of enterprises, including running a newspaper.

After moving to New York City in 1834, he discovered his calling in the "show business." He established a popular show whose main draw was Joice Heth, a black ex-slavewoman who was promoted as being 160 years old and the nurse of a baby George Washington. In 1841 Barnum bought an existing museum that became Barnum's American Museum; its natural history exhibits, memorabilia, and oddities entertained and educated millions. It burned to the ground in 1865. A new museum was built three years later, but was also razed by fire.

Barnum was 60 by the time he moved into circuses. His Grand Traveling Museum, Menagerie, Caravan, and Circus (also known as "The Greatest Show on Earth") covered five acres and toured America. He is also remembered for bringing Swedish opera star Jenny Lind to the US. Despite paying her $1,000 a night, Barnum made a large profit on the tour.

In later years he turned to politics, being elected to the Connecticut legislature in 1865 and serving two terms, fighting unsuccessfully for a seat in Congress, and in 1875 becoming mayor of Bridgeport, Connecticut. He died in 1891.

Barnum's books include The Life of P.T. Barnum: Written by Himself *(1854, with later revisions),* The Humbugs of the World *(1865), and* Struggles and Triumphs *(1869). He intentionally put his autobiography into the public domain, and by the end of the nineteenth century it was said to be second only to the New Testament in terms of copies in print.*

1921

Your Invisible Power

"There is nothing unusual or mysterious in the idea of your pictured desire coming into material evidence. It is the working of a universal, natural Law... Everything in the whole world, from the hat on your head to the boots on your feet, has its beginning in mind and comes into existence in exactly the same manner. All are projected thoughts, solidified."

"Once a thing seems normal to you, it is as surely yours, through the Law of growth and attraction, as it is yours to know addition after you have learned the use of figures."

"On previous occasions, when making my mental picture, I had felt that I was waking up something within myself. This time there was no sensation of effort. I simply counted over the twenty thousand dollars. Then, in a most unexpected manner, from a source of which I had no consciousness at the time, there seemed to open a possible avenue through which the money might reach me."

In a nutshell

What we visualize tends to come into being. Use this invisible but logical power to turn any desire into reality.

In a similar vein

Rhonda Byrne *The Secret* (p 58)
Charles Fillmore *Prosperity* (p 98)
Esther Hicks & Jerry Hicks *Ask and It Is Given* (p 152)
Catherine Ponder *Open Your Mind to Prosperity* (p 218)

CHAPTER 5

Genevieve Behrend

The older prosperity manuals are often the best, and Genevieve Behrend's writings provide a charming entry point to the genre. It is fascinating to sit down with *Your Invisible Power* after reading contemporary manifestation and "law of attraction" books like *The Secret* and *Ask and It Is Given*, as you realize that many of their ideas are not new, with Behrend having studied and written about this material 80 years previously.

Behrend was the only known pupil of Thomas Troward (1847–1916), a former judge in the Punjab of British India who in his spare time had studied the world's sacred books and become a metaphysical philosopher. He was a master, according to Behrend, of "the laws governing the relation between the individual and the Universal Mind." In addition to his celebrated Edinburgh lectures, highly praised by philosopher William James, Troward is best known for his book *The Creative Process in the Individual*, which argues that the fulfillment of our individual personalities is vital for the evolution of the universe. His thinking was seminal in the emergence of the New Thought movement and Ernest Holmes' "Science of Mind."

Troward's work was not easy reading, however, and Behrend took it upon herself to simplify his ideas for a larger audience. In the manner of Florence Scovell Shinn (see commentary in *50 Success Classics*), who also lived in New York in the 1920s, Behrend's short book combines spiritual principles with anecdotes of her work to help people appreciate their abundant nature.

Compared to its modern counterparts, *Your Invisible Power* is more focused on visualization to achieve desires, and is also distinguished by its concept that every person is "God in miniature." In practical terms, this means that when you have feelings of lack, you have just forgotten your connection to "Divine abundance."

Create order through visualization

Behrend's first point is that visualization actually brings order to your mind. The universe, and the Mind behind it, is perfectly ordered, and your use of vivid imagination allows this order to be expressed.

We only have airplanes and telephones, she notes, because someone first imagined that such things should exist. All great advances are a triumph of principle over current circumstances or "reality." Reality is a blurry concept when you consider that all things are first created in the mind; at the moment of their imagining they are already part real.

When the Wright brothers were designing and experimenting with their flying machines, these early craft were just the current expression of a perfect image of flight already created. After each failure, it is said that one brother would say to the other, "It's all right, Brother, I can see myself riding in that machine, and it travels easily and steadily." With such strong images always in front of them, their success in creating the first workable airplane took on an air of inevitability.

As Behrend puts it, "In visualizing, or making a mental picture, you are not endeavoring to change the laws of Nature. You are fulfilling them." A strong mental image summons the "mysterious but unfailing law of attraction," which allows things to manifest according to what you have imagined.

Exploit the power of strong images

Behrend notes, "Everyone visualizes, whether he knows it or not." We all create our futures first in the mind before they are played out in physical reality. This creates the wonderful opportunity of being able to choose those images.

There is nothing weird or strange about the process. The laws of visualization, attraction, and manifestation are the natural way everything is created. As examples, she mentions railway magnate James J. Hill, whose railroad stretching from one coast of America to the other was built in his mind years before the first track was actually laid; and the millionaire Australian grazier James Tyson, who made the deserts "blossom as the rose." Even when he was working for a few shillings a day as a bushman, she notes, he "simply kept his thought centered upon the idea of making fences and seeing flowers and grass where none existed at that time."

Yet what Hill and Tyson did we all do to achieve a goal. The image of what you want is strong enough to pull you into action. Behrend refers to a rather beautiful statement from St. Paul in the Bible to sum up what she is saying: "The worlds were formed by the word of God. Things which are seen are not made of things which do appear."

Expressions of divine abundance

The Great Architect of the Universe contemplated Himself as manifesting through his polar opposite—matter.

Behrend goes to some lengths to explain the theology behind what she describes as the "law of attraction." As the above quote indicates, there is a Creative Power, Universal Mind, or God that generates the universe and that, for completion's sake, likes to see thought manifested in physical form. Human beings are like the Creative Power in miniature, also able to turn thoughts into reality, literally to make our own worlds in the same way that God has total command over the universe.

Human beings exist so that the Universal Mind can be differentiated, expressed in an endless variety of personalities. Therefore, by visualizing and then bringing something into form, you are fulfilling God's will for you to be unique and powerful. You fulfill your personality by creating something out of nothing.

Behrend notes that some people feel that it is "too material" and not spiritual enough to visualize things that you want to happen. Yet the deliberate manifesting of what you want is exactly what God intended for you to do. God creates with total ease and joy; so should you.

Manifest money

People visited Behrend at her New York rooms. Some wanted to manifest money, others sought to be healed in some way. Many were desperate. Some were about to lose their business, others' wives had left them. Behrend would calmly assert to each that they had not been separated from their "good"; that this was only an illusion. To bring back their happiness or wellbeing, what they first had to do was reconnect to the "Universal Substance" or God.

Behrend recalls a man who was about to lose the beloved home where he had grown up in the American South. Creditors were about to foreclose and he did not know what to do. She quietly affirmed to him that the same Universal Power that brought him into the world "did so for the purpose of expressing its limitless supply through him." Nothing could cut him off from this Source, and the feeling of lack he was experiencing had no truth. She told him, "Infinite substance is manifesting in you right now."

The following week, just before she was about to deliver a lecture, Behrend received a message from the man. Money had come through in a miraculous way, and he had been able to telegraph an amount sufficient to pay off the mortgage. "Please tell the people this afternoon," he wrote, "about this wonderful Power."

You may feel ashamed to ask for what you want, but in these moments remember Behrend's idea that you are simply a smaller version of the Universal Mind or God. It is your nature to constantly desire and bring into being new things. Therefore, she writes, "Do not fear to be your true self, for everything you want, wants you."

How Behrend manifested $20,000

People often asked Behrend what led her to study "mental science" and the laws of prosperity. She always welcomed these inquiries, since she believed that a person who claimed to know psychological truths should have first tested them on themselves.

After her husband died she was bereft, but had been left enough money to live on. She wandered the world, but without inner contentment or direction. She studied Christian Science for a while, and even met Mary Baker Eddy, the movement's founder, but did not stick with it. A friend invited her to meet Abdul Baha, the seer and son of the founder of the Baha'i faith, who told her that she would "travel the world over seeking the truth, and when [she] had found it, would speak it out."

Her ephiphany came she discovered a book containing Troward's lectures. In her state of mind she immediately fell on a certain passage, which promised that, because each person's mind is "a center of the Divine Mind," we can experience contentment and perpetual growth in the manner of God. At that point Behrend resolved to study with Troward, but realized she would need more money than she possessed to do so. She was then in New York and Troward was in Cornwall, England.

Behrend began a visualization routine every night and morning of counting out twenty $1,000 bills, and seeing herself buying her ticket to London, traveling on the ship, and being accepted as Troward's pupil. She constantly affirmed to herself "My mind is a center of Divine operations," yet did not think about how she would actually get the money (she had no idea; it seemed such a large amount). Instead, she would "let the power of attraction find its own ways and means."

Thanks to this work in faith and visualization the money did materialize, coming from a source she would never have thought of. In only about six weeks, it had gone from being an image in her mind to the reality of her bank account.

You will have to get the book to find out how Behrend did actually come to be Troward's pupil; it is a long story that involves solving a cryptic line from the Bible and a Parisian astrologer.

Believe you already have it

Reflecting on the achievement of her aim, Behrend recalls the Biblical promise, "All things whatsoever thou wilt, believe thou hast received, and thou shalt receive." That is, when the idea of receiving something becomes quite normal to you, it will happen as surely as night follows day.

Anticipating readers' doubts, she asks: How you can proclaim faith in something when you do not have that faith? In such times, she says, you have to recall and observe what faith does. Recall your state of mind when you simply had to bring something into being—and you did—and create that state of mind again. She observes:

> *Your inhibition of all doubt and anxiety enables the reassuring ideas to establish themselves and attract to themselves "I can" and "I will" ideas, which gradually grow into the physical form of the desire in your mind.*

By deliberately choosing positive thoughts, you set in train the attraction of more "can do" thoughts, which can only result in positive, powerful action. The clarity of what you are visualizing, combined with your relaxed faith, makes you more open to receive the ideas and opportunities you need to achieve your goal. At the end of the book Behrend provides suggestions on "How to Pray or Ask." All these suggestions follow the idea of "Ask, believing you have already received, and you shall receive."

Final comments

The critical view of books like *Your Invisible Power*, even more so their modern equivalents, is that they pander to our materialistic side. Is it really a good use of our visualizing powers, for instance, to manifest a new BMW? This, however, would be missing the point. What you ask for is not really important in the larger scheme of things; much more significant is the discovery that you are a "co-creator" in this universe, able to bring almost anything into being if you develop a relaxed belief in its coming. With this knowledge you can never be a victim of circumstances, but rather a center of power.

Some readers will feel that *Your Invisible Power* has too much spiritual mumbo-jumbo in it, but this simply reflects Behrend's efforts to convey Troward's complex theology. A Christian who had a major influence on the development of Mental Science, his thinking was in fact based squarely on reason, and he resolutely opposed any kind of occult learning. The goal of Behrend's writing was to help people develop a "magnetic mind" that can draw desired things or circumstances to them. Whether you choose to believe that these processes are purely physiological or involve spiritual forces is up to you. What matters more is whether they work, and you won't know if they do until you try them in your own life.

Genevieve Behrend

Born in 1881, information is scant on Behrend's early life except that she was a native of Paris and one of her parents was Scottish.

Between 1912 and 1914 she immersed herself in Troward's teachings, and on her return to New York City she established the "School of the Builders," lectured, and gave advice to people in need. She later established another school in Los Angeles, lectured widely on Mental Science, and became well known through radio broadcasts. She died in 1960.

Behrend's other book is Attaining Your Heart's Desire *(1929).*

2007

The Little Book of Common Sense Investing

"Successful investing is all about common sense... Simple arithmetic suggests, and history confirms, that the winning strategy is to own all of the nation's publicly held businesses at very low cost. By doing so you are guaranteed to capture almost the entire return that they generated in the form of dividends and earning growth."

"[The] stock market is a giant distraction that causes investors to focus on transitory and volatile investment expectations rather than on what is really important—the gradual accumulation of the returns earned by corporate business."

In a nutshell

If you invest in stocks at all, put your money in a fund that automatically owns a little bit of every company listed. Over time, it is a sure and almost worry-free way to accumulate wealth.

In a similar vein

Warren Buffett *The Essays of Warren Buffett* (edited by Lawrence Cunningham; p 46)
Benjamin Graham *The Intelligent Investor* (p 134)
Peter Lynch *One Up on Wall Street* (p 186)

CHAPTER 6

John C. Bogle

Despite his tremendous wealth, along with Warren Buffett John Bogle is something of a financial maverick. He made his name as the founder, in 1976, of the first ever stock market index fund, the Vanguard 500, which he grew to be the second largest fund provider in the world. In 2004, *Time* magazine included him as one of the "world's 100 most powerful and influential people," and in 1999 *Fortune* named him one of four "Giants of the 20th century" in the investing field.

So what is an index fund? Essentially baskets of all the major stocks listed in a certain market, these funds usually track an established index such as the Standard & Poor's 500 (S&P 500, established 1926), comprising the 500 largest corporations in America, or the Dow Jones Wilshire index, which takes in close to 5,000 stocks.

Traditional index funds never do any trading, or buying and selling of stocks, as regular managed funds do, but simply buy once and keep. This can make them seem very boring. However, the lack of trading excitement is easily made up for by their remarkably good long-term records. Investing is really about common sense, and the basic arithmetic in support of index fund investing, Bogle asserts, is irresistible. They make the apparently complex world of finance simple, and the case for them is "compelling and unarguable," he says.

As we would all like as much certainty as possible when investing in stocks, *The Little Book of Common Sense Investing* makes intriguing reading.

Who are you making rich?

For the average punter, Bogle says, the stock market is a loser's game. Why? First, we have a misplaced faith in financial experts, who not only do no better than we collectively do ourselves but often perform worse; secondly, we do not realize the huge eroding effect on our funds of money managers' fees and the tax inefficiency of their way of operating. Those who always win are the "financial croupiers"—brokers, investment bankers, money managers, and so on who rake in over $400 billion a year. As Bogle puts in, in a casino "the house always wins."

Thanks to speculation, returns from the stock market vary greatly, much more so than the output of the economy itself, but the costs of investing stubbornly remain. You do not pay lower fees to your fund managers when they have a bad year or decade. We naturally like to think of the compounding increase in the value of stocks we hold, but we often don't understand the compounding of investment costs (fund joining and operating fees, taxes levied on transactions, and so on). Mutual fund fees range from 0.9 percent of assets to 3 percent, with an average of 2.1 percent. While these do not appear high at the beginning (1.5 percent of $100,000, for instance, does not seem exorbitant), over time these costs can erode a potential fortune.

Bogle provides some further facts. Between 1980 and 2005 the US stock market averaged a return of 12.5 percent a year. In the same period, the average mutual fund only returned 10 percent, thanks to costs of 2.5 percent. Index funds, in contrast, have costs averaging only 0.2 percent. You can imagine what the difference in costs makes over the long run: In that 25-year period, a $10,000 investment in the S&P 500 directly or an index fund tracking it would have grown to $170,800. The same money in a managed mutual fund would have come to only $98,200. That is a huge difference, thanks in no small measure to the difference in costs.

Apart from the cost difference, how does the actual performance of regular funds and index funds compare? In the period 1995–2005, index funds returned a compound profit of 194 percent, while managed mutual funds returned only 154 percent. Again, a massive difference.

Stay still and prosper

You may think that your mutual fund is expertly turning over stocks frequently to make the most of your money, but in doing so it is also spending your money, because each transaction has costs both in terms of taxes and management. You can be sure that someone is getting paid a lot for calling the buys and sells. To justify their fees, fund managers have to be seen to be "doing something," but as Warren Buffett has observed, "For investors as a whole, returns decrease as motion increases."

Because index funds invest automatically across the board, they do not need layers of analysts or managers. As they do not trade but simply buy and hold, they avoid all the usual costs built up by frequent transactions. The longer you hold, the less risk there is, because you have left speculation (with all its costs and fluctuations of fortune) behind and have become an owner of businesses. Bogle's recipe is very simple: "[Once] you have bought your stocks, get out of the casino and stay out."

Invest in capitalism, not in the casino

Stock market investors can easily forget that they are investing in the ingenuity, innovation, and productive power of companies, which in America over the last 100 years have enjoyed a 9.5 percent return on their capital. When you compound this rate of return over many years, you get astounding results. Over a decade, a dollar invested becomes $2.48, over two decades $6.14, three decades $15.22, four decades $37.72, and over five decades $93.48—from a single dollar. Of course, you have to adjust this for inflation, which significantly reduces the purchasing power of your money decades hence, but over an investment span of 30 years, for example, an investment of $100,000 in corporate America through an index fund would still become worth over $660,000 in current real (spending power) terms.

Bogle notes that the gains of the stock market, measured over time, almost exactly match the gains made by American business itself. The average return on stocks is 9.6 percent, while return on capital invested directly into businesses averages 9.5 percent. He observes that, "in the long run, stock returns depend almost entirely on the reality of the investment returns earned by our corporations." The stock market may overvalue companies for as long as a decade, then the next decade might undervalue them. But there is always "reversion to the mean," with the underlying worth of the companies behind the stocks being revealed.

Bogle asserts that the stock market is a "giant distraction," Shakespeare's proverbial "tale told by an idiot, full of sound and fury, signifying nothing." Driven in the short term by emotions, thanks to this irrationality no one can ever know for sure which way they will turn. It is a fool's game to try to guess. However, you can be surprisingly sure about the long-term productivity of business, and by avoiding the game of "picking winners" and simply investing in the whole stock market, you know you will reap the results of business growth. Bogle recalls investor Benjamin Graham's analogy: "In the short run the stock market is a voting machine... [but] in the long run it is a weighing machine."

Bet on the numbers, not on people

Bogle's question is: Why are people paying *more* money for a way of investing that has *worse* returns?

Unfortunately, most of us do not know any better. We are advised to invest in managed funds under the illusion that there are some "star funds" or "star managers" who will earn us great returns. However, even when some funds do better than others, their performance is almost never maintained (just as you can't maintain a win on the horses for ever). Great returns, as Burton Malkiel pointed out in his book *A Random Walk Down Wall Street*, are often sheer luck. We are stupid enough to invest based on past performance, which is not only no guarantee of future performance, but almost predicts future worse performance.

Fund managers are human beings and get excited by the direction markets seem to be taking. Like anyone, they have a tendency to buy stocks at their peak and not buy them when they represent best value. There is none of this risk entailed in having a stake in an index fund that automatically tracks the market overall.

In the long term, all gains and losses in the stock market are balanced. It is a zero-sum game. However, if you invest in the game overall, you will win. As Bogle expresses it: "Don't look for the needle—buy the haystack."

The secret's out

As the founder of the world's first index fund, Bogle of course has a vested interest in promoting this type of investing, but he supplies plenty of evidence (placed in boxes headed "Don't take my word for it") from academics and major figures in the finance world to support his case. These include:

- Peter Lynch, legendary manager of the Fidelity Magellan Fund, noted in *Barron's* magazine that mutual fund performance was getting worse, and that "The public would be better off in an index fund."
- Mark Hulbert, editor of the *Hulbert Financial Digest*, wrote: "You can outperform more than 80 percent of your fellow investors over the next several decades simply by investing in an index fund—and doing nothing else."
- The *Economist* magazine noted that managed funds "charge their clients big fees for the privilege of losing their money."
- Warren Buffett's partner in Berkshire Hathaway, Charlie Munger, is quoted as saying: "The poor guy in the general public is getting a terrible product from the professionals."
- Tyler Mathisen, editor of *Money* magazine, having been critical of "boring" index funds like Bogle's, has admitted he was wrong: "Gunning for average is your best shot at finishing above average... Indexing should form the core of most investors' fund portfolios."

Final comments

Bogle describes the shift to put money in index funds as a "revolution." Indeed, what he says undermines the whole edifice of modern equity finance, based as it is on the belief that you can "pick winners," and that you must pay people a lot of money for their expertise. For many years his strategy made Bogle a lone voice. It was 1984 before a second index fund started up after his own, yet now there are around 580 in the United States alone. Some, ironically, are "managed index funds," which means that they choose stocks in only some industry sectors that pay more dividends or may grow more quickly, and therefore try to beat the market. Bogle takes a dim view of them, as they significantly increase costs and risk compared to a traditional index fund. He also predicts that returns on stocks will be subdued in the years ahead, which is another reason to stick with traditional indexers, since managed funds will keep charging the same costs whether they do well or not.

With 18 chapters and over 200 pages, *The Little Book of Common Sense Investing* is not that little and can seem repetitive—but in a way that affirms rather than annoys. Reading it is like having a fireside chat with one of the masters of investing, except that you may not be able to sleep having listened to his powerful message. His detractors, he notes, have said that the only thing going for him is his ability to state the obvious, but in a financial world of promotion and chicanery, perhaps putting your trust in the "relentless arithmetic" of index fund investing is the smartest thing you can do.

Though the book is about the American market, if you live outside the US there is likely to be a choice of index funds operating in your part of the world. Wherever you are, the principle remains the same: In stock investing, avoid the complex and instead "profit from the magic of simplicity."

John C. Bogle

Born in 1929 in Verona, New Jersey, Bogle graduated from Blair Academy before attending Princeton University, where in 1951 he received an economics degree. After graduating he began working at the Wellington Management Company in Pennsylvania. He rose to become chairman of that company, and in 1974 left to start Vanguard.

Other books include Common Sense on Mutual Funds *(1993),* John Bogle on Investing *(2000), and* The Battle for the Soul of Capitalism *(2005), which argues for higher ethical standards in American finance.* The Little Book of Common Sense Investing *is dedicated to Paul Samuelson, an economist and Bogle's mentor at Princeton. See also* John Bogle and the Vanguard Experiment: One Man's Quest to Transform the Mutual Fund Industry, *by Robert Slater (1996), and* The Bogleheads' Guide to Investing *by Taylor Larimore, Mel Lindauer, and Michael LeBoeuf (2006).*

Bogle and his wife Eve live in Valley Forge, Pennsylvania.

2002

Losing My Virginity

"...you're trying to create something that is original, that stands out from the crowd, that will last and, hopefully, serve some useful purpose. Above all, you want to create something you are proud of. That has always been my philosophy of business. I can honestly say that I have never gone into any business to make money."

"I may be a businessman, in that I set up and run companies for profit, but, when I try to plan ahead and dream up new products and new companies, I'm an idealist."

In a nutshell

Don't be afraid to be different. On entering any new field or an industry, aim to really shake it up and provide new value.

In a similar vein

Felix Dennis *How to Get Rich* (p 68)
Peter Drucker *Innovation and Entrepreneurship* (p 80)
Conrad Hilton *Be My Guest* (p 164)
Anita Roddick *Business as Unusual* (p 238)
Howard Schultz *Pour Your Heart into It* (p 248)

CHAPTER 7

Richard Branson

Everyone knows who Richard Branson is: the entrepreneur famous for the Virgin brand name, the adventurer who has crossed oceans in a hot air balloon, and, more recently, the philanthropist knighted by the Queen of England.

What most of us know about Branson comes from snippets on television and newspaper articles, but there is a reality behind the image that only a good autobiography reveals. There are hundreds of "how I did it" stories by well-known businesspeople, but *Losing My Virginity* is one of the best. This is thanks to the rich material Branson has to draw from (he is an inveterate note taker and diarist, and his scribblings over a 25-year period enabled the book to be written), but also because he manages to avoid self-aggrandizement.

This commentary covers the 572-page updated 2002 edition, which, whether you are an aspiring entrepreneur or not, is a fantastic read. The book demonstrates that being different is not an obstacle, but almost a requirement, in achieving prosperity.

"You will either go to prison or become a millionaire" (1)

Born in 1950, Branson enjoyed a happy childhood, with parents who considered their children equals and who often set challenges to make them self-reliant. Though decidedly upper middle class, the family never had a great deal of money, and Branson's mother was always thinking up ways to earn extra income from cottage industries in the garage.

At the private school he attended, Stowe, Branson was considered a bit slow and lazy. He was in fact dyslexic and admits that by age 8 he still couldn't read and was hopeless at maths and sciences. As British schools glorify sportspeople, he channeled his energies into doing well on the field. When he left school the headmaster said to him, "You will either go to prison or become a millionaire."

Branson's first entrepreneurial success was a national magazine for students, which included interviews with Mick Jagger and John Lennon. He admits he did not go into the venture to make money, more as a fun enterprise. In fact it did not make money, but was kept going with the help of his friends and a bit of advertising.

Branson's clique were all obsessed with music, and he hit on the idea of selling records cheaply through mail order, particularly ones that were not stocked in the high-street stores. The business mushroomed, but a postal strike made Branson realize how vulnerable it all was. He began looking around for a retail space.

"You will either go to prison or become a millionaire" (2)

The first Virgin record store became a hangout for young people, and was the first to cater for the youth market exclusively. Many more stores followed around Britain.

The early days of Virgin were anything but regular. The business was run not from office quarters but basements, church crypts, and houseboats, with plenty of hangers-on helping out, only some of whom were earning the standard Virgin salary of £20 a week. Branson never obeyed the business rule not to work with your friends; most of the Virgin inner circle for the first 15 years were people who had grown up with him. Though there were inevitably fallings out, this accidental management strategy was remarkably effective.

In an atmosphere of free love and plenty of drugs, someone had to be getting up early and worrying about paying the invoices and salaries, and Branson was unusual in his coterie for not indulging much, preferring instead "to have a great time and keep my wits about me." Behind the barefooted, long-haired hippy was a businessman who wanted to make a difference.

Though his chain of record shops was growing, with all the overheads it was actually losing money. Branson accidentally reached a solution to the problems that would almost fulfill the bad part of his headmaster's prophecy. He began buying records wholesale, saying they were to be sold in Belgium and thus escaping hefty UK domestic sales duties. After three trips taking the records across the English Channel to imaginary buyers, which he then sold at great profit back in the Virgin stores, his activities were discovered by Customs and Excise. To escape jail Branson had to pay back three times the amount that he had not paid in duties (£60,000 in 1971, a great deal of money). Under tremendous pressure he somehow met the payments from store earnings, but the experience burned him and he resolved never to do anything approaching illegality again. Barely 21, he was growing up fast.

Entering the big time: Music

Fond of the idea of having his own record label whose acts could be promoted through the Virgin stores, Branson scraped together enough money to buy an old manor house in Oxfordshire, which he slowly converted into a recording studio.

The first act Virgin signed was an unusual choice. A young musician called Mike Oldfield had spent months perfecting a recording that had no vocals and lots of bells and other unusual instruments. This was a bizarre choice for what was intended as a rock music label, but it paid off. *Tubular Bells* was one of the biggest-selling albums of the 1970s and it bankrolled

Virgin's early years in the business. The label later attracted the Sex Pistols, Culture Club, Phil Collins, Human League, and other stars to its fold, and by the early 1980s had become a label to contend with. Branson had achieved his wish for a "vertically integrated" music company, in which the Virgin stores, including the famous Virgin Megastores, could promote the bands that Virgin Music had signed.

Entering the big time: Airlines

With his focus on the music industry, Branson had never considered starting an airline. But when he received a proposal to establish a transatlantic service to compete with British Airways, he could not resist. Against the better judgment of his advisers, he called Boeing in Seattle and negotiated to lease a 747 for a year, "just to see" if the whole idea would work. Virgin Atlantic was soon a reality, aiming to satisfy the demand that Laker Airways had tapped before British Airways had forced it out of business.

Virgin Atlantic almost never got off the ground. On the inaugural flight, a flock of birds flew into one of the uninsured engines, ruining it at a cost of £600,000. This brought the company over its overdraft and it came close to being bankrupted. Only an emergency recall of cash from Virgin Group's overseas operations got it through. Between 1984 and 1990 Virgin Atlantic remained tiny, with only a handful of planes.

The fuel price jump brought on by the first Gulf War was a major obstacle, as was the sudden loss of passengers after the events of September 11, 2001. Virgin also had to contend with a "dirty tricks" assault from British Airways, which saw the new airline as a threat that had to be crushed, whatever the means. As it soaked up more and more cash, Branson's bankers were losing patience and he was led to a painful realization: either sell Virgin Music and keep Virgin Atlantic flying; or lose the airline and leave the Virgin brand name in tatters, not to mention costing thousands of people their livelihood.

Again, in spite of the good advice of family and friends, Branson took the decision to sell Virgin Music, which he and his team had spent 20 years developing. It was a harrowing decision, particularly as he had just signed the Rolling Stones, marking the culmination of the label's rise. He had "lost his virginity." But the sale brought in £560 million, or $1 billion, and gave Branson the freedom to chart to course of the Virgin group of companies without bankers yapping at his heels. His share of the sale, he noted, gave him money "beyond his wildest dreams."

The Branson style

Branson notes that no matter what people may tell you, there is no "recipe" for business success that can be applied to any field. There is, however, a Branson style of doing business that might be instructive for the aspiring entrepreneur.

The secrets of his success can be boiled down to the following:

- Thinking big and taking calculated risks. He notes, "My interest in life comes from setting myself huge, apparently unachievable, challenges and trying to rise above them."
- Being less stressed than others by uncertainty.
- Trying to prove people wrong.
- Having the simple belief that "you can do it."

Branson's main criterion for entering a new market or industry is that it be fun. There has to be room to shake up stodgy markets and provide something new. Unfortunately, this often involves being the minnow trying to take on corporate whales.

During the war with British Airways, there were many rumors that Virgin Atlantic was about to go bankrupt. At one point it owed £55 million to various banks and Branson had to do a tremendous juggling act to keep things afloat. He writes, "It sometimes seems to me that I have spent all my life trying to persuade bankers to extend their loans." Since the Virgin Group has always reinvested profits back into its businesses, it has never had a cash cushion like established corporations, so there was always the danger of the money running out. Every record deal Branson made seemed like putting the company on the line, and it was only in the mid-1990s that he could relax a little.

Branson's reflection on these difficult years provides good advice for anyone in business under financial pressure: "However tight things are, you still need to have the big picture at the forefront of your mind." Whenever he found himself in a difficult spot and his advisers suggested shrinking back a little and playing it safe, this was the point where he would actually go out on a limb.

Other insights include:

- Branson generally makes his mind up about people and new business proposals "within about 30 seconds." Though a business plan has to be good, he ultimately goes on gut instinct.
- He is not a fast talker or a great public speaker, and admits that it often takes him time to answer a question properly: "I hope that people will trust a slow, hesitant response more than a rapid, glib one."
- He hates criticizing people who work for him, and the lowest points of his working life have been when he has had to let people go. He always tries to get someone else to do this instead!
- He admits that many of his successes were not his own ideas (he did not even come up with the name Virgin). Despite the image of a lone entrepreneur, like any great company Virgin was really built by a core of trusted managers and advisers.

- Virgin has no huge corporate headquarters, but buys houses in British and American cities for staff to work from. Branson saw a lot of his two children when they were growing up because he literally worked from home. He and his wife Joan lived on a London houseboat until they were well into their 30s.

Final comments

What is amazing about Branson is the number of his achievements that have nothing to do with business. A large portion of the book, and some readers will feel the most exciting part, relates to his various efforts to break hot air ballooning and ocean powerboat world records. Why has he felt compelled to go off on such adventures (which have brought him close to death several times) when he is already someone—with his wealth, success, and happy family—who "has it all"? His answer is simply that it adds another dimension to his existence and makes him feel alive.

One of the interesting aspects of the book is the soul-searching that Branson undertook when he turned 40. Was he going to spend his life creating and building companies? Surely there was something more. For a time, he considered selling off his assets and going to university to study history. Today, however, he puts much of his nonwork energies into philanthropy. A friend of Nelson Mandela, Bill Clinton, and other luminaries, he has put time and money into helping people with HIV/AIDS, protecting African wildlife, seeking peace in Northern Ireland, and addressing global warming.

Yet it is through his companies that Branson has changed people's lives the most, continually seeking ways to deliver new value to the public, whether through low-cost flying, mobile phones, or cheaper credit cards. At the time of writing, Virgin Galactic is on track to be the first company to offer commercial passenger flights into space. This enterprise fulfills Branson's business criterion of only going into fields that are fun and exciting, yet where there is also money to be made. What could be a better definition of a prosperous life?

1997

The Essays of Warren Buffett

"We intend to continue our practice of working only with people whom we like and admire. This policy not only maximizes our chances for good results, it also ensures us an extraordinarily good time. On the other hand, working with people who cause your stomach to churn seems much like marrying for money—probably a bad idea under any circumstances, but absolute madness if you are rich."

In a nutshell

Don't invest in stocks, invest in the businesses behind them.

In a similar vein

John C. Bogle *The Little Book of Common Sense Investing* (p 40)
Benjamin Graham *The Intelligent Investor* (p 134)
Peter Lynch *One Up on Wall Street* (p 186)
Adam Smith *The Wealth of Nations* (p 260)

CHAPTER 8

Lawrence Cunningham

Currently the second richest person in the world after Bill Gates, Warren Buffett is also arguably the most successful investor of all time. Countless books have been written about him, but *The Essays of Warren Buffett* (edited by Lawrence Cunningham) is the only compendium of writings from the Sage of Omaha himself.

Cunningham's book is a carefully chosen selection of Buffett's famous annual letters to shareholders in Berkshire Hathaway, the fantastically profitable holding company that he has managed since the 1970s with partner Charlie Munger, achieving an average annual return of 25 percent over the last 25 years. Though it still owns large stakes in many publicly listed companies, it also buys outstanding private companies, which in 2006 had collective revenues of close to $100 billion.

Apart from a youthful apprenticeship with his mentor Benjamin Graham (see commentary p. 134) when he lived in New York, Buffett has always lived in Omaha, Nebraska, and his approach to investing is a long way from Wall Street in every sense. His letters to shareholders are eagerly anticipated because they contain many simple nuggets of wisdom, often delivered through amusing anecdotes or pithy sayings. (He once, for instance, ruefully apologized for the expense of maintaining a private jet, which he dubbed "The Indefensible.")

The following are some themes that emerge from his writings.

Look for underlying value

For Buffett, the key to winning in the stock market does not lie in predicting the market's direction, but in knowing the value of businesses, irrespective of their current quoted price. He criticizes investment advisers who waste their time making forecasts about the economy, when it is much more important to find good businesses that will remain good for years to come.

He also dismisses efficient market theory (EMT), which holds that there is no point analyzing and calculating the value of a business because the stock market, working with perfect efficiency, always reveals a company's value through its share price. In fact, he believes, prices only reflect value most of the time, and having total faith in them prevents people from actually trying to understand businesses. Buffett quotes Benjamin Graham: "In the short run, the market is a voting machine, but in the long run it is a weighing machine."

Stock-market prices for companies are driven by emotion, not truth, and the truth about a company lies in its operating results rather than its current stock price or its glossy forecasts. Berkshire often makes its best acquisitions when fear is at its highest or sentiment about the market at its lowest. For the investor in fundamentals, these are times to buy.

Markets are risky, good businesses are not

Buying stocks is generally seen to be about taking risks, but the Buffett way reduces risk to a bare minimum. Noting that many of his family members and close friends have invested the majority of their net worth in Berkshire Hathaway, he comments:

> *I've never believed in risking what my family and friends have and need in order to pursue what they don't have and don't need.*

There is no point in losing a night's sleep over a stock play just to gain a bit more. Better to be so sure about an investment that the ups and downs of its stock price will not worry you. You know the company's intrinsic worth and that the market will sooner or later recognize this. This is the essence of value investing.

Buffett famously does not invest in industries that he does not fully understand. He was widely criticized for not entering the technology stocks boom of the late 1990s, instead buying companies that produced boring things like paint, bricks, and carpets. His golden rule is to invest only in your "circle of competence," areas you know something about, where you can understand how a company makes its money. A quote from Thomas Watson of IBM sums up Buffett's philosophy: "I'm no genius. I'm smart in spots—but I stay around those spots." Like everyone else, he appreciates the growth to the economy that new ideas and technologies bring, but as an investor he notes:

> *our reaction to a fermenting industry is much like our attitude toward space exploration: We applaud the endeavor but prefer to skip the ride.*

Lessons for the small investor

Many other lessons for the small investor can be drawn from Buffett's essays, including:

- Invest only in companies whose earnings will surely be higher in the future than they are now.

- Look for companies that have a "durable competitive advantage." Even if their stock price goes up and down, this advantage will naturally see them outperform other stocks.
- When you do buy a stock, buy it for the long haul ("If you aren't willing to own a stock for ten years, don't even think about owning it for ten minutes.")

Buffett likes to invest in what he calls "the Inevitables," companies whose products will still be bought 10, 20, or 30 years from now, and whose brand is so famous it gives them the lion's share of a market. Berkshire Hathaway has had large holdings in Coca-Cola and Gillette for many years because although elements like distribution, manufacturing processes, and product innovation will evolve, people will still be drinking Coke and needing to shave for their investment lifetimes, and they will turn to the trusted names.

His attitude is: If you find a small number of companies with a strong competitive advantage and at reasonable prices, why diversify? Paradoxically, putting more of your money into a smaller number of carefully chosen stocks means that you can relax. In any given year, Berkshire Hathaway may make only a handful of investments in the stock market, sometimes none at all. Often, Buffett notes, the smartest investment move is inactivity:

> *Charlie and I decided long ago that in an investment lifetime it's too hard to make hundreds of smart decisions... Therefore, we adopted a strategy that required our being smart—and not too smart at that—only a very few times. Indeed, we'll now settle for one good idea a year. (Charlie says it's my turn.)*

Buying for keeps

Along with its investments in the stocks of large corporations, Berkshire Hathaway has bought many smaller companies outright, such as Borsheim's Fine Jewelry, See's Candies, and Nebraska Furniture Mart. These are often family enterprises lovingly built up over many years. The owners wish to realize some gains for all their hard work, yet do not want to sell to just anyone. When Berkshire Hathaway steps in everyone wins: The fund gets a fantastic business that will keep growing indefinitely, while the owners usually stay in place to keep running it, doing what they love. By selling to Buffett they receive guarantees that the business will not be merged with another, sold off, broken up, or moved from its home-town base.

Having owners with a strong emotional attachment to their company generally suggests the company will have honest accounting, respect for customers, pride in the product, and loyal and effective management in place; in short, integrity. Buffett remarks, "After some mistakes, I learned to go into business only with people whom I like, trust and admire." This strategy can be a remarkably good filter for making investment decisions.

Once Buffett buys a company he intends to keep it, even if it goes through rough patches and does not contribute much to Berkshire Hathaway's bottom line. In the meantime, the fund tries to get the problems fixed. Buffett tells the CEOs of each company he buys to run the business as if:

- They own 100 percent of it.
- It is the only asset their family owns or will ever own.
- It can't be sold or merged for at least 100 years.

This is an outlook that runs counter to the approach of just about every other investment company, but as Buffett wrote in his 1985 Annual Report:

No matter how great the talent or effort, some things just take time: you can't produce a baby in one month by getting nine women pregnant.

Berkshire Hathaway, he notes, has "the longest investment horizon to be found in the public-company universe."

Investors in his fund are expected to hold on to their stock for many years, even passing it on to relatives after their death. In the fund's *Owner's Manual*, Buffett writes:

We hope you instead visualize yourself as a part owner of a business that you expect to stay with indefinitely, much as you might if you owned a farm or apartment house in partnership with members of your family.

The company's annual meeting in Omaha is designed for the faithful, part information and part entertainment, and attracts thousands of stockholders from around the world.

Final comments

Though most of the essays in the book are a few years old, their basic lessons have not dated. Buffett established his investing style decades ago, and while it has undergone refinements, the philosophy remains: Work with people you like and trust, and as long the financial fundamentals are also good, prosperity will take care of itself. We have a tendency to think that anything related to business or money requires us to be hard nosed, but basic to Berkshire Hathaway's fortunes has been developing a system for finding people who *care*.

Interestingly, Buffett is well known for not going along with most other tycoons in calling for lower corporate taxes. He is quite happy to pay the US rate of 35 percent because he feels that, in a capitalist society that rewards financial success above all others, it is fair that he is required to give a decent proportion back in the form of redistributed wealth to people whose success is not related to money, such as nurses and teachers.

What will happen when Buffett dies? His vast fortune is already being divested into the Bill and Melinda Gates Foundation (see p. 105), but this does not mean that Berkshire Hathaway will be wound up. On the contrary, he and Munger have created a set of "business genes," a way of doing business that will outlive them no matter who is actually running the company. Ultimately, their greatest legacy may not simply be the enrichment of shareholders or the money that is given away, but demonstrating an investing philosophy that anyone can follow to their profit.

Though not really an easy read for beginner investors, with a little effort to understand the financial terms a purchase of *The Essays of Warren Buffett* will be amply rewarded. Readers can supplement it with more recent Buffett letters found on the Berkshire Hathaway website, and for an excellent portrait of the man himself, Roger Lowenstein's biography *Buffett: The Making of an American Capitalist* (Random House, 1995) is recommended.

2006

The Secret

"The greatest teachers who have ever lived have told us that the law of attraction is the most powerful law in the Universe."

"It is the law that determines the complete order in the Universe, every moment of your life, and every single thing you experience in your life... You are the one who calls the law of attraction into action, and you do it through your thoughts."

"People who have drawn wealth into their lives used The Secret, whether consciously or unconsciously. They think thoughts of abundance and wealth, and they do not allow any contradictory thoughts to take root in their minds... Whether they are aware of it or not, their predominant thoughts of wealth are what brought wealth to them. It is the law of attraction in action."

In a nutshell

You are a powerful magnet, attracting into your life the equivalent of whatever you are strongly feeling or thinking about.

In a similar vein

Genevieve Behrend *Your Invisible Power* (p 34)
T. Harv Eker *Secrets of the Millionaire Mind* (p 86)
Charles Fillmore *Prosperity* (p 98)
Esther Hicks & Jerry Hicks *Ask and It Is Given* (p 152)

CHAPTER 9

Rhonda Byrne

At a low point in her life, with her father recently deceased and her business close to collapse, Rhonda Byrne's daughter gave her a copy of Wallace Wattles' *The Science of Getting Rich*. The ideas in this New Thought classic (see commentary in *50 Success Classics*) seemed to run counter to everything she believed, but she could not stop thinking about it. Over the next few months she implemented its messages in her life with transformative effect, personally and financially.

Believing she had found a "secret" that should be more widely known, Byrne began developing the idea for a film, taking advantage of her connections and knowledge as a television producer. She raised money to visit the United States and interview every teacher, writer, or speaker who seemed to know about this secret. Made for only $3 million, the film did not have the cinema or television release intended, but this turned out to be a blessing in disguise. It became a word-of-mouth hit as an internet download, and DVD sales began to explode; over two million copies have sold in the US alone.

The surprise is that the book is not just a spinoff marketing afterthought to capitalize on the film's success, but a powerful work in its own right that has actually sold more copies. *The Secret* is a long homage to the thinkers and authors that have inspired Byrne: from New Thought legends Charles Haanel, Robert Collier, Wallace Wattles, and Genevieve Behrend, to contemporary self-growth gurus such as Denis Waitley, Jack Canfield, and Neale Donald Walsch. In between, there are quotes from Einstein, Jung, Emerson, and other "great minds" who she says knew about "the Secret."

The book follows the structure of the film in featuring the thoughts of particular teachers interspersed with narration. However, it goes into more detail on many points, and has much more of Byrne's own commentary and examples from her life.

The law of attraction and how it works

The "secret" that Byrne felt she had discovered was the "law of attraction." In essence, this law says that whatever you think about or put your attention on becomes reality in your life. You attract things, people, and situations that are of a similar "vibration" to you. The universe is essentially energy, and all energy vibrates at a certain frequency. And each person is vibrating at a particular frequency, existing as an energy field within larger energy fields.

According to Byrne (and this is where she goes beyond mainstream science), your "vibration" is determined by your thoughts and feelings. Think of yourself as a transmission tower, she says, broadcasting frequencies of thoughts into the universe, beyond space and even time. Change your frequency, via a change in your thoughts, and you can become virtually a new person who attracts different people and circumstances into your life.

The law is said to work whether you know about it or not, or believe in it or not. Yet once you do, an amazing possibility emerges: You can "think your life into existence." In observing the incredible imbalance of wealth on our planet, Byrne offers this as the reason: People who are wealthy think only thoughts of more wealth. "They only know wealth, and nothing else exists in their minds." Even most people who have made a fortune then lost it become wealthy again before long. This is because they remain focused on abundance all the time, despite current circumstances. The law of attraction *must* deliver to them the equivalent of their dominant thoughts.

Naturally, when people discover this law, they worry about the effects that their negative thoughts will have. But as Michael Bernard Beckwith, one of the teachers in *The Secret*, notes, affirmative thoughts are many times more powerful than negative ones. He suggests you "proclaim to the Universe that all your good thoughts are powerful, and that any negative thoughts are weak." There is thankfully a time delay or buffer between your thoughts and their coming to fruition, which allows you some space to refine what you really want.

Use the creative process

The "creative process" is the specific way in which you can use the law of attraction to obtain what you want. It involves three steps:

- Ask the universe—you must be crystal clear about what you want.
- Believe—act, speak, and think as though you have already received what you have asked for.
- Receive—feel great that it is coming to you. Feeling good sets up the necessary vibration to manifest the desire.

Asking for what you want is, Byrne writes, is "like placing an order from a catalogue." You place the order once, then wait expectantly for the item to arrive. When buying from a catalogue you do not place an order, then place another one in case the first one doesn't arrive. Ask once, and do so as if you know what you have asked for is on its way.

Remember that the universe does not strain in its creation of anything. Think about grass: It grows effortlessly. In the same way, you manifest your desires easily when you are relaxed and have a knowing and joyful sense of expectation. Action that you take that is inspired by meditation or happens through the law of attraction is effortless—and a lot more powerful—than trying to do anything by force.

To receive more easily, Byrne instructs, do things now that align you with what you want. If you want a new car, go for a test drive. If you want a particular house, inspect it and picture it as yours. Otherwise, these things will remain "out there," separate to you.

You don't need to know how

You do not have to know *how* the universe will provide what you want, you just require the faith that it *will*.

In *The Secret* Jack Canfield, co-creator of the *Chicken Soup for the Soul* book series, provides a good analogy: When driving at night from California to New York, you don't need to see all the way from one coast to another. All you need is for your headlights to show you the next 200 feet in front, and you will get there. In life, you have to trust that you will be "shown the way." Most people, he observes, never ask for what they want because they cannot see how it could possibly come to them.

If you keep wondering about the "how," the message you are giving out to the universe is doubt. In contrast, when you have a relaxed belief, the universe corresponds to that vibration. You have to "believe in the unseen." In response, the universe will rearrange events and circumstances so that what you imagine to be real becomes real. It always, says featured author Bob Dooley, "knows the shortest, quickest, fastest, most harmonious way between you and your dream."

Feel love and gratitude

To make the law of attraction really work in your life, Byrne writes, you have to increase the amount of time during which you are feeling good. Living in a state of love and gratitude for everything around you creates a vibration that can only attract more good things and situations into your life.

The book includes many quotes from Charles Haanel, author of *The Master Key System*. Haanel taught that the law of attraction is really another name for love. Have frequent thoughts of love, and you will be superb at manifesting anything you want. It is vital to elevate how you feel in any moment, since when you have negative feelings you are blocking all the good that the universe wants to give you.

Byrne tells readers: "If you only do one thing with knowledge of The Secret, use gratitude until it becomes your way of life." You can't receive more into your life, be it a house, a car, or a new spouse, while you are ungrateful about what you already have. Thoughts of "not enough" mean that "not enough" will continue to be your reality. As her hero, Wallace Wattles, remarked, "Many people who order their lives rightly in all other ways are kept in poverty by their lack of gratitude."

Affirming that you are surrounded by plenty ensures that plenty more comes your way. Give thanks for everything when you get up in the morning and before turning in at night, and watch your outlook on life and circumstances change. Instead of thinking that life is a struggle, start believing that things come easily to you.

How much do you want to earn?

Byrne notes, "To attract money you must focus on wealth." Obvious? In fact most people focus on not having enough, and that becomes reflected in their circumstances. After she had read Wallace Wattles, Byrne knew that the universe would provide for her. Her vibration had gone from resistance to attraction of her good, and the good came pouring in. "The shortcut to anything you want in your life," she reiterates, "is to BE and FEEL happy now!" In such a state of mind, it is easy to believe that we already have what we want, and the universe responds quickly and often dramatically to our convictions.

To illustrate her point, in the chapter "The secret to money," Byrne includes another anecdote from Jack Canfield. He recalls the advice of Clement Stone, a great motivator and businessman, who told him to set a big goal for himself that would "blow his mind" if he achieved it. At the time Canfield was earning $8,000 a year, so he made it his goal to earn $100,000 a year. He taped a made-up $100,000 bill to his ceiling and every day visualized what it would be like to have the money. For a month, nothing happened. Then, he had what he describes as "a one-hundred-thousand-dollar idea." He had published a book, and worked out that if he sold a certain number of copies he would earn his money target. In a supermarket, he saw the popular *National Enquirer* magazine and had the thought of getting his work featured in it. A few weeks later he gave a talk and afterwards a woman interviewed him who also wrote freelance for the *Enquirer*. Her subsequent article helped the book to take off.

Did Canfield "attract" his $100,000? Not quite—that year he earned $92,327. But it was close enough, his wife reasoned, to try the process out on a larger scale; why not go for $1 million? In due course, for his first *Chicken Soup for the Soul* book Canfield received a check from his publisher for over $1 million.

Final comments

Is the law of attraction really a secret? You may think it is all mystical rubbish, but in the Bible it is expressed in the statement "To him that hath, more will be given." That is, feelings of abundance in the first place only attract more abundance. Feelings of lack have a corresponding effect. Why this should happen is a mystery, but whether you decide to believe in Byrne's law or not, it cannot be denied that there are millions of examples in which a person's convictions, backed up by strong emotion, have been translated into reality.

The Secret includes a quote attributed to Buddha: "All that we are is the result of what we have thought." Again, this is a rational, rather than a mystical, concept. The circumstances you find yourself in today, if you are not happy with them, are not "you." They are simply the result of all that you have thought and done in the past, and your future can be totally different. If most of your thinking is negative and rooted in feelings of lack, it is logical that this outlook is expressed in real life. As one of the teachers in *The Secret* notes, the only reason anyone is not living the life of their dreams is that they are thinking more thoughts about what they *don't* want than what it is they *do* want.

The majority of people who buy *The Secret* probably do so with an improvement of their finances in mind. However, there are also chapters on health and relationships, and how using the law of attraction can change the world. The book and the film may be seen as works of marketing genius that have made their creator millions, but plenty of people testify to their powerful effect, attracting many intelligent people who are interested in the link between mind and physical manifestation.

Rhonda Byrne

Born in 1952, Byrne has spent many years working in the Australian television industry, with production credits including The Don Lane Show, What's Cooking, The World's Greatest Commercials, *and* Sensing Murder.

The Secret *was part funded by Australia's Channel 9, but once made the network was reluctant to air the film, considering it would appeal to only a niche audience. This forced Byrne's production company to focus on internet downloads of the film to recoup the investment.*

Sales of The Secret *book were boosted by the author's appearances on the* Oprah *and* Larry King Live *television shows. Though based in Melbourne, Byrne has relocated to Los Angeles to make* The Secret 2, *a film with Hollywood studio funding.*

1889

The Gospel of Wealth

"This, then, is held to be the duty of the man of Wealth: First, to set an example of modest, unostentatious living, shunning display or arrogance; to provide moderately for the legitimate wants of those dependent upon him; and after doing so to consider all the surplus revenues which come to him simply as trust funds, which he is called upon to administer... in the manner which, in his judgment, is best calculated to produce the most beneficial results for the community... doing for them better than they would or could do for themselves."

"The man who dies rich thus dies disgraced."

In a nutshell

The wealth creator has a moral obligation to enrich the lives of others in whatever way they can.

In a similar vein

Joel T. Fleishman *The Foundation* (p 104)
Conor O'Clery *The Billionaire Who Wasn't* (p 92)
Muhammad Yunus *Banker to the Poor* (p 286)

CHAPTER 10

Andrew Carnegie

It might be a nice difficulty, but it is a difficulty nonetheless: If you are incredibly rich, what will you do with all your money when you die?

When in 1901 he sold his huge iron and steel interests to financier John Pierpont Morgan, personally receiving over $225 million, Andrew Carnegie became the richest individual of his age. The son of a poor Scottish linen weaver, he was the classic American immigrant success story who, in addition to possessing great judgment and drive, also admitted he had been in the right place at the right time.

Carnegie's family had settled in Pittsburgh, then a cradle of America's industrial revolution, and as a young man he held jobs in the country's emerging telegraph and railroad industries. Later, as a captain of industry, he was sharply criticized for keeping wages low and hours long (the famous Homestead strike in 1892 at one of his plants resulted in the deaths of ten men), yet he also kept with him a European sense of the "public good," spending the last part of his life working out how to give his money away for the greatest benefit.

The Gospel of Wealth, as it became known after publication in Britain, was an essay originally published in the *North American Review*. It became famous across the Atlantic when former British Prime Minister William Gladstone helped organize its publication in the *Pall Mall Gazette*. Even today its influence is out of all proportion to its length, running as it does to no more than a few thousand words. Bill Gates, Warren Buffett, and duty-free billionaire Chuck Feeney have each been inspired by the essay to give away the larger part of their fortune during their lifetime.

Freedom, inequality, and wealth

Carnegie begins his essay by noting the huge differences in wealth in the modern world. He does not, as you might expect of an "enlightened capitalist," decry the disparity; in fact he applauds it, noting that today's poor person is much better off than the poor of the past. They can afford what would have once been thought of as luxuries even to royalty.

Furthermore, he writes, this great inequality is the natural way of the world, a demonstration of the self-evident principles of survival of the fittest and advancement of the best able. Luck certainly plays a part, he admits, in the fortunes of men, but in a free society the people of ability and ambition naturally prosper while others lag.

All this, according to Carnegie, is a given. But the big question facing capitalism is this: If it leads to great wealth being concentrated in the hands of a few, what should be done with all the excess? Even though some people have been "born lucky" in terms of attributes, it is also true that whatever they create through enterprise cannot be achieved without the public's patronage. Therefore, he reasons, great wealth ultimately belongs to the society that has helped create it.

What to do with it

Noting the obvious—that you can't take it with you when you die—Carnegie goes through the ways in which a rich person can get rid of their fortune. They can leave it to their family; bequeath it to the public on their death; or dispense and distribute it during their lifetime.

History shows that large fortunes are more of a burden than a boon to those who inherit them. Though some heirs turn out to be exemplary stewards of the family resources, without an incentive to work hard most children of the wealthy tend to lead mediocre lives, and some are downright destroyed by their money. Naturally, Carnegie comments, magnates want to leave their wives and daughters well provided for, but they should think hard about leaving much to their sons.

As a general rule, he notes, most fortunes are passed on not because of thoughts of the welfare of children, but because of family pride. Much better, he feels, to distribute your fortune during your lifetime, using the same imagination and diligence that you display in creating it. This means avoiding the typical philanthropist's path of giving it away to charity, instead working actively yourself to ensure maximum social benefit for your bucks.

Where to spend it

In another, related essay, Carnegie lists some areas that are deserving of entrepreneurial largesse. They include universities, libraries, parks, museums and art galleries, hospitals, concert halls, swimming baths, and churches. He observes that wealth, "passing through the hands of the few, can be made a much more potent force for the elevation of our race than if it had been distributed in small sums to the people themselves." That is, people on their own cannot be trusted to make the best use of money, but give them a noble institution or needed facility and they will use it to good ends. Carnegie himself became famous for his endowment of public libraries (close to 5,000 around the world) and funding of institutions devoted to peace (he pulled out all the stops to try to prevent the First World War).

New York City had already been endowed with the Astor and Lenox libraries, which were combined (with further funds from Samuel J. Tilden) to create the famous New York City Public Library. Carnegie takes his hat off to other philanthropists in this mold, mentioning Tilden, Cooper, Pratt, Stanford (endower of Stanford University), and the Vanderbilt family, who built the university named after them while they were in their financial prime.

Final comments

Wealthy people are always eager to find ways around the biblical line "It is easier for a camel to go through the eye of a needle than for a rich man to enter the kingdom of heaven." Carnegie, however, did not dispute the warning, wryly noting that it "betokens serious difficulty for the rich." His own gospel, he believed, expressed the full intent of Jesus's words in its recognition that a person who dies rich "dies disgraced."

Some have viewed Carnegie's attitude as paternalistic. Yet he honestly believed that individuals, including himself, counted for little in relation to the progress of humanity overall. But history does not usually forget great givers, and many of the monuments built to serve the apparent pride of their capitalist donors are still around, continuing to elevate and inspire. Carnegie set the modern standard for big-time philanthropy, and beyond the millions of lives enlightened by his libraries and other institutions, this is perhaps an even greater legacy.

Andrew Carnegie

Born in Scotland in 1835, Carnegie moved with the family to the US when he was in his early teens. His first job, at 13, was in a cotton mill, followed by work as a telegraphist and a railway clerk. He quickly rose through the ranks at the Pennsylvania Railroad Company before launching himself as an iron manufacturer in Pittsburgh. When the Civil War erupted, he was asked to take charge of US government railways and telegraphs. He was a republican and opposed slavery, and this provided an opportunity to serve the cause.

After selling his iron and steel works, Carnegie spent his retirement years at his beloved Skibo castle in Scotland. He died in Lenox, Massachusetts in 1919.

A keen writer, his books include An American Four-in-Hand in Britain *(1883),* Round the World *(1884),* Triumphant Democracy *(1886),* The Empire of Business *(1902),* James Watt *(1905), and* Problems of To-day: Wealth, Labor, Socialism *(1907). Carnegie also inspired Napoleon Hill's research into successful American businessmen, which led to the writing of* Law of Success *and* Think and Grow Rich.

2006

How to Get Rich

"The bottom line is that if I did it, you can do it. I went from being a pauper—a hippy dropout on the dole, living in a crummy room without the proverbial pot to piss in, without even the money to pay the rent, without a clue as to what to do next—to being rich. And I am certainly no business genius, as my rivals will happily and swiftly confirm."

"After a lifetime of making money and observing better men and women than I fall by the wayside, I am convinced that fear of failing in the eyes of the world is the single biggest impediment to amassing wealth. Trust me on this. If you shy away for any reason whatever, then the way is blocked. The gate is shut—and will remain shut."

In a nutshell

Be willing to fail in public, and you have jumped the hurdle holding most people back from getting rich.

In a similar vein

Richard Branson *Losing My Virginity* (p 46)
T. Harv Eker *Secrets of the Millionaire Mind* (p 86)
Conrad Hilton *Be My Guest* (p 164)
Anita Roddick *Business as Unusual* (p 238)

CHAPTER 11

Felix Dennis

Felix Dennis is best known as the British owner of magazine titles including *ComputerShopper*, *PCWorld*, *Maxim*, and *The Week*. With interests on both sides of the Atlantic, he has a fortune estimated at $1 billion.

With all this money, what was his purpose in writing a book? Amid a plethora of rosy "you can do it!" motivational books, he felt there was an absence of honest insights into what entrepreneurs really think and feel on their way to the top—and the costs that are incurred in reaching it. *How to Get Rich* devotes as many words to Dennis's mistakes and disasters as to his triumphs, and rather than being about how to get rich quick, it concerns "Knowledge learned the hard way." He is very clear that he has not written a self-improvement tome that whips the reader into an inspired frenzy, and yet this is an inspiring book.

To write it, Dennis retreated to a cottage on his estate on the Caribbean island of Mustique. Usually he goes there to compose poetry, but felt it worth his time to put forth his wisdom about what had made him one of Britain's wealthiest (and most colorful) businesspeople. *How to Get Rich* is an entertaining, rollicking read that many people (even those not much interested in money) finish in a day or two thanks to its humor and fast pace. Dennis never went to university, but the text is littered with quotes from great thinkers and doers such as Bacon, Shakespeare, Churchill, and Kipling, along with his own excellent verses on money and life.

What are the chances?

What are the odds of actually getting rich? Dennis notes that only a tiny percentage of people in his native Britain could be considered really wealthy. To be included in the *Sunday Times* Rich List of the wealthiest thousand people in the country, in terms of population you have only 17 chances in a million. Not as bad as the lottery, but not that encouraging either.

But don't let this get you down, because large chunks of the population (and this applies to most countries) "either have no desire to be rich or have chosen professions that rule them out of the race." Five million people in the UK (out of 60 million) work for the government in some way. None of them is ever likely to be rich on their civil service wages.

Dennis asks: Among the people you socialize with, see on the street, work with, are any of them really dedicated to becoming rich? Only maybe 1 or 2 percent ever are. Plenty of people are ambitious, but this drive is usually channeled into career success, not on amassing money *per se*.

Is it worth it?

Dennis enjoys five homes, three estates, luxury cars, and private jets (he does not own them because "If it flies, floats or fornicates, *always* rent it—it's cheaper in the long run"), has an art collection, a valuable library, cellars of fine wine, and chauffeurs. He has never learned to drive, and when he was young told friends, "You don't understand. I was born to be driven."

Yet all his chasing after money took its toll. Working 16 hours a day led him to drugs, prostitutes, and general debauchery, and delayed him from beginning his other much-loved career as a poet, which he took up in his 50s. At one point Dennis describes himself as a "coked-up, overweight, cigarette-smoking, malt-whisky-swilling idiot with too much money," a veritable Keith Richards of the business world. He only came to his senses after a stay in an American hospital where he almost died from Legionnaire's disease. Eventually, he handed over much of the running of his businesses to others and sorted out his personal life, but he admits he should have done this a lot sooner.

The other not-so-nice element of seeking to be rich is how others see you. To get rich, Dennis writes, you have to grow a mental armor that protects you against the snickering, mockery, and envy of others who do not want you to succeed. Even friends and family will often say they want you to succeed, yet if you do so it may just expose their own timidity, and at a deeper level they may actually be pleased if you don't.

You have to see obtaining wealth as a game that you can laugh about, or it will destroy you and your health. There are more important and serious things in life, so you must know when to step back.

So why do it?

Money does not make you happy, Dennis notes, but people continue to believe that it will. When he points this out to friends who are not rich, they respond that while this might be the case for him, money definitely would make *them* happy.

Money, Dennis confesses, "quite definitely improved my sex life." This is because money equals power, and power is an aphrodisiac. He quotes author James Baldwin: "Money, it turned out, was exactly like sex. You thought of nothing else if you didn't have it, and thought of other things if you did."

On a more serious note, Dennis examines other reasons for seeking great wealth, recalling F. Scott Fitzgerald's famous comment, "Let me tell you about the rich. They are different from you and me," and Ernest Hemingway's famous riposte, "Yes, they have more money." Dennis sides with Fitzgerald, noting that what wealth really gives people is *confidence*, whether from the pride of making money or having been born rich. The paradox is that you need loads of confidence in yourself in the first place to become rich, although this is something that you can learn or fake.

Money can also give you something else valuable: control over your time. Though you may have an army of financial advisers and employees, you are still not obliged to be in a certain place at a particular time each day. You can sit on an island in the Caribbean writing poetry if you want to.

This does not mean that the pursuit of wealth suits everyone. Only pursue wealth, Dennis warns, if you have an inner need to do so. Do not mistake mere desire for compulsion. You can't get rich by being half-hearted about it—you must commit.

What it takes

Dennis deals with the common reasons people put forward for not taking risks to get rich. The usual excuse of the young is that they don't have enough experience or capital, and older people claim that they don't want to jeopardize the career they have built so far or can't afford to put at risk the security of their families.

If you believe in these excuses, he notes, then you are destined not to be rich. He has always had a lot of people working for him who he knows are smarter, but they also fear losing what they have gained, so they will never go out on the proverbial limb as required to really enrich themselves. And yet, your family will not love you any less if you decide to "seize the day"; it is really you that is stopping yourself. The hardest thing, in business as in life, is actually taking the first step. There always seems to be so many reasons not to. Yet as German philosopher Wolfgang Goethe wrote: "There is one elemental truth, the ignorance of which kills countless ideas and splendid plans: that the moment one commits oneself, Providence moves all."

You may be stopped from action by the fear of embarrassment or failure. Yet if you are not willing to fail, you will forever be bound in circumstances that involve little risk. And with little risk there are only small rewards. Dennis is blunt: "If you cannot face up to your fear of failure, you will never be rich." This is not just one factor you must consider. Rather, it is "the single biggest impediment to amassing wealth."

Fear rules us, so if you can rule your fear you can chart your own destiny. Don't let the "horrible imaginings" that Shakespeare wrote about rule your life. Life goes quickly, and the clock is ticking.

Ownership is everything

Dennis quotes John Paul Getty: "The meek shall inherit the earth, but not the mineral rights." If you really want to be rich you must own something, preferably your own company and preferably 100 percent of it. Dennis recalls the many brilliant publishers and managers of large magazine companies who at the end of their careers are worth no more than a few million, just because they didn't own anything. In contrast, he once made $1 million in one day by selling to a rival a magazine that he had not even published yet. Easy? Yes, but the fact is it was his to sell in the first place. You can forgo intelligence, skill, talent, and a winning personality, but if you own things, you can be rich.

Employees get a lot less because they don't risk much; they have pensions and sick pay and so on, and are protected by a lot of laws. The majority of people want three things more than they want money: job security, job satisfaction, and power. If you expressly want to be rich you have immediately separated yourself from the "loyal lieutenants" who fill the world's workplaces.

Dennis's first couple of years in business were nightmarish, a depressing slog to raise money in the face of commercial extinction. Friends had steady, well-paid, and even interesting jobs, yet he was not even able to buy a round of drinks in a pub. But he remembered Winston Churchill's comment "When going through hell, keep going," and the prospect of otherwise being a wage slave drove him on.

He had his first (unlikely) publishing success in 1974 with *Kung-Fu Monthly*, a hit all over the world for ten years. The key, he believes, was thinking big. Not many magazine publishers in Britain at the time were prepared to fly economy-class around the world cutting deals with people they didn't know. Importantly, Dennis did not just license the magazines, but put up his own capital in partnership with local firms. This was more risky, but because he was also an owner, it brought greater rewards.

Ideas are cheap, it's their execution that makes you rich

In his chapter "The fallacy of the great idea," Dennis notes that ideas cannot be patented. They are worthless unless they are implemented well and profitably. He mentions Ray Kroc, who did not invent McDonald's, but turned the initial restaurant into a perfect system of fast, reliable food at low prices in a clean environment that could be replicated endlessly around the world. Who became rich? Not the original McDonald brothers but Kroc. Many wealthy people become so through emulating a great idea that has already proven itself. This is a surprisingly underused path to wealth.

Final comments

Warning: This book will actually turn off many a reader from the pursuit of riches. It is in fact quite a dark portrait of wealth. Dennis is explicit about the downsides, with the tunnel vision and time usually required for first-generation wealth often coming at the cost of close relationships and family.

Life is pretty comfortable for most people in well-off countries. Why give yourself trouble by insisting on going out on your own? Rather melodramatically, but perhaps truthfully, Dennis writes: "Somewhere in the invisible heart of all self-made wealthy men and women is a sliver of razored ice... If you do not wish it to grow, then quit any dreams of becoming wealthy now."

If you do dare to try, and want real advice that is not overblown, "you can do it" inspiration, *How to Get Rich* is one of the best guides around for what you may be in for. If you can ride the rollercoaster, Dennis often points out, and can banish or control your fears, you will discover that "the world is awash with money with your name on it, waiting to be claimed."

He provides plenty of examples from the magazine world to prove his points, but it is the generic lessons that will interest most readers. For all his attempts to mark his book out as "anti-self-improvement" and "telling it like it is," in fact it underscores all the things you read about in motivational titles: believe in yourself, go the extra mile, think big. Dennis's conclusion is simple: Anyone can become rich, but you must be prepared to pay the price.

At the end of the day he does not take wealth, or his mad pursuit of it, too seriously, and counsels the reader not to either. If you start to believe you are "king of the world" when you get a bit of success, it won't be long before you wind up in hospital or prison. Think big about your dreams and your work, he says, but in your personal life, *act small.*

Felix Dennis

Dennis was born in Kingston-upon-Thames, London, in 1947. His parents divorced when he was a toddler and his mother took an accounting qualification to provide him and his brother with a brighter future. He was thrown out of school at 15, played in R&B bands, and attended Harrow College of Art. He became one of the founders of the infamous satirical magazine Oz, *and in 1971 was imprisoned on obscenity charges. Dennis was given a shorter sentence than the other two editors because the judge considered him "less intelligent."*

He started his publishing company in 1973, the first title a comic that only broke even. In the same year he co-authored a biography, Bruce Lee: King of Kung-Fu, *which thanks to Lee's death became a bestseller. Dennis established the first computer magazines in the UK (*Personal Computer World *and* MacUser*), the sale of which in the mid-1980s made him wealthy. He also co-founded a computer mail order business, MicroWarehouse, that later went public. Dennis Publishing today owns 19 magazines in the UK including* Auto Express, PC Pro, Viz, *and* The Week, *and recently divested itself of its American titles including* Maxim, Blender, *and* Stuff.

Dennis has had three volumes of poetry published, A Glass Half Full, Lone Wolf, *and* When Jack Sued Jill. *He other main interest is establishing the Forest of Dennis, a large broadleaf forest in central England.*

1992

Your Money or Your Life

"Financial independence is being free of the fog, fear and fanaticism so many of us feel about money."

"The shift from an ethic of growth to an ethic of sustainability will require nothing less than for each one of us to transform our relationship with money and the material world."

"So much dissatisfaction comes from focusing on what we don't have that the simple exercise of acknowledging and valuing what we do have can transform our outlook."

In a nutshell

By living on less, you can actually enjoy life more.

In a similar vein

Paul Hawken, Amory B. Lovins, & L. Hunter Lovins *Natural Capitalism* (p 146)
Jerrold Mundis *How To Get Out of Debt, Stay Out of Debt, and Live Prosperously* (p 196)
Dave Ramsey *Financial Peace Revisited* (p 228)
Marsha Sinetar *Do What You Love, the Money Will Follow* (p 254)
Lynne Twist *The Soul of Money* (p 278)

CHAPTER 12

Joe Dominguez & Vicki Robin

In the 1960s, Joe Dominguez worked on Wall Street as a financial analyst and institutional investment adviser. At the age of 31 he retired and did not work for money again. Yet he did not make a "killing"—his nest egg was $71,000 (around $400,000 in today's money)—but simply worked out how much he would need not to have to work again, while still having a reasonable lifestyle.

Dominguez was surprised to find that his personal experiment, which was one of the things that attracted his co-author and partner Vicki Robin to him, also interested many people in the circles he moved in. His discussions with friends about the role of money in their lives, and their ability to live comfortably and meaningfully on very little, grew into a seminar and audio program that spread across America and around the world.

Your Money or Your Life was described by the *Los Angeles Times* as "the seminal guide to the new morality of personal money management," and as one of the first books of the "simple living" movement has continued to be popular. Far from being outdated, its message that we all live on the same planet and therefore must be responsible stewards of its resources has never been more relevant.

How much do you really need?

Philosopher John Stuart Mill once noted that "Men do not desire to be rich, only to be richer than other men." Financial independence is as much psychological as material freedom, involving shedding your past assumptions about what is "enough" for you to live happily and well.

Money is often tied to social expectations: the right house in the right suburb, the right schools and colleges, exotic vacations. Big incomes often equal big expenses. Many people's existing "financial maps" have led them into a mire of dependency.

Through questioning people who came to their training courses, Dominguez and Robin found that whatever their incomes were, people always thought they would be happier with more money. If only they had an amount equal to double what they had now, they believed, they would be happy.

These days people tend to think of themselves more as "consumers" than "citizens." As Dominguez & Robin note:

We moderns meet most of our needs, wants and desires through money. We buy everything from hope to happiness. We no longer live life. We consume it.

The "rat race" involves working to buy luxuries that you don't have enough time to enjoy. According to the authors' "fulfillment curve," no matter how much more money you earn, it does not lead to increased enjoyment or satisfaction with life. In fact, if you are able to reduce your expenditure and "declutter" your life you are likely to experience an *increase* in satisfaction. It is very easy to fall into a bad cycle of debt, spending, and consuming, when all you really want, they suggest, is a reasonable level of comfort and security—a simpler lifestyle. When you simplify your life, you tend to spend less than you earn, and this alone can bring peace of mind.

Get off the treadmill

People think about money in different ways—as power, as security, as happiness, as evil—but is it really any of these? The basic mistake people make is imagining money as external to themselves, something that they struggle for and that will magically give them wellbeing and personal worth. Dominguez and Robin come up with another definition of money. It is something you *trade your life energy for*. For most people, this "something" is paid work.

Most adults spend the majority of their waking hours at work, getting ready for work, traveling to and from work, and winding down from work. Given the time this eats up, it is no surprise that we identify ourselves so much with our occupation. Though most of us have to work to earn money, do we really have to earn as much as we do for a fulfilling life?

If you are honest about all the time that goes into having your job, not just being in the office, your hourly wage rate will need adjusting. The job that you thought paid you $30 an hour might actually be paying you only $15. Not just commuting to work and the purchase of expensive work clothes, but all the "convenience" costs for the time you don't have to do things yourself, such as bought meals, laundry services, along with "escape entertainment" and expensive vacations that you would not feel the need for if you actually loved the work you do. The thinking goes "I work damn hard, I deserve the best," so you spend a lot on things that can make up for the misery of working.

Often, the key to getting in control of your finances is not earning more, but adjusting your lifestyle. Simple things like living close to where you work can dramatically increase your free time and cost you less. Also, it may be possible to retire much earlier than you think if you adopt a "simpler living" philosophy.

Time, not money

What do people want more of? Generally, it is more time, not more money. Surveys have indicated that people feel hostage to their jobs, and would rather work four days a week for less money. Dominguez and Robin observe:

> *Our jobs have replaced family, neighborhood, civic affairs, church and even mates as our primary allegiance, our primary source of love and site of self-expression.*

The high price of "success" is that (even in 1990, when *Your Money or Your Life* was being written) 54 percent of Americans believed they had less free time than they did five years previously. In the quest to earn more we have forsaken the time to enjoy family, friends, community, spending time in nature, watching movies, or whatever really fulfills us, yet leisure is not a commodity, it is an intrinsic part of life. We should not have to sell our souls to have free time. It is not a selfish thing, but allows for self-development and devoting yourself to the higher good.

What are you really worth?

Dominguez and Robin provide a nine-step process for getting back in control of your money and your life. The first step is to work out how much you have earned in your life to date. In doing this, you have to be honest and include all tips, gifts, and under-the-counter money, as well as all wages from jobs.

Many people find that they have underestimated how much they have earned in total, and coming up with a large figure can be very empowering. This is particularly true of people who are currently not working, such as mothers who thought they "were not worth much."

Readers are asked to calculate the value of all their assets, then work out the total of all liabilities, including all debts, loans, and bills outstanding. In doing such a balance sheet you will arrive at your net worth in financial terms, which is obviously not to be understood as your *self*-worth. The figure you come up with may give rise to feelings or blame, guilt, anger, or compassion, but it is important not to blame yourself. The object is to get an accurate picture of the role of money in your life so that you are able to change your financial map for the future.

The truly rich are frugal

"Frugal" is now a very unfashionable word, yet it is a trait that built nations. It derives from the Latin *frux*, meaning fruit or virtue, and *frui*, meaning to enjoy or use well. Therefore, frugality does not actually mean going without, but enjoying what you have!

Too often people don't want a thing for its use but for the power or success it symbolizes. But to have something modest and use it often, taking good care of it, can be a source of much pride and happiness. As Dominguez and Robin note:

Frugal people... get value from everything—a dandelion or a bouquet of roses, a single strawberry or a gourmet meal... To be frugal means to have a high joy-to-stuff ratio.

They point out that often "the difference between prosperity and poverty lies simply in our degree of gratitude." It's not about being a tightwad, but about getting maximum enjoyment out of resources.

Your Money or Your Life provides lots of great tips for becoming frugally minded, including:

- Never go shopping on the spur of the moment ("He who hesitates saves money").
- Don't go shopping as a form of leisure ("Needs expand to encompass whatever you want to buy on impulse").
- Use what you have longer. Using everything for 20 percent longer can save you a lot over a year.
- Love materials. Learn more about them and what they need to stay in good shape.
- Pay with cash. You spend on average 23 percent more if you are using cards.

Record every cent

Another of the book's nine steps is to write down every amount, small and large, that comes into or leaves your hands. Why be so zealous?

In doing this, the authors argue, you become conscious of the role of money in your life, with nothing hidden: "Since money has a direct correlation to your life energy, why not respect that precious commodity, your life energy, enough to become conscious of how it is spent?"

You will discover which of your expenses are unfulfilling ones, and which are truly worth the exchange of your life energy. They make the point that pursuing sustainability is not just a "hippie green thing," but makes economic sense. For example, buying a good coat that lasts ten years will be a lot cheaper than buying a new one every two or three years to have the latest look. When buying food, purchase stuff that has less packaging; as well as being more likely to provide real sustenance and enjoyment, it will probably cost less and go further.

Final comments

You do not have to choose between "your money" and "your life." As this book tries to demonstrate, they should never be put in separate boxes. There are ways in which your working self, your money self, and your role as a family member, friend, neighbor, and citizen can all be reconciled. Life is not just about making as much as you can and spending it before you die, but being in control of your finances so that you have plenty of time to enjoy family and friends and pursue personal interests. Surely this is real prosperity.

Your Money or Your Life was well ahead of its time in talking about the effect on our planet of overconsumption. No matter how rich or "civilized" we have become, we still need clean air, water, and fertile soil to survive.

The book is an antidote to getting brainwashed by the consumer culture, and some readers will disagree with its contention that economic growth is a philosophy to be dispensed with, yet Dominguez and Robin are not anticapitalist. Later chapters on long-term growth and protection of your savings through financial instruments such as bonds are well worth reading. Readers will also enjoy the brief portraits scattered throughout of people who have adopted the principles in *Your Money or Your Life* and how it transformed their lives.

Joe Dominguez

Born in 1939 in Spanish Harlem, New York City, Dominguez grew up financially poor. He worked for ten years on Wall Street before retiring in 1969.

The film Affluenza *(1997), which looked at rampant materialism in America, is dedicated to Dominguez, who died of cancer in Seattle in 1997, aged 58.*

Vicki Robin

Born in 1945 in Long Island, Vicki Robin graduated with honors from Brown University, Rhode Island. After an early career in film and theater in New York, she met Dominguez. They worked as volunteers on a range of projects such as helping young people with drug problems. In 1984 they founded the New Road Map Foundation (www.newroadmap.org), a Seattle-based, volunteer-run nonprofit body that promotes "a humane, sustainable future for our world" with a focus on reducing consumption. All royalties from Your Money or Your Life *go to the foundation.*

The New York Times *called Robin the "prophet of consumption-downsizers," and she remains a central figure in the simpler living movement. She has served on a presidential taskforce on consumption and population, and is Chair of the Simplicity Forum (www.simplicityforum.org), a leadership group promoting personal choices that can help save the planet.*

1985

Innovation and Entrepreneurship

"Entrepreneurship is neither a science nor an art. It is a practice."

"Entrepreneurship is not 'natural'; it is not 'creative.' It is work… Entrepreneurial businesses treat entrepreneurship as a duty. They are disciplined about it… they work at it… they practice it."

"Effective innovations start small. They are not grandiose. They try to do one specific thing… Grandiose ideas, plans that aim at 'revolutionizing an industry,' are unlikely to work."

In a nutshell

The purpose of entrepreneurship is to deliver new satisfaction and value, and it is built on "unexpected successes" that are quickly capitalized on.

In a similar vein

Richard Branson *Losing My Virginity* (p 46)
Conrad Hilton *Be My Guest* (p 164)
Guy Kawasaki *The Art of the Start* (p 174)
Anita Roddick *Business as Unusual* (p 238)
Howard Schultz *Pour Your Heart into It* (p 248)

CHAPTER 13

Peter Drucker

Over 20 years since its publication, *Innovation and Entrepreneurship* is still the landmark work on a subject that, before Drucker, had benefited from little real analysis.

At the beginning, Drucker is clear that his book is not about the psychology or character of entrepreneurs. It is not the mysterious "flash of genius" so often ascribed to the wealth creator that interests him, but actions and behavior: how innovation and entrepreneurship can be boiled down to a system that can be learned and applied by anyone. Drucker was unusual among business gurus for working with people in all types of organizations including labor unions, girl scout bodies, science labs, churches, universities, and relief agencies. His message was: Wherever you work, there is huge scope for changing how you do things in ways that can make a massive difference.

Drucker began teaching innovation and entrepreneurship in the mid-1950s, and *Innovation and Entrepreneurship* represents three decades of testing his ideas. Many of the examples are drawn from his own experience as a consultant, or from the experience of people he taught. Though some of it is now dated, overall this is a timeless work that should be read by any aspiring entrepreneur or organization starter.

It's management, stupid

At the beginning of *Innovation and Entrepreneurship* Drucker draws attention to a mystery: Why, in the US economy from 1965 to 1985, despite inflation and oil shocks, recessions and major job losses in certain industries and government, did huge growth occur in jobs? These jobs—40 million of them—were not created by large corporations or government, but mostly by small and medium-sized businesses. Most people explained the growth in terms of one phrase: "high tech."

In fact, only around 5 million of the new positions came from the technology field. The key "technology" driving jobs growth, according to Drucker, was not widgets and gadgets, but entrepreneurial *management*. The force of the entrepreneur, he suggests, is always greater than the current state of the economy. Even the famous Kondratieff waves—cycles of technology and production that are meant to drive economies—did not explain a lot of economic growth.

Management, or how things can be done better, is best appreciated as a "social technology," as much as a discipline like engineering or medicine. Drucker notes that the huge success of McDonald's was in large part due to better management of a service that had previously been run by Mom and Pop owners. Everything—the product, the time it took to make it, the way it was made, the way it was sold and served—was refined and standardized beyond belief. This was not "high tech," Drucker observes, it was doing things in a different, better way, and in the process creating new value.

What is an entrepreneur?

"The entrepreneur," wrote French economist Jean-Baptiste Say in 1800, "shifts economic resources out of an area of lower and into an area of higher productivity and greater yield." This was the original definition and the best, Drucker maintains.

Entrepreneurship is not a personality trait, it is a feature to be observed in the actions of people or institutions. Entrepreneurs in health, education, and business work in basically the same way. Essentially, they don't just do something better, they do it *differently*.

Classical economics says that economies tend towards equilibrium—they "optimize," which results in incremental growth over time. But the nature of the entrepreneur is to "upset and disorganize." He or she is a wildcard that generates wealth through the process that economist Joseph Schumpeter described as *creative destruction*. This involves dealing with uncertainty and with the unknown, and having the ability to exploit and respond intelligently to change. It is a misconception, Drucker says, to think that everyone who starts a new business is being entrepreneurial. People do take a risk in opening a shop or a franchise, but they are not really creating anything new, not creating a new type of value for the customer.

The risk myth

Drucker asks: Why does entrepreneurship have the reputation of being very risky, when its purpose is simply to shift resources from where they yield less to where they yield more? In fact, it is less risky than just "doing the same thing better"; in following this course it is easy to miss out on new opportunities totally and run an enterprise into the shoals almost without noticing. Embracing change and assiduously trying out different things are actually the best way to invest resources. Drucker points to the amazingly successful record of continually innovating high-tech companies—Bell Lab, IBM, 3M (today we would add Apple)—to see that this is true. Entrepreneurship is only risky, he observes, when so-called entrepreneurs "violate elementary and well-known rules." It is not risky when it is systematic, managed, and purposeful.

He notes:

Entrepreneurship is not "natural"; it is not "creative". It is work... Entrepreneurial businesses treat entrepreneurship as a duty. They are disciplined about it... they work at it... they practice it.

Entrepreneurship can exist in large organizations, and in fact Drucker says they must become entrepreneurial if they are to have a long-term future. General Electric in America and the retailer Marks & Spencer in the UK are both big companies that have strong records of creating new value. The big expansion in American universities from the original elite college system was driven by entrepreneurship: finding new "customers" for higher education by providing new worth and relevance. This was not a case of taking great risks, but rather identifying opportunities.

How to be an innovator

According to Drucker, innovation is "whatever changes the wealth-producing potential of already existing resources." The best innovations can be alarmingly simple, and often have little to do with technology or inventions. For example, there was nothing technically remarkable about creating a metal container that could be easily offloaded from a truck onto a ship, but the advent of container shipping as a standardized system of moving things around the globe was an innovation that quadrupled world trade.

Many of the greatest innovations are some kind of social value creation, such as insurance, the modern hospital, buying by installment, or the textbook. Were it not for the humble textbook, which emerged in the mid-seventeenth century, universal schooling would not have been possible, and if US farmers had not had access to installment purchasing, the surge in agricultural productivity would not have happened. This financial innovation allowed them to become much more productive today, instead of having to wait years to afford a purchase.

Drucker suggests that science and technology are actually the *least* promising of all the sources of innovation, generally taking the most time to realize any benefits and costing the most. In reality, anything that takes advantage of an unexpected change in society or a market is actually quicker, easier, or more likely to result in success.

The entrepreneur is on the lookout for:

- "the unexpected": an unexpected success, failure, or event (see below)
- incongruities: between things as they ought or are said to be, and how they actually are
- problems with an existing process for which no one has provided a solution
- changes in how an industry or market operates that take everyone by surprise
- demographic (population) changes
- changes in "perception, mood or meaning"

The unexpected success

Drucker includes several fascinating examples of the "unexpected success" and the extent to which those involved were able to take advantage:

- New York department store Macy's did poorly for several years because it considered itself primarily a fashion store and was downplaying the growing effect of appliance sales on its bottom line. To the company's directors, these sales were an "embarrassing success." Only later, after it had accepted the place of appliance sales as a bona fide part of its image and range, did the store again prosper.
- Many antibiotics developed for humans can be used on animals, yet when vets tried to buy these drugs they met resistance from the manufacturers. Allowing the drugs to be sold for animal use was beneath them. But another firm bought the rights to the drugs and marketed them specifically to vets, as a result creating the most profitable segment of the pharmaceutical industry.
- IBM and Univac initially made computers aimed at the scientific market. Both were surprised by the interest from business users. IBM steamed ahead, though, when it "lowered itself" to sell to the business market.
- After television began, everyone "knew" that book sales in America would plummet; no one would be bothered to read again when they could enjoy television instead. In fact the opposite happened: Book sales boomed. Yet it was not the traditional bookstore owners who took advantage of this. Large book chains were established not by book lovers, but by experienced retailers who worked out which titles generated most profit per feet of bookshelf.

Changing your whole direction to take account of an unexpected success requires humility. If you are a company that has staked its reputation on a particular quality product, but a cheaper, less grand product has booming sales, it is difficult not to view it as a threat because, as Drucker puts it, "The unexpected success is a challenge to management's judgment."

The customer is everything

Most people associate innovation with a "bright idea," like the zipper or the ballpoint pen. But Drucker notes that barely one in five hundred of these "bright ideas" ever covers the costs of their development. On its own, innovation is not worth a great deal. It is only when it meets the market through the catalyst of entrepreneurial management that you start to create things of great value. An innovation is much more than a technological advance; it is "an effect in economy and society," something that changes the way people do things. Real innovation is always about the end customer.

For example, British company De Havilland produced the first passenger jet plane, but US companies Boeing and Douglas took the industry lead because they created ways for airlines to finance such expensive purchases. Dupont did not just invent Nylon, it created new markets for its product in areas as diverse as women's hosiery and underwear, and automobile tires. The innovator must figure out the market and system of delivery of their product, or the markets will be taken away from them.

You can't do market research on people's reactions to things that don't yet exist. In this sense innovation will always be a risk, but it becomes less risky when you remain open about how, and by whom, your innovation will be used. People do not buy products, but what the product does for them. The purpose of innovation is to provide satisfaction where before there was none.

Final comments

Drucker always seemed to be years, if not decades, ahead of anyone in his field, and *Innovation and Entrepreneurship* was, perhaps remarkably, the first to treat the subject in a systematic, nonsensational way. It is an endlessly fascinating work that should bring new rigor to your thinking about ways to create new value. Get it for the many examples and elaboration of themes that there is not enough room to cover here. One particularly useful chapter relates to the "dos and don'ts" for starting any new venture.

Peter Drucker

Drucker was born in Vienna in 1909 and his father was a civil servant in the Austro-Hungarian empire. After leaving school he went to study in Germany, obtaining a doctorate in public and international law at Frankfurt University. He worked as a journalist in London, before moving to the United States in 1937, becoming an American citizen in 1943.

From 1950 to 1971 Drucker was a business professor at New York University, and in 1971 he was appointed Clarke Professor of Social Science and Management at Claremont Graduate University in California, a position he kept until his death.

He wrote 39 books and was also a columnist for the Wall Street Journal *from 1975 to 1995. His 1946 book* Concept of the Corporation, *based on a study of the inner workings of the General Motors Corporation, made him well known. Other titles include* The Practice of Management *(1954),* The Effective Executive *(1966), and* Post-Capitalist Society *(1993). In 2002, when he was in his 90s, Drucker was awarded the Presidential Medal of Freedom by George W. Bush. He died in 2005.*

2005

Secrets of the Millionaire Mind

"[Just] as there are 'outer' laws of money, there must be 'inner' laws. The outer laws include things like business knowledge, money management, and investment strategies. These are essential. But the inner game is just as important."

"Whatever results you are experiencing in your life, whether you are positive or negative, rich or poor, they are just a reflection of your inner world. To change the visible, you must change the invisible."

"Let me put it bluntly: anyone who says money isn't important doesn't have any! Rich people understand the importance of money and the place it has in our society... poor people validate their financial ineptitude by using irrelevant comparisons. They'll argue, 'Well, money isn't important as love'... What's more important, your arm or your leg? Maybe they're both *important."*

In a nutshell

To obtain your desired outer results, you must first master the inner game of wealth.

In a similar vein

Rhonda Byrne *The Secret* (p 58)
Michael E. Gerber *The E-Myth Revisited* (p 128)
Mark Victor Hansen & Robert G. Allen *The One Minute Millionaire* (p 140)
Joe Karbo *The Lazy Man's Way to Riches* (p 168)
Robert Kiyosaki *Cashflow Quadrant* (p 180)
Thomas J. Stanley & William D. Danko *The Millionaire Next Door* (p 266)

CHAPTER 14

T. Harv Eker

In his 20s Harv Eker was a "success junkie" who had read all the self-improvement books and been to all the seminars. He had tried and failed at several businesses, and kept wondering when he was going to "make it." "I had heard of this thing called profit," he ruefully notes. "I just never saw any of it."

In desperation, he began to examine his deepest thoughts about himself. Even though he had professed a desire to become rich, he recognized that in reality his fear of failure was greater. Was he destined to be a struggler? The third time he moved back in with his parents, one of his father's friends—who happened to be wealthy—gave Eker some advice. He too had been a "disaster" until he learned a vital truth: Rich people think differently to the average person. Copy the way they think, and you will be ready to become rich yourself.

Eker studied the psychology of wealth creation and success, and learned mental techniques and strategies to recondition his mind to think in a rich person's way. He learned that rich people do not "hope for the best"; they do not get sidetracked by "better" opportunities; they play to win and do not give up in tough times. So, when he opened a fitness products store, borrowing $2,000 on his credit card, he swore to himself he would not quit until he left the business as a millionaire. In two-and-a-half years he created a chain of 10 stores, of which he sold 50 percent to a large company for $1.6 million.

Secrets of the Millionaire Mind is a brash, flashy volume that nevertheless contains a treasure trove of pointers to the wealth mindset. The first part of the book relates to Eker's own rise, but it is Part Two, "Seventeen ways rich people think and act differently from poor and middle class people," that readers may find most compelling.

What's your financial blueprint?

From sporting goods, Eker changed career to became a business trainer. In seminars he discovered something interesting: Half the people attending would get what he was saying and act on it to achieve success. For the other half, not much would change. He realized that he could teach the practical tools of business success until the cows came home, but unless a person's whole mind changed toward the acceptance of wealth and being a creator of wealth, they would get nowhere. Not until they mastered *both* the "inner game" and the "outer game" of wealth would their lives be transformed.

According to Eker, we all have a "financial blueprint," formed when we are young, which dictates the level of wealth we will reach in life. What we are told about money or learn from observing our parents all gets filtered into our subconscious to create a basic mental-financial reality. Most people are not aware of this, and their adult logic about money is usually tripped up by deeper and more powerful feelings that govern what they actually do.

Eker and his wife, for instance, had totally different money blueprints, and as a result they were always fighting about finances. She had grown up believing that women don't have money, therefore when their husbands give them money they must spend it—*all* of it. To her, money meant pleasure. Eker's own fundamental belief, having grown up poor, was that money meant freedom—the more you accumulated, the freer you would be. Imagine the clash of these two blueprints! Yet if you do recognize each other's blueprints and bring them into alignment, relationship miracles can happen.

You're worth it

Many people subconsciously believe that they are not worthy to receive abundance, that money is related to some perceived flaws in their personality, or they have some notion that being poor is more "spiritual." Some people's money blueprints set them up to earn only a certain amount, whether it is $20,000 or $500,000. They will rise to this amount and go no further, since this is the figure they believe they are worth.

But these beliefs are made-up stories that can be replaced with the new belief of "I *am* worthy." You must acquire the mindset that you can be wealthy without having to prove anything. There is so much money swishing around the world, Eker notes, yet poor people believe that there is a limited amount to go around and that you have to struggle for your piece of the pie.

Rich people, in contrast, believe that new wealth is continually created, and that there is a limitless supply of money. Become a great receiver, a "money magnet," Eker says. Celebrate any money that comes to you, no matter how small, and the universe will give you even more.

It makes the world go round

Do you believe that "money just isn't that important"? People have said this to Eker at his seminars. Eventually they admit that they are having financial "challenges" or some other euphemism. Eker's conclusion: "If you don't think money is important, you simply won't have any."

According to Eker, poor and middle-class people try to play down the importance of money compared to other things, particularly love, but to be happy and fulfilled you must have both. "What's more important," he asks, "your arm or your leg? Maybe they're both important." Rich people value love as much any anyone, but they are not afraid of admitting just how important money is.

When Eker moved his family to a wealthy part of San Diego, they were nervous about how they would be received by their neighbors. In fact they were blown away by the generosity and kindness of the "millionaires next door." "Needless to say," he notes, "my old, conditioned belief that rich people were greedy snobs dissipated in the light of reality." Now, he says, the kindest, nicest, and most generous people he knows are also the wealthiest.

Never complain, act

Eker's golden rule for wealth and life is "never complain." What you focus on always expands, therefore if you complain about problems they will only grow. Complaints are, he unceremoniously remarks, a "crap magnet," and he challenges the reader not to complain even once in a seven-day period, including mental complaints. He has been amazed at how many lives this small exercise has transformed people's attitudes.

What has this got to do with wealth? Poor people have a habit of blame, complaint, and justification. Their financial or life situation is always the fault of the economy, their upbringing, their spouse, or something else. Rich people, on the other hand, believe that their life is to be shaped according to their will. They never consider themselves victims. If something needs to change, they take it upon themselves to act.

You can keep a set of behaviors that keeps you in mediocrity, Eker remarks, but just remember that "every time you blame, justify, or complain, you are *slitting your financial throat*." Adopt the rich way of experiencing the world, which is a joyful focus on opportunities and action.

Commit to be rich

The universe, Eker remarks, acts like a big mail-order service that delivers to you what you desire. But it doesn't work if you are sending out mixed messages. You are on the road to wealth as soon as you work out exactly what you want and unequivocally *commit* to being rich. Once you do, Eker notes, the universe has a way of doing what it can to support you. The vast majority of people never do these two simple things, and their finances show it.

The road to wealth is "not a stroll in the park," he remarks. This means that to become rich you have to get good at handling problems, even welcoming bigger ones into your life. Rich people are solution oriented; they are determined to be bigger than their problems, because they know that this is how you advance in life. When Eker finally succeeded in business, he put it down to one thing: committing to succeed no matter what. This conviction enabled him to surmount obstacles that his earlier self would have crumbled under before. He learned the simple truth that poor people remain so because they are beaten by their problems, while the rich become rich because they defeat them. Poor or middle-class people would *like* to be rich, wealthy people are *committed* to being rich. Between the two mindsets is a world of difference.

Get paid for your results, not your time

Rich-minded people become rich because they do not want to have any ceiling on what they can earn. They prefer to earn money based on their results, whether through commissions, royalties, or having their own business.

Poor people don't have this results outlook, and as a result prefer to get paid a guaranteed amount for their time only. The only problem is that your time is limited. No matter how much you get paid an hour, you only have a certain number of hours. Rich people, in contrast, create things or systems that can earn money for them independently of their time input. This may be creating a business employing other people, a business system like a franchise that can be sold, or investments that produce income from capital.

Eker observes that, "Rich people focus on their net worth. Poor people focus on their working income." The modern world is based around people going to college or training school, working hard, and obtaining a secure working income. But go to any country club, he suggests, and you won't find people conveying their delight that they just got "a raise and a cost of living allowance increase." No, they will be saying things like "Sue just sold her business, she's now worth twelve million" or "Chris has cashed in his stock options for five million." Instead of annual income, they discuss each other's *net worth*. By focusing on your net worth, above and beyond your earnings, your whole financial picture will begin to change.

First admit you don't know, then learn

Secrets of the Millionaire Mind provides some simple, almost-too-obvious advice: Poor people are focused on spending their money. Rich people are focused on making it, keeping it and investing it. Another way of saying this is that wealthy people are not smarter than poor people; they just have different and more supportive money habits. If you are not currently managing money well, it just means you were not programmed to do so. Eker notes that in school he was not taught Money Management 101, but the War of 1812, "which of course," he comments, "is something I use every single day." But once he learned money management, he was able to become rich.

Many people offer him the excuse: "I don't have any money to manage." Yet the way of the universe is that if you manage what you do have well, you will get more. Perhaps the greatest obstacle people have to becoming rich is that they "think they already know" about money, yet it is precisely your version of what is right that has led you to your current financial status. No one is ever born knowing how to manage money, Eker remarks. There is nothing holding you back from wealth except your own ignorance.

Final comments

If you are affronted by the brazen pursuit of wealth you might not like Eker's style, but it is worth reminding yourself of his point that love and money are both very important dimensions of life. Therefore, you are being disingenuous if, in the same way you work on having more love in your life, you do not work on having more money.

Some readers will be turned off by the fact that *Secrets of the Millionaire Mind* is used as a tool to sell Eker's other products, such as his "Millionaire Mind Intensive Seminar." But this self-promotion does not take away from the book's content, and as Eker himself notes, people who are immediately turned off by something that is "sold" to them are unlikely to be rich. Those with a millionaire mindset understand the role of promotion to both educate, and be educated in, new ideas. At any rate, with a price tag of less than $20 you may look back on the purchase of this book as a bargain. Notwithstanding all the other great prosperity titles, you could become wealthy by reading this one alone. There is a lot of powerful wisdom in fewer than 200 pages.

T. Harv Eker

Eker grew up in Toronto. His parents were European immigrants who arrived in Canada just after the Second World War with only $30. As a teenager he did odd jobs including selling newspapers, and after graduating from school he went to New York University, but stayed for only one year. He lived in several US cities, but none of the businesses he started met with success until he opened a retail fitness store, then one of the first in America.

Secrets of the Millionaire Mind *was his first book and reached no. 1 on the* New York Times *bestseller list. Eker's Peak Potentials Training organization offers a variety of wealth and personal development seminars.*

2007

The Billionaire Who Wasn't

"Chuck Feeney has been ahead of his time. By giving away his fortune, personally overseeing that it is put to the best use, and determining that Atlantic Philanthropies should spend itself out of existence, he ensured his personal legacy as the champion of giving while living."

"He never seemed to feel entitled to the things that went with being rich. By dispossessing himself of the trappings of wealth, he removed a temptation to think that wealth made him better than anyone else."

In a nutshell

Building a fortune is one thing, but seeing it put to good use while you are alive is an even greater satisfaction.

In a similar vein

Andrew Carnegie *The Gospel of Wealth* (p 64)
Joel T. Fleishman *The Foundation* (p 104)
Howard Schultz *Pour Your Heart into It* (p 248)
Lynne Twist *The Soul of Money* (p 278)

CHAPTER 15

Conor O'Clery

In 1988, *Forbes* magazine's annual list of America's most wealthy listed Charles F. Feeney as the 23rd richest American alive, with a personal worth of $1.3 billion, greater than that of Rupert Murdoch or Donald Trump. In fact, four years earlier Feeney had secretly given away almost his entire fortune to a philanthropic trust. He had retained enough to live on for the rest of his life, but no longer even owned a house or a car. He was, as Irish journalist Conor O'Clery phrases it in this powerful biography, "the billionaire who wasn't."

O'Clery had been introduced to Feeney while covering the New York financial world for the *Irish Times*, and when the true story was later revealed about the extent of Feeney's giving, he agreed to cooperate on a biography if it would mean that the philosophy of "giving while living" would be spread. O'Clery followed his subject around the world and talked to colleagues, family, and friends to gain insights into what drove one of history's biggest, and most fascinating, philanthropists.

The Billionaire Who Wasn't is two books in one: the remarkable story of duty-free retailing and its leading company, DFS, whose extraordinary growth and profits paralleled the rise of jet travel; and that of Feeney himself, businessman, linguist, and traveler, who took the needs of the world on his shoulders and became a model philanthropist.

Looking for opportunities

Charles Feeney was born into an Irish-American family in blue-collar New Jersey in 1931. His father was an insurance underwriter and his mother a nurse who liked to perform secret acts of charity. The family was lucky enough to make ends meet even through the Great Depression.

Charles was a bright boy and had a talent for making money from odd jobs. After graduating from high school he signed up for the US Air Force, first training as a radio operator in Texas before being stationed in Japan. Working in signals intelligence, he privately studied and became fluent in Japanese, and stayed on after the Korean War broke out.

After the war, Franklin D. Roosevelt's GI Bill gave Feeney the opportunity to go to university, and he chanced on an article on Cornell University's School of Hotel Management in upstate New York. It sounded interesting and he applied. When his acceptance came it was a big deal for the Feeneys, as no member of the family had ever been to university, and certainly not an Ivy League one like Cornell.

The hotel school was a breeding ground for entrepreneurs, and to help pay his way Feeney became the "sandwich man," selling sandwiches around campus at night when there were no burger joints or other places to eat. Graduating in 1956, to his mother's dismay he turned down offers to work for major hotel chains in favor of traveling. After winning a few thousand dollars in Nevada casinos he sailed to France, taking language courses and then organizing a summer camp for the children of US Navy staff on the French Riviera. There he met an Englishman selling duty-free liquor to American sailors (who were not allowed to drink while on board, but could have bottles shipped back to their homes in the US). Feeney caught up with a fellow Cornell graduate, Bob Miller, who was then working at a Ritz hotel in Spain, and the pair set up their own duty-free business. Neither would know at the time that their partnership (with the later addition of two more partners) would survive and become one of the most profitable in business history.

Their company, Duty-Free Shoppers or DFS, bid for and won the rights to run the first duty-free concessions at Honolulu and Hong Kong airports, followed by airport stores in Toronto, San Francisco, and Los Angeles. In the late 1960s and early 1970s most companies' stock prices experienced huge falls, but DFS was becoming a cash bonanza to its four partners, Feeney, Miller, Alan Parker, and Tony Pilaro, who by 1977 were receiving combined annual dividends of over $30 million. Feeney pocketed $12 million one year, $18 million the next, and as the 1980s began his annual share of the dividend was over $23 million, all in cash and tax free. DFS revenues continued to grew at a rate of 19 percent through the decade (with its Honolulu store alone turning over $400 million a year) and it became the largest liquor retailer in the world.

Ego-less giving

Though his family (including his French wife and five children) enjoyed homes around the world, from the south of France to Hawaii to New York, Feeney himself became increasingly uncomfortable with his wealth, and continued to fly economy-class and wear a $15 dollar watch. Casually and sometimes shabbily dressed, he was anything but the image of a wealthy businessman, and taught his kids to be self-reliant and unselfish, providing them with their own spending budgets to manage. He starting giving money away in an unstructured fashion, initially to Cornell (which he believed had given him so much) and to his children's school in Nice.

Feeney's lawyer and confidant, Harvey Dale, suggested he read Andrew Carnegie's famous essay on wealth and giving (see commentary p. 64) and also introduced him to Maimonides, a Jewish philosopher who wrote about *tzedakah* or giving, the highest level of which aimed to help people achieve self-sufficiency and was carried out anonymously. This sort of ego-less giving, also promoted in other religions, had a great effect on Feeney. Already not the sort of person to "blow his own horn" and get his name stuck on buildings, he resolved to become an anonymous donor.

Feeney's Atlantic Foundation, first registered in Bermuda in 1982, was unusual for a charitable foundation in comprising not simply a large sum of money, but actual ownership of companies and assets. Feeney made sure his wife and family had plenty to live on and kept the houses, but almost his entire fortune, including his 38.75 percent share in DFS, was transferred irrevocably to the foundation. He personally was left with less than $5 million, enough to continue his travels around the world and pick up restaurant tabs without having to worry. Though he would control the foundation's giving—mainly for education, health, aging-related issues, and social justice ends—he was no longer a rich man.

The spending begins

With his proud Irish heritage, Feeney traveled in Ireland a great deal in the 1980s. This was before the country's great economic boom and he wanted to do something to help. He began spending hundreds of millions of dollars on universities in both Ireland and Northern Ireland, setting them up to provide top-quality graduates when the economy finally leapt ahead. Atlantic also poured £75 million (which the Irish government was forced to match) into the university research sector, then among the weakest in Europe. The effect was transformative, with 46 research programs or institutes created and a reversal of the research brain drain to other countries. Yet all this was done in total secrecy, with the money received only on condition they did not seek to find out who the donor was.

Feeney's foundation also began contributing funds ($30 million over five years) to the Northern Ireland peace process, meeting Sinn Féin leader Gerry Adams and providing an office for the party in New York out of his own pocket. This inevitably brought accusations that Feeney was "funding the IRA" when it leaked out he was a donor, but Atlantic carefully funded projects on both sides of the conflict and its intervention became a great fillip to peace. Gerry Adams considered Feeney's role "pivotal" and a "brilliant investment."

Coming out

Feeney sold his stake in DFS in 1996 to the luxury goods company Louis Vuitton Moët Hennessy. All $1.62 billion of it was now to be spent by his foundation in his lifetime. After the sale, Feeney and Alan Parker sent checks to longstanding staff members in the company amounting to almost $40 million. The recipients, who were not expecting to gain anything, were astounded. As O'Clery notes, "It was an almost unheard-of act of generosity in the corporate world."

Feeney's largesse through the Atlantic Foundation (now Atlantic Philanthropies) was revealed to the world the following year by the *New York Times* under the headline: "He Gave Away $600 Million and No One Knew." The story noted that the foundation was now the fourth largest in America, behind Ford and Kellogg but bigger than Rockefeller and Mellon.

Emptying the coffers

On what is Atlantic spending its money? Overall, it has given 2,900 grants amounting to $4 billion. In the US this has included $600 million to Cornell University, $125 million to Stanford University, which Feeney's son attended, but also amounts to smaller institutions that Feeney has noticed needed upgrading and whose students were disadvantaged.

In keeping with the global outlook of its founder, Atlantic's tentacles of generosity spread around the world. Ashamed at what America did to Vietnam in its war there, Feeney's foundation has injected lot of money into improving healthcare and hospitals in the country, and establishing or restoring libraries, schools, and universities.

Feeney has also become Australia's most generous philanthropist, pouring millions into universities there. As in Ireland most are state funded, and his strategy has been to provide an initial third of monies needed, which are then matched by the university and government. Atlantic has also given millions for healthcare in Cuba (a challenging task given Feeney is an American citizen) and to AIDS-prevention work and several universities in South Africa.

The organization supports "civil society" organizations such as Amnesty and Human Rights First, has helped groups opposing the death penalty, and given donations to maintain nonprofit public broadcasting. Driven by Feeney's left-of-center politics (he opposed the Iraq war and George W. Bush's election to the US presidency in 2004), the foundation is considered "progressive."

Feeney's intention is that Atlantic's coffers will be emptied in his lifetime, and a target has been set for 2016. Given that, as of 2007, its endowment is around $4 billion, this means spending $400 million a year. Part of the "problem" of spending it all is that the foundation's investments have been spectacularly successful and it keeps growing in size. From 1980 to 2000, for instance, it averaged an annual return of 29 percent, thanks in part to smart investments in the technology field.

Final comments

As a business biography alone O'Clery's book is valuable, showing that huge money can be made from very simple business models. DFS's success could be put down to four men in a room working out what they would bid for airport duty-free concessions, and winning them. Once established, profits came easily. Feeney insisted that luck played a big role in the company's fortunes, that it reaped the benefits of being the first trusted brand in a fast-growing new field. Yet *The Millionaire Who Wasn't* is also peppered with his advice to others always to "think big" (in both business and philanthropy), and in his restless desire to build a great business even the other partners admitted that Feeney had been the driving force.

Today, Feeney travels the world with his second wife, former secretary Helga Flaiz, constantly seeking out new and better uses for his foundation's money and visiting potential donors in their offices instead of making them come to him. Many grants stem from things Feeney reads about in local newspapers on his travels, as much as formal proposals. He gains satisfaction from observing an eye operation to save someone's sight in a hospital he has funded, or anonymously watching students work in a library he helped establish.

O'Clery notes the irony of a man whose fortune was built on selling luxury goods, but who "would not be seen dead with a Louis Vuitton briefcase," and who once attended an important meeting with Irish prime minister Bertie Ahern wearing a pair of glasses "held together by a paper clip that stuck up like an aerial." Seamus Heaney, Ireland's Nobel Prize-winning poet, described Feeney as a modern-day St. Francis whose self-renunciation—combined with Medici-like largesse—has provided opportunities and happiness for millions. Whereas Bob Miller, his former partner, lives in luxury homes and socializes with European royalty, Feeney stays in bolthole apartments rented by his foundation, takes buses and taxis instead of limousines, and prefers to mix with normal people. His children note that he is generally a happy man, who would probably have been less happy if he had tried to hold on to his pile of money.

Conor O'Clery

Born in Belfast, O'Clery has a degree from Queen's University, Belfast. He has worked for the Irish Times *for 30 years in various reporting and editing roles, including stints as a foreign correspondent in London, Moscow, Washington, Beijing, and New York, and has twice been awarded Journalist of the Year in Ireland. He has also written for* The New Republic *and* Newsweek.

Other books include Daring Diplomacy: Clinton's Secret Search for Peace in Ireland *(1997) and* Panic at the Bank: How John Rusnak Lost AIB $700 Million *(with Siobahn Creaton, 2002).*

1936

Prosperity

"The unfailing resource is always ready to give. It has no choice in the matter; it must give, for that is its nature. Pour your living words of faith into the omnipresent substance, and you will be prospered though all the banks in the world close their doors. Turn the great energy of your thinking toward 'plenty' ideas, and you will have plenty regardless of what men about you are saying or doing."

"The spiritual substance is steadfast and immovable, enduring. It does not fluctuate with market reports. It does not decrease in 'hard times' nor increase in 'good times.' It cannot be hoarded away to cause a deficiency in supply and a higher price... It is ever the same, constant, abundant, freely circulating and available."

"The anxious thought must be eliminated and the perfect abandon of the child of nature assumed, and when to this attitude you add the realization of unlimited resources, you have fulfilled the divine law of prosperity."

In a nutshell

All wealth begins and ends with God, therefore gratitude for what you have is the master key to prosperity.

In a similar vein

Rhonda Byrne *The Secret* (p 58)
Napoleon Hill *The Master-Key to Riches* (p 158)
Catherine Ponder *Open Your Mind to Prosperity* (p 218)

CHAPTER 16

Charles Fillmore

Book titles that aim to define their subject often fall short of the mark. Samuel Smiles' *Self-Help* (1859), which launched the modern literature on the subject, is an exception. Another is Charles Fillmore's *Prosperity*, which although by no means the first title in the area is one of its great books.

Written in the depths of the Great Depression, *Prosperity* is a sort of triumphant victory song that celebrates the never-ending flow of "universal abundance," often in the face of apparent lack and hard times. Many will find it too old-fashioned, ethereal, or Christian for their liking, while others will see it as the most inspiring of all prosperity writings. Either way, all serious students of the subject should have it in their library.

Fillmore and his wife Myrtle founded the Unity spiritual movement, which has been instrumental in raising the profile of prosperity consciousness as a concept. Written when he was in his 80s, the book represents a lifetime of Fillmore's wisdom as a thinker and a writer, and is his best-known work.

Intelligence and the abundance of "nothingness"

In the early part of the book, Fillmore is keen to bring science into his spiritual reasoning. He notes the view of scientists of his time that the "ether" or atmosphere was not nothing, but

> *charged with electricity, magnetism, light rays, X rays, cosmic rays, and other dynamic radiations... it is the source of all life, light, heat, energy, gravitation, attraction, repulsion... it is the interpenetrating essence of everything that exists on the earth.*

In other words, he writes, "science gives to the ether all the attractions of heaven without directly saying so." Whether you call it space, the ether, spirit, God, or the heavens, the essential nature of this alive but nonphysical substance is to give; out of it all things come.

Prosperity in every sphere of life, from love to money to health, will result when you are attuned to this substance, relying on it rather than on the apparent solidity of matter and circumstances. Pour your faith into its reality and it will bring forth everything you need to prosper. This substance is the source of your supply, not conditions or people.

In having this faith, Fillmore observes, you have to forget any previous ideas about what is possible. God or spirit operates at a totally different level to matter, and physical form only comes into being as the result of what it intends. The universe is not a set of "blind mechanical forces." Rather, it is "persuaded and directed by intelligence."

The invisible supply

The implication, Fillmore says, is that the more you understand matter, money, and possessions as emerging from the universal spiritual flow, the less need there is for you to grasp after things and treat them as solely yours.

People must begin to consider themselves as "common heirs to the universal resource that is sufficient for all." He is not suggesting that you embrace communism, simply that you recognize your ability to create what you need and, after the fashion of the universe itself, not hoard but keep giving. Anyone who uses this knowledge of the invisible supply for what they might "get out of it" will be disappointed. Though they may seem to prosper at first, their selfish outlook will lead to no good in the end. The paradox of true prosperity is that the more you appreciate it as a force designed to lift up everyone, the more naturally your own good will arise.

Bless what you have

If you do find yourself low on funds, Fillmore says, praise and bless whatever you have and imagine it growing larger. When you eat, be grateful for the food in front of you as the embodiment of universal substance. Do not think about yourself, your interests, or your gains and losses, but think larger thoughts about an endlessly renewable supply and the good of all.

By blessing what you have, you put the law of increase into motion. All things in matter or spirit are connected, and by focusing on what is physically in front of you, you can imagine more of it coming into being. This is exactly what Jesus did with his loaves and fishes miracle, and what the widow did in the prophet Elisha's day when she turned her small amount of oil into enough to keep the lamps burning through the night.

Recognize the importance of thoughts and words

Prosperity cannot happen, Fillmore notes, while you continue to entertain poverty-stricken thoughts. Each thought draws more to it of the same type, leaving no room for the truth of prosperity to become part of your mindset.

You may discount your casual thoughts and ideas, but he warns that they "are the eternal realities from which we build our life and our world." Talk only of prosperity and it will become your reality. Say this to yourself, he suggests:

I am God's offspring, and I must think as God thinks. Therefore I cannot think of any lack or limitation.

Let God order your life and finances

Fillmore observed that many people live in the "real world" for six days of the week, then leave a bit of room for God on Sundays. For them, it is not right to bring spirituality into the marketplace.

If you are really to prosper, however, you must take a leap of faith and allow God into all areas of your life. He writes:

This mind of the Spirit will guide you in perfect ways, even in the minute details of your life, if you will let it do so. But you must will to do its will and trust it in all your ways. It will lead you unfailingly into health, happiness, and prosperity, as it has done and is doing for thousands, if and when you follow it.

Give up striving

Nature does not need to strive and neither do you. In one of his more beautiful passages, Fillmore observes:

We do not have to work laboriously in the outer to accomplish what the lily does so silently and beautifully. Most of us rush around trying to work out our problems for ourselves and in our own way, with one idea, one vision: the material thing we seek. We need to devote more time to silent meditation and like the lilies of the field simply be patient and grow into our demonstrations… these substance ideas with which we are working are eternal ideas that have always existed and will continue to exist, the same ideas that formed this planet in the first place and that sustain it now.

Things come to you easily when you live in a state of love and gratitude. Dwelling on thoughts of Spirit, God, and love leads you to everything you need, plus a host of blessings you never even expected or wanted.

More prosperity principles

Among Fillmore's many other insights are:

- You don't have to know how the prosperity law works scientifically. All you must do for it to work is to have a time of silence once a day in order to concentrate on the source from which all things come. Recognition of it, gratefulness for it, and faith in it is enough for it to work for you.
- You never prosper by trying to get anything out of anyone, or trying to "win" in a trade or bargain. Instead, "Hold steadily to the law of equity and justice that is working in and through you, knowing for a certainty that you are supplied with everything necessary to fulfil all your requirements."
- Don't be anxious. People who hunger to be good and righteous are always fulfilled. If you put Spirit first, you should not be ashamed about picturing what

you need and knowing it is already coming to you—now. If doubts creep in, say, "I trust Omnipotence… I know that God does provide for the fulfilment of His divine idea, and I am that divine idea."

- Don't simply ask God for riches. Instead, like Solomon—the richest man of his age—ask for wisdom, for ideas. People from all over the world visited Solomon for advice and brought gold with them. Great judgment, given as a gift from God, is a basic ingredient of prosperity.
- Some believe that poverty can be a blessing—that it is God's will for us to have hard times as well as good times so that we can appreciate things more. But this is not the way of God at all: His nature is eternal giving and new creation, and it is up to us to attune ourselves to this reality.
- Whatever talent you have you must use it fearlessly, not letting anything stand in your way. To bury your talent goes against the prosperity law. Don't focus too much on your present conditions, only on what you are on your way to becoming.
- Give away 10 percent of all money that comes to you: "There is nothing that keeps a person's mind so fearless and so free to receive the good constantly coming to him as the practice of tithing."

Final comments

Today, bestsellers like *The Secret* have made prosperity consciousness a household concept, but in 1930s America, when the evidence pointed only to the reality of hard times, it took courage and moral leadership to affirm the ideas contained in Fillmore's book.

There is something very comforting and inspiring about *Prosperity*. It is the book to read when you feel overwhelmed by your financial problems, as it shows you that ultimately the source of all wealth is nonmaterial. Most of the time you may be focused on the routines of working, spending, and saving, when the real source of prosperity, the infinite spiritual "substance" from which all matter comes, awaits your attention. If you can go into a quiet place and be still, you will be reminded of this source and worry less about where the money will come from. Fillmore asked out loud to the reader, "Is this an impractical utopia?" His answer was that you could not know until you tried out his concepts in your life.

Some readers won't like the many references to the Bible, but Fillmore was a founder of the very undogmatic Unity church and in fact his explanation of the spiritual laws of prosperity goes beyond any single religion.

He intentionally never copyrighted his books so that they could be made free forever, a gesture that underlined his belief in plenty. You can freely download *Prosperity* from the internet (see the Credits section for details).

Charles Fillmore

Born on an Indian reservation in Minnesota in 1854, the son of a trader, in his late teens and 20s Fillmore worked as a printer's apprentice, mule-team driver, and assayer.

In 1884 he and his wife Myrtle moved to Kansas City, where they invested in real estate but lost all their money. They began attending classes on New Thought philosophy and its ideas on the healing powers of the mind, which seemed to cure Myrtle of her tuberculosis and Fillmore of the leg injury that he had received as a boy.

In 1889 they began a silent prayer group and established a new journal, Modern Thought, *followed by* Unity *magazine two years later. Based in Kansas City, over the next few decades the Unity organization grew to include a radio station, a vegetarian restaurant, a business magazine, and, in 1906, ordained ministers. In 1929 it relocated to land at Lee's Summit, Missouri, where Unity Village is still the world headquarters for the Unity church.*

Myrtle Fillmore died in 1931 and Charles in 1948.

2007

The Foundation

"There are thousands of foundations actively working for the betterment of society here in the United States and around the world. And behind each foundation stands a wealthy individual or family that chose to declare 'enough is enough,' and then gave away a significant portion of their wealth for the benefit of the wider community rather than hoard it, invest it, or spend even more of it on personal pleasures."

In a nutshell

Private wealth in the form of foundations is a valuable "third force" in changing the world.

In a similar vein

Andrew Carnegie *The Gospel of Wealth* (p 64)
Conor O'Clery *The Billionaire Who Wasn't* (p 92)
Lynne Twist *The Soul of Money* (p 278)
Muhammad Yunus *Banker to the Poor* (p 286)

CHAPTER 17

Joel T. Fleishman

In 2006, the usually low-profile world of philanthropy hit the headlines. Warren Buffett, the second richest person in the world, announced that he would be giving away the bulk of his fortune. Though the scale of the donation was remarkable ($31 billion), the real surprise came from the way it would be distributed. Buffett would not create his own foundation, but instead give his money to the Bill and Melinda Gates Foundation, which itself already had $32 billion. Buffett's reasoning was that, although he had been brilliant at making money, he did not believe he would be as good at giving it away. The Gates foundation was already set up and had goals he approved of, so it made sense to entrust his money to it; a typically smart and humble move by the world's greatest investor.

Vehicles for giving

In *The Foundation* Fleishman notes that the modern foundation was pioneered by Andrew Carnegie (see commentary p. 64), whose systematic funding of thousands of public libraries and establishment of institutions devoted to peace have had great and often unmeasured benefits for millions of people.

Most people have heard of the Ford and Rockefeller Foundations, thanks to their famous donors, but they are only the tip of an iceberg. Fleishman, who has worked in and around foundations most of his life, notes that there are 68,000 in America alone. While most are small, in 2003 46 had assets of more than $1 billion, and 64 had assets of between $500 million and $1 billion. In 2005 they made combined annual grants of more than $33 billion. (The Bill and Melinda Gates Foundation is mandated to give out more than a tenth of this total, $3.5 billion, every year.)

These are amazing figures, and Fleishman is clearly a believer in the power of foundations to do good. At a sociological level, he argues that they are an important "third force" separate to government and business. Yet while governments have an electorate to answer to, and businesses must make account to their shareholders, foundations are not really accountable to anyone. To fulfill their potential, he suggests, they will have to become more focused and less secretive.

Why give wealth away?

In a book drawing on 45 years of studying, working with, and running foundations, Fleishman asks the obvious question: Why do rich donors want to divest themselves of their wealth?

He includes a quotation from the autobiography of John D. Rockefeller, *Random Reminiscences of Men and Events* (1909). Noting that you can only get so much happiness from nice meals, big houses, and fine clothes, Rockefeller wrote: "As I study wealthy men, I can see but one way in which they can secure a real equivalent for money spent, and that is to cultivate a taste for giving where the money may produce an effect which will be lasting gratification."

While creating a foundation can be used by the donor as a way to better their public image (Fleishman notes that the announcement of the Gates Foundation came in the midst of Microsoft's antitrust battle with the US government), on the whole this is not the case, as many donors have good reputations in the first place and genuinely want to "give something back." They consider themselves lucky people, and simply wish to confer on others some of the advantages they have enjoyed.

What foundations do

What foundations do is as diverse as the personalities of their founders. Some are politically liberal, some conservative; some like taking risks, others do not. They can be variously a driver, a partner, or a catalyst, depending on the amount of involvement or money they put into a certain goal or project. Many were set up to support specific institutions (e.g. the Duke tobacco family's endowment of Duke University, or rail magnate Leland Stanford's founding of Stanford University), while others have a very broad remit to promote "the well-being of mankind throughout the world" (the stated aim of the John D. Rockefeller foundation).

Rockefeller's money was used to build the University of Chicago and the Rockefeller Institute of Medical Research (now Rockefeller University), which produced a vaccine for yellow fever, and was also put toward research work to improve agricultural output in developing countries. The "Green Revolution," which allowed Pakistan and India to grow enough food to ward off mass starvation, was spearheaded by Rockefeller agronomist Normal Borlaug, who won the Nobel Prize in 1970 and was credited with saving over a billion lives. The Ford and Kellogg Foundations have also been instrumental in helping to increase agricultural yields in poor countries.

Andrew Carnegie's money built 1,681 libraries in America and 2,509 around the world, set up Carnegie-Mellon University and the Carnegie Endowment for International Peace, funded the US National Bureau of Economic Research, and was behind the Public Broadcasting Commission that led to the establishment of the PBS television network and US National Public Radio. Gunnar Myrdal's famous report on race issues, *The American Dilemma*, was financed by the Carnegie Corporation, as was the research that led to the making of *Sesame Street*, the first truly educational kids television show that helped millions of disadvantaged children become literate.

Foundations do not often start great new movements or ideas, but allow them to expand and flourish. The Ford Foundation helped to expand Muhammad Yunus's Grameen Bank in Bangladesh (see commentary p 286), providing for thousands more micro-credit loans to the "poorest of the poor." The Alfred P. Sloan Foundation, which seeks to increase public understanding of science, put up money for the acclaimed plays *Copenhagen* and *Hubbell*, and the Ford Foundation provided start-up money for the Mexican-American Legal Fund and other minority legal defense organizations. Billionaire financier George Soros's foundation has been involved in a long-term institution-building effort to create "open societies" in the former eastern bloc states.

The aims and achievements of some of the larger foundations include:

- Kaiser Family Foundation—healthcare for people without insurance.
- Robert Wood Johnson Foundation—created by one of the three brothers of Johnson & Johnson fame, funds programs to counter tobacco and obesity.
- Atlantic Philanthropies—mainly education, health and aging, and social justice, established by duty-free king Chuck Feeney (see commentary p 92).
- Rosenwald Fund—Julius Rosenwald spent his clothing fortune building almost 5,000 schools for black children in the American South.
- Annie E. Casey Foundation—Annie E. Casey was the mother of Jim Casey, who started the messenger service that became the UPS Corporation. Gives grants for programs to help disadvantaged children and youth.
- Andrew Mellon Foundation—established by the eponymous banker and industrialist, provides chairs, fellowships, and grants to sustain studies in the humanities; builds libraries in Central and Eastern Europe.
- Henry Luce Foundation—the famous publisher's foundation honors his wife Clare Boothe Luce by giving awards to women studying science, engineering, and mathematics.
- Howard Hughes—the billionaire aviator's Medical Institute has produced four Nobel Prize winners and a number of significant advances and discoveries.
- Commonwealth Foundation—funding for social work, hospice care, geriatrics, and gerontology.
- William and Flora Hewlett Foundation—the HP founder's focus is on alternative dispute resolution, while the David and Lucille Packard Foundation promotes sustainable energy use in China.

Not all foundation work has been praiseworthy. Both the Carnegie and Ford foundations were involved in eugenics programs that sought to create a scientific basis for differences between racial types, and the Rockefeller Foundation was behind syphilis experiments conducted on Alabama prisoners without their consent between 1932 to 1972.

On the whole, though, foundations have made and continue to make a great positive impact, often getting behind issues that seem too risky or expensive for governments to tackle.

Proving their worth

The issue that Fleishman has (along with plenty of politicians and journalists) is that foundations are not really accountable to anyone. But why should they be, if they were established wholly through a private fortune?

His answer is that they receive significant taxpayer-funded support and protection. In the United States foundations do not pay tax on income or appreciation, and pay only a "federal foundation tax," which is usually only 1 or 2 percent of their assets. Thus the government forgoes money that otherwise might have been collected and redistributed to taxpayers; also, because giving by the general public is tax deductible (individuals give over $20 billion a year to foundations in the US), the Treasury loses out on revenue it otherwise would have received through taxing higher incomes.

Fleishman estimates that around $20 billion is lost in tax every year by giving foundations special status. However, as foundations give away $32 billion a year, there is a net benefit of $12 billion to society. But does the money spent generate real, focused social value? The US Congress has become more interested in this issue, and in the last few years attempts have been made to raise the minimum amount that foundations have to pay out every year (currently 5 percent of assets per annum). Apart from basic financial documents that need to be submitted to the Internal Revenue Service, foundations have little accountability for how they are run, who they employ, and how much salary is paid to staffers.

Fleishman's argument is that these bodies can't just settle for "doing good." They must get more rigorous about where their money is most efficiently and usefully deployed, tackling society's most urgent problems, and they must set goals and benchmarks for their own performance. Society strikes a bargain with foundations: They get tax exemption, but in return they have to prove their worth to the tax-paying public.

The future of philanthropy

All the surplus wealth that society generates has to go somewhere. As Fleishman notes, new and rich foundations are springing up every day. In the 30-year period to 2009 there will likely be a doubling in their number.

Yet the traditional foundation seems to be giving way to "venture philanthropists"—newly rich, often very young tycoons, such as eBay founder Pierre Omidyar and Google's Larry Page and Sergey Brin—who want to bring the same entrepreneurial abilities to solving social problems that they did to building businesses. Many are opting for a mixture of profit and nonprofit vehicles to achieve their goals.

Another trend is strategic partnerships. The Sloan, Rockefeller, and Gates foundations, for instance, have combined to fund the International AIDS Vaccine Initiative, and the Gates and Rockefeller foundations have formed the Alliance for a Green Revolution in Africa, which will team decades of Rockefeller expertise in agronomy with Gates money. Such a combining of strengths could produce a new wave of charitable value for millions.

Final comments

Based on extensive interviews and detailed case studies, *The Foundation* is the best-researched contemporary guide to its subject. Though it is focused on US foundations, these do account for the vast majority of the world's private charitable wealth. Fleishman points out that America's charitable dispensation will grow hugely in the twenty-first century, with one estimate being $41 *trillion* between now and 2050. We are thus entering a golden age for philanthropy, but with hopefully a greater emphasis on measurable results.

Amid all this giving, it is easy to forget where the money came from and to take for granted the many great scientific advances, social programs, and institutions that foundation money has bought. Legislators and others have a right to demand more accountability from these organizations, but they should not go too far, as Fleishman rightly suggests. Many of their most potent results have emerged from the ability to act freely, while still staying true to the vision of the founding donors.

Joel T. Fleishman

Fleishman is Professor of Law and Public Policy at Duke University in North Carolina, a post he has held since 1971, and is also Director of the Samuel and Ronnie Heyman Center for Ethics, Public Policy and the Professions. He has a Master of Laws degree from Yale University.

From 1993 to 2001 Fleishman was president of the Atlantic Philanthropic Service Company (now Atlantic Philanthopies, the foundation of Chuck Feeney, see commentary p. 92), and is currently a trustee of The John and Mary Markle Foundation and chairman of the board of trustees of the Urban Institute. He is a director of Polo Ralph Lauren Corporation and Boston Scientific Corporation.

1962

Capitalism and Freedom

"The great achievement of capitalism has not been the accumulation of property, it has been the opportunities it has offered to men and women to extend and develop and improve their capacities."

""The great advances of civilization... have never come from centralized government... Newton and Liebnitz; Einstein and Bohr; Shakespeare, Milton and Pasternak; Whitney, McCormick, Edison and Ford; Jane Addams, Florence Nightingale, and Albert Schweitzer; no one of these opened new frontiers in human knowledge and understanding, in literature, in technical possibilities, or in the relief of human misery in response to governmental directives. Their achievements were the product of individual genius, or strongly held minority views, of a social climate permitting variety and diversity."

In a nutshell

The free market, not government, ensures protection of individual rights and standards of quality, and delivers extraordinary prosperity to those who seek it.

In a similar vein

Ayn Rand *Capitalism* (p 234)
Adam Smith *The Wealth of Nations* (p 260)

CHAPTER 18

Milton Friedman

Capitalism and Freedom, a major work of twentieth-century economics and political philosophy, opens controversially. Friedman asserts that John F. Kennedy's famous statement in his inaugural address as United States president—"Ask not what your country can do for you, ask what you can do for your country"—was not worthy of the role of an individual in a free society.

Government, Friedman writes, should not be the patron of an individual, nor should that person consider themselves a servant of the government. In a real democracy the nation exists only for the will of the people; governments are a means toward an end, nothing more.

Capitalism and Freedom is a reiteration of what Scottish economist Adam Smith (see commentary p. 260) said less than two centuries before: Left to their own devices and free of excessive government control, people prosper and create civilized communities. Yet in the twentieth century, in the face of various socialist experiments and growing state intervention in western countries, Friedman's reminder became an urgent one. Making a clear connection between economic freedom and political freedom, he showed that free markets were not a luxury but the very basis of personal and political liberty.

How free markets protect

Historically, political freedom has followed the emergence of free markets and capitalist institutions. This is because, Friedman notes, a healthy private economy naturally provides a check on the power of the state.

For instance, even though they were officially persecuted, in medieval times Jews still thrived because they could operate as merchants. The Puritans and Quakers were only able to relocate to America because they had built up funds in the comparatively free market of Britain, despite being lumbered with other restrictions.

Where monopolies and trading restrictions are rife, so is special treatment of one social, racial, or religious group over another; the ability to "keep people in their place" remains. In a genuinely free market, economic efficiency is separated from irrelevant characteristics such as skin color or faith. "[The] purchaser of bread," Friedman remarks, "does not know whether it was made from wheat grown by a white man or a Negro, by a Christian or Jew." Further, a businessperson who favors one group over another will be at a market disadvantage to a businessperson who does not, and one who is blind to differences among suppliers will have more choice from whom to buy and hence lower costs.

During the period of blacklisting of Hollywood actors and screenwriters as a result of Senator McCarthy's anticommunist witchhunts, many writers continued to work anyway, often under assumed names. Without an impersonal market that created a demand for their services, they would have lost their livelihood. In a communist society, Friedman notes, such a situation would be impossible since all of the jobs are controlled by the state. In another example, Winston Churchill was prohibited from speaking out against Hitler on BBC radio in the years after the German Chancellor came to power, because the matter was deemed too controversial. It is unlikely this would have happened had the BBC not been a government monopoly. Friedman's message: Governments often seek to protect citizens from all sorts of things, failing to see that the "invisible hand" operating in free and open markets—for goods, labor, and information—somehow manages to offer much greater protections of personal liberty.

The idea that free markets do this was the exact opposite of what intellectuals were saying through most of the twentieth century. The individual was seen to be vulnerable in the face of corporate power and to need governmental protection. This view evolved out of the horrors of the Great Depression, which was considered to be a terrible failure of the markets. In fact, as Friedman argues in *Capitalism and Freedom*, the Depression was largely a failure of government.

Meddling in the market

Both full employment and economic growth have been put up as reasons governments should have more control over the economy. The Great Depression, people invariably say, is surely evidence of the inherent instability of markets left to their own devices.

In fact, Friedman says, the Depression was caused by government mismanagement. The US government's Federal Reserve System, through clumsy use of the levers of the monetary system (specifically, not increasing the money supply in the wake of bank collapses), turned what would have been a contraction lasting a year or two into a catastrophe. The "mistakes of a few men" caused untold misery to millions, which could have been avoided if the market had been truly left to itself. Though he accepts that it is the role of government to create a stable monetary system, the responsibility is a grave one and should be severely limited.

In his chapter on fiscal policy, Friedman observes that Keynesian government spending to kick-start stagnant or depressed markets is simply "economic mythology" and is not proven by empirical studies. For every $100 spent there may be a $100 effect, but the real consequence is a growth in government spending, and however well intentioned it may be, most of it is inefficiently allocated.

Progress via people, not governments

There is never any shortage of "good reasons" why government should get involved in curing market or social ills. Sometimes the good intentions are matched with impressive achievements. Friedman applauds, for example, the creation of a US national freeway system, the building of major dams, its public school system, and some public health measures.

However, most of the advances in the American people's standard of living have arisen from their ingenuity and have nothing to do with government. Prosperity has come despite all the laws and "projects," not because of them. Generally, excess regulations "force people to act against their immediate interests in order to promote a supposedly general interest."

Friedman famously includes a list of areas of government intervention that he believed were not justifiable. These include tariffs and import quotas, subsidies to farmers, rent controls, minimum wages, regulation of industries including banks, transport, and radio/television, social security programs making people put aside a certain amount of money for retirement, public housing, licensing of occupations, and conscription in peacetime.

While all these policies sound good in theory, in truth they often have the reverse effects than those they intended. For instance, the minimum wage was partly aimed at alleviating the poverty of African-Americans; what actually happened was that the unemployment rate of teenage blacks shot up. Public housing was designed to alleviate poverty; instead, it concentrated poverty in pockets. Social security policies were intended to provide a safety net for those unable to work, but instead created dependants who might otherwise have contributed to the economy. Friedman's damning conclusion: "Concentrated power is not rendered harmless by the good intentions of those who create it."

There are really only two ways in which a society can organize economic activity, Friedman writes:

- through centralization and coercion
- through facilitating a marketplace for the trade of goods and services

The drive toward centralization usually begins in a spirit of goodwill, but before too long power becomes more important, and "the ends justify the means." Coercion and violence are considered a small price to pay for a glorious dream of equality.

In a free country, however, free discussion and voluntary cooperation are the means for achieving anything. This may be a slower way to achieve ends, but it is surer and less dangerous. The beauty of markets is the way they allow unanimity without conformity; a direction emerges, but no one has been *made* to do anything.

Freedom first, equality second

Friedman argues that inequality is always less in capitalist countries. Many will disagree with this, pointing to the vast gaps between, say, a corporate executive earning $10,000 a day, and someone who works in a shop earning $20,000 a year. Yet even a low-paid person in a capitalist economy, he points out, is better off than the privileged classes were a century ago. They do not have to engage in backbreaking labor, medical care is vastly improved, they have at least basic education, they live with modern plumbing and heating, and they have cars, television, radio, telephones, and entertainment, all of which the rich and royal of previous times could only have dreamed about. Even if individuals do not seem to do well out of capitalism, they still benefit in many ways. In contrast, in stratified social systems and communism the "goodies" always seem to go only to those at the top.

The heart of liberal philosophy, Friedman writes, is people having equal rights and equal opportunity. It does not mean that there should be equal wealth. If everyone grows richer in a capitalist system, this is a welcome by-product of freedom, but it is not its purpose. The purpose of a free, capitalist system is the freedom of the individual. What they do with that freedom is their business.

Final comments

In the Preface to the 1982 edition, Friedman notes that, although there were signs of change, America and other western countries still had a long way to go in reducing the weight of government. Ronald Reagan and Margaret Thatcher were among his admirers and sought to keep government small, but neither actually managed to reduce the level of government spending. Today, farm protection is still high, free trade is still an aim rather than a reality, and in most countries government spending as a share of gross domestic product has remained the same or grown. Despite endless evidence to the contrary, it seems that governments still believe they know what is best for the people.

The Economist described Friedman as "the most influential economist of the second half of the 20th century... possibly all of it." His influence did not just lie in what he said, but in the fact that he was able to say it to noneconomists. Until the publication of *Capitalism and Freedom* he was little known outside the academic world, but the book (which has sold over half a million copies) raised his public profile, as did his 300 columns in *Newsweek* magazine and his popular *Free to Choose* television series.

Capitalism and Freedom may shift your beliefs about economic morality. You may have assumed that the government that intervenes to "help" people the most is morally superior, but Friedman shows how free economic and political systems ensure the dignity of the individual in a myriad of often unforeseen ways.

Countries fashioned after the ideas of Adam Smith and Friedman should in theory be monsters of selfish consumerism. But as Friedman pointed out, people want to be free not just so they can get rich, but to live according to deeply held values. Prosperity is not just about making money, but about the freedom to live the way you want.

Milton Friedman

Born in 1912 in Brooklyn, New York, Friedman was the youngest child of Jewish immigrants from what is now the Ukraine. They moved to New Jersey when he was still a baby and ran a dry goods store. He graduated from high school before he was 16, winning a scholarship to Rutgers University where he studied mathematics and economics, then another scholarship for a Master's degree at the University of Chicago, received in 1933. At Chicago he met his future wife and collaborator, Rose Director, and studied under distinguished economists Jacob Viner and Frank Knight.

Unable to find an academic job during the Depression, Friedman worked as an economist in the Roosevelt administration. At this time he believed in Keynesian economics, but later came to the view that government fixing of wages and prices only hampered America's recovery. During the Second World War he worked at the Division of War Research at Columbia University, receiving his PhD in 1946. In the same year he accepted a teaching position at the University of Chicago, where for the next 30 years he formed the center of the Chicago School of libertarian economics.

In 1964 Friedman was an adviser to Barry Goldwater in his campaign for the US Presidency; he later advised Richard Nixon. His ideas were influential in the acceptance of fluctuating exchange rates and the floating of the dollar. Friedman won the Nobel Prize for Economics in 1976 and the Presidential Medal of Freedom from Ronald Reagan in 1988. He died in 2006.

Other works include his magnum opus, A Monetary History of the United States, 1867–1960 *(with Anna Schwartz, 1963), and* Free to Choose: A Personal Statement *(with Rose Friedman, 1980).*

2005

The World Is Flat

"It is now possible for more people than ever to collaborate and compete in real time with more other people on more different kinds of work from more different corners of the planet and on a more equal footing than at any previous time in the history of the world—using computers, e-mail, fiber-optic networks, teleconferencing, and dynamic new software."

"Wealth and power will increasingly accrue to those countries, companies, individuals, universities, and groups who get three basic things right: the infrastructure to connect with this flat-world platform, the education to get more of their people innovating on, working off of, and tapping into this platform, and, finally, the governance to get the best out of this platform and cushion its worst side effects."

In a nutshell

Technological advance is creating a "level playing field" in which previously marginalized people and countries can play a competitive role in the world economy.

In a similar vein

Milton Friedman *Capitalism and Freedom* (p 110)
Paul Zane Pilzer *God Wants You to Be Rich* (p 214)
Adam Smith *The Wealth of Nations* (p 260)

CHAPTER 19

Thomas Friedman

In 2004 Friedman, a prize-winning foreign affairs columnist and author of a book on globalization, *The Lexus and the Olive Tree*, went to Bangalore—India's Silicon Valley—to learn why Indians had begun to take over information technology and other service work that had once been done within the borders of America and other rich countries.

He discovered that India was becoming a major player not just in outsourced IT, but also in areas such as accounting and radiology. In east Asia he found a similar story. Despite the two countries' uneasy historical relationship, Japan had begun outsourcing data-entry and software-development services to China, especially Dalian, China's own Silicon Valley. In the United States, Friedman was surprised to discover that JetBlue airlines was "homesourcing" its flight-reservation services to housewives working out of their homes in Salt Lake City, Utah.

These and many other examples convinced him that fairly recent developments in information technology had leveled the world's playing field, creating a new "flat" global economy that was allowing individuals and small organizations to compete—and collaborate—with each other like never before. Globalization was not simply making goods and services cheaper for those living in the rich world, but was enriching the providers, wherever they lived.

The World Is Flat was first published in 2005 and became a worldwide bestseller. Because of continued technological and market developments and the need to explore their implications in further depth, a second edition was published in 2006, followed by yet another edition with new chapters in 2007. At over 600 pages the book is packed with hundreds of ideas, examples, and anecdotes that are not possible to summarize here. However, the themes below try to give you a taste.

How the world flattened

In setting the scene, Friedman goes back to the origins of globalization to show that "flattening" has been going on for a long time. He divides the process into three eras. Globalization 1.0 spanned 1492 to 1800 and was about countries exploring global opportunities, beginning with Columbus's "discovery" of America. Globalization 2.0, from around 1800 to 2000, involved a shift toward companies becoming the major players in the world economy. Very recently, starting around 2000, Globalization 3.0 has enabled individuals to compete and collaborate globally, including many more non-westerners.

A handful of key factors, or "flatteners," enabled Globalization 3.0 to develop. On the political front, the key event was the fall of the Berlin Wall in 1989, which "tipped the balance of power across the world toward those advocating democratic, consensual, free-market-oriented governance, and away from those advocating authoritarian rule with centrally planned economies." This development helped moved the world toward being perceived as "a single market, a single ecosystem, and a single community."

In technology, the popularization of personal computers was pivotal. Starting in the mid-1990s, the power of PCs was greatly leveraged by the global connectivity provided by the internet, the World Wide Web, and the Netscape web-browsing interface. In addition, a massive overinvestment by telecommunications companies in global fiberoptic lines meant it suddenly became very cheap to communicate and send large files from anywhere to anywhere. India took full advantage of this cheap infrastructure in its array of ingenious outsourcing solutions.

This connectivity was further leveraged by workflow software, enabling projects to be divided into pieces and completed in different parts of the world, then seamlessly reintegrated. In addition, Web search engines such as Yahoo! and Google gave everyone access to a universe of real-time information at their fingertips. It was expected that this would allow existing media companies to "push" their content easily to millions more. In fact, the more powerful effect was individuals uploading their own content to the Web through avenues such as blogging, Wikipedia, and podcasting. These developments were further enhanced by what Friedman calls "steroids," additional technologies such as wireless connectivity that let people work and utilize information outside the normal workplace.

The convergence of these changes around the year 2000 led to entirely new forms of commerce. India became a major hub for outsourcing services, China became a leading offshore manufacturer for the world market, and companies like Wal-Mart and Dell pioneered hyperefficient "supply chaining" involving intricate global networks for manufacturing and distribution. The convergence, Friedman writes, was no less than "the most important force shaping global economics and politics in the early twenty-first century."

The rest of *The World Is Flat* explores the implications of these changes.

A new world of work

The flattening process is moving some jobs to other countries and is eliminating others altogether. However, novel categories of jobs will emerge to make optimal use of the new flattened platform. These will include "collaborators," who coordinate efforts horizontally within and between companies; "synthesizers," who integrate disparate areas of knowledge in innovative ways; "explainers," who can explain complex matters to any audience; "personalizers," who create value by providing the human touch to services and products; and "green people," who have the knowledge and skills to fix environmental problems.

These new types of jobs build on existing knowledge but require different ways of deploying it. Friedman notes:

> *it was never good to be mediocre in your job, but in a world of walls, mediocrity could still earn you a decent wage… In a flatter world, you really do not want to be mediocre or lack any passion for what you do.*

In short, a flattened world is bringing a shakeout of traditional ways of working, in which only those who love what they do and provide unique value will really prosper.

True education

As jobs shift and competition intensifies, Friedman comments, education will provide the key to adding value. It must become central to a society's functioning, combining traditional teaching with product wizardry, and must flow over the conventional borders of work, school, and home. If you are not constantly learning, you can be sure that someone doing a similar job to yours *is*.

Education must again revolve around genuine passion and curiosity, so that the vital habit of self-education is developed. A core of technical knowledge will always be needed, but Friedman astutely points out that full development of potential will also require generalist, liberal arts education and encouragement of right-brained thinking. This allows people to "connect the dots" between disciplines, leading to enhanced creativity and innovation.

Role of government

Friedman suggests that, in a flattening world, the role of government will essentially be to ensure that markets are free, taking away current forms of protectionism that—to their long-term economic detriment—insulate people from the real world. In an active sense, governments will need to focus on promoting a physical and social context that enables people to make the most of a new flat-world platform, while limiting its drawbacks. They will need to invest heavily in both conventional physical infrastructure such as roads and sanitation, as well as high-tech infrastructure such as fast broadband access for everyone. In social terms, they must maintain the rule of law, so that human interactions can happen in an atmosphere of trust. At the same time, red tape will need to be cut so that innovation is not hindered. To help individuals keep up with intensified competition and adapt to shifting job markets, measures such as allowing for portable job benefits and supporting lifelong learning will also be important.

Ireland is offered as an example of highly successful government involvement. In the space of one generation, reforms such as free college education, national healthcare, and courting foreign investment have made it the second richest country (per capita) in Europe, ahead of Germany, France, and Britain. Nine of the world's top ten pharmaceutical companies, and seven of the ten top software companies, now have operations in Ireland, and Dell is its top exporter. Once, the country's greatest export was its people. Now, heavily invested in, they are its greatest asset.

Culture matters

The link between culture and economic success is often seen as a complex and sensitive issue, but Friedman is not afraid to jump in with the view that "invisibles" like openness to innovation, adaptability, frugality, tenacity, patience, and hard work make all the difference to a nation's success. Furthermore, as technology knocks down the walls around countries, the benefits or drawbacks of these cultural differences are exposed.

Friedman is more ambivalent about how flattening will affect culture itself, and perhaps rightly so, given the lack of precedents for such intensified global cultural contacts and mixing. On one hand, flattening could promote cultural diversity, for example by allowing individuals to "upload" their local culture to the world. On the other, given the cultural dominance of the US in technology and the media, flattening could lead to a degree of cultural homogenization. Either way, the genie is out of the box. The key issue is how individuals, businesses, and governments adapt so they can flourish according to their own goals.

Interestingly, despite his focus on technology, Friedman stresses the importance of personal qualities for prospering in the new landscape. He notes that, in a flattening world, "the most important competition is now with yourself—making sure that you are always striving to get the most out of your imagination, and then acting on it." Imagination, vision, hard work, tenacity—these seem to be the constants in the achievement of personal and economic success, and in a world in which technology is the great leveler, they become even more valuable.

Final comments

The World Is Flat is a captivating read that, true to Friedman's trade, often feels like a series of interlinked magazine articles. He is a prolific generator of words, and it will take you a long time to get through the whole book.

Its bold theme, combined with Friedman's high profile, has attracted plenty of criticism, including:

- Its thesis appears to rely on information and opinions gleaned by "talking with friends in high places" (Friedman seems to be able to get interviews with anyone on the planet), which may be acceptable in journalism but is not sufficient as the basis of a work of political economy.

- The book is suffused with a value system based on a belief in free markets and American cultural and economic dominance.
- The power of multinational corporations, and the adverse consequences of their profit-centered focus, are underestimated.
- Prospects seem dim for the true participation of regions such as Africa, and even rural India and China, in a flattening world. (As Friedman himself notes, the high-tech sector accounts for only 0.2 percent of the Indian population; Bangalore is not India.)

While these points may be valid, they do not render the book's broad thesis inaccurate. The fact is, we do live in a more connected world, and even though certain regions seem to have been left behind, it does not cancel out the long-term trend. History may be the best guide here. Britain's industrial revolution, for instance, was centered in its main cities, and if you ventured into the countryside you may not have noticed any great change. But it was happening nevertheless, and in a generation or two the society and economy were transformed, making it the wealthiest country on earth.

The World Is Flat does not say that flattening will make everybody in every country rich. It does say, however, that with access to technology there are now opportunities that did not exist even ten years ago for people to engage in the world economy. This must be a positive development.

Thomas Friedman

Born in 1953 in Minnesota, Friedman has a bachelor's degree in Mediterranean studies from Brandeis University, and a Master's degree in Middle Eastern studies from Oxford University. As a journalist his focus has been the Middle East, first with United Press International, then with The New York Times. *His work has been awarded three Pulitzer prizes. Friedman has also hosted several documentaries for the Discovery Channel.*

Previous books include From Beirut to Jerusalem *(1989),* The Lexus and the Olive Tree: Understanding Globalization *(1999), and* Longitudes and Attitudes: Exploring the World after September 11 *(2002).*

Married with two daughters, Friedman lives in Bethesda, Maryland.

1992

Hard Drive

"Gates was immediately hooked. Whenever he had free time, he would run over to the Upper School to get more experience on the system. But Gates was not the only computer-crazed kid at Lakeside. He found he had to compete for time on the computer with a handful of others who were similarly drawn to the room as if by a powerful gravitational force. Among them was a soft-spoken, Upper School student by the name of Paul Allen, who was two years older than Gates.
Seven years later, the two classmates would form Microsoft, the most successful startup company in the history of American business."

In a nutshell

In your field of work, see what can be achieved by "setting the standard." With a big, clear vision in place, you can make the most of any opportunity that comes your way.

In a similar vein

Richard Branson *Losing My Virginity* (p 46)
Peter Drucker *Innovation and Entrepreneurship* (p 80)
Anita Roddick *Business as Unusual* (p 238)
Howard Schultz *Pour Your Heart into It* (p 248)

CHAPTER 20

James Wallace & Jim Erickson

Bill Gates is today best known for being the richest man in the world, thanks to the astounding success of the company he co-founded. But what do we really know of Gates the person, and what is the secret of Microsoft's success?

There are now many Gates biographies, but *Hard Drive: Bill Gates and the Making of the Microsoft Empire*, written by two Seattle journalists, still gives the best insights into the early years of Microsoft and what it was like to work under its CEO. This is a fantastic read, better than many novels. If you are about to start a business, it may expand your thinking of what you should aim for.

At another level, if you use a Microsoft operating system or application, it is fascinating to learn of the long road that was taken before these products seemed easy to use. Although this was a company that grew incredibly fast, it was still almost 15 years before Windows became a household name.

The book was written in 1992 and covers only Microsoft's first 15 or so years, but these were the most interesting and the most instructive in terms of lessons for the wealth creator.

Seeing the future—and acting on it

It is well known that Gates started Microsoft with friend Paul Allen when he was only 19, having dropped out of Harvard. However, by this time he was already an expert programmer, having spent the previous few years working on a primitive computer at school. When still in his final year, he was offered a job (with Allen) at $165 a week to debug the computer system of a defense contractor. His school, the enlightened, expensive Lakeside in Seattle, allowed him to take a whole semester off to accept the posting.

The pair had talked about starting their own software company for years, and shared a vision that almost everybody would some day have their own personal computer (this was in the age when computers filled whole rooms and were so expensive, only corporations and the military had them). Why should they not be the ones who provided the software programs?

Gates' parents, however, expected him to go to college. At Harvard, he wanted to find people who were smarter than he. Disappointed, he spent a lot of time playing poker in addition to doing some maths courses, but it was still a fruitful time. The authors note, "At Harvard, Gates read business books like other male students read *Playboy*. He wanted to know everything he could about running a company, from managing people to marketing products."

When Allen saw an article in *Popular Electronics* about a new "personal computer" that was being made by a company called MITS in New Mexico, he and Gates realized they had to make their move. They flew south and convinced the hardware firm that they could write a software program that would actually make the Altair computer usable by enthusiasts.

Relocating to Albuquerque, in a great hurry they tailored a version of the BASIC programming language for the Altair. Gates put everything into the new business, taking only a few days off during its first two years. However, it soon became obvious that the real value in the computer was its software, and Gates and Allen were eager to sell their program to other firms. Eventually they were able to wiggle out of the contract with MITS and became free to sell versions of BASIC to other companies. Amazingly, these included big names such as General Electric and National Cash Register. The tiny outfit began to make real money.

Later, after Microsoft had relocated to Seattle to be nearer Gates' parents, he confessed to a fellow programmer his two ambitions:

to design software that would make a computer easy enough for his mother to use and to build a company bigger than his dad's law firm.

By 1981, having made an agreement with its Goliath, IBM, Microsoft had already fulfilled the second aim.

Customers first, profits second

Potential clients coming to Microsoft headquarters frequently thought that Gates was the office boy. At 25 he still looked 17, and often wore a pizza-stained t-shirt he had slept in the night before. But once the youthful CEO started talking, Wallace and Erickson note, clients forgot his age. Clearly a master not only of the technical stuff but of the business of the computer industry, he even wrote his own contracts, taking clauses from corporate law textbooks.

In his zeal for customers Gates went for market share first, often quoting too low for the work involved and imposing ridiculous timeframes on his programmers. Yet his ethos of satisfy the customer first, profits second, meant that the company raced ahead of its competitors. In the early days, Wallace and Erickson write, "Gates sustained Microsoft through tireless salesmanship," making cold calls and haranguing potential buyers until they relented. In an echo of Michael Gerber's advice of "work on your business, not in it" (see commentary, p. 128), Gates, although an excellent programmer, was always slightly more inspired by the business of Microsoft and where it could go than the actual products themselves.

He was an intense communicator, willing to tear a person to pieces on some intellectual, business, or programming point. Yet he was also able to listen and change his mind in a hurry if the facts pointed that way. Microsoft hired people in his image: very high IQ, passionate, willing to work around the clock. When a deadline loomed, the whole company would be forced into a frenzy, pulling all-nighters to meet deadlines. His habit of making it onto planes just before the gates closed was symbolic of a larger outlook of taking things to the edge. It was at this edge, he once commented, "where you most often find high performance."

Windows of wealth

Microsoft's informal company motto was "We set the standard." Not just an empty morale booster, it reflected the prizes that would go to the firm that established proprietary industry standards for systems and applications. And by designing software "easy enough for [Gates'] mother to use," the company would find a universal audience for its products. In the famous Windows operating system, the two visions came together. Consider, however, the long and rocky path to its achievement:

- The initial version took 30 of the company's best programmers two years to create and test. Hundreds of screaming fits preceded the launch date.
- Once released, it was a commercial and critical flop. An improved version still did not set the world alight.
- Windows 3.0, released in 1990, finally delivered on the system's initial promise, selling 3 million copies in its first year alone.
- Even including the many elements that it lifted from Apple's "graphical user interface," Windows was seven years in the making.

Today powering 90 percent of the world's personal computers, Windows may have revolutionized personal computing, but marketing played a vital part in its establishment as the industry standard.

For this job Microsoft hired Rowland Hanson, head of marketing for Neutrogena. In the cosmetics industry the brand is everything, and Hanson felt that in the computer industry too, having good software was only half of the battle. To be really successful, Microsoft had to have its name connected with its products. People had to want not just programs, but *Microsoft* programs. Hanson's goal, the authors says, was "to make Microsoft the Sara Lee of the software industry."

After the success of Windows 3.0, Windows did indeed became a famous brand with an equally famous logo. It has been an astonishing cash cow for

Microsoft, with the Vista system the latest incarnation. By setting the standard, even if that standard was considered by many not to be the industry's best, Microsoft found (to IBM's chagrin) that the real money was in the "soul" of a machine—its software—rather than bits of metal and molded plastic.

Final comments

Was there something special about Gates himself that enabled Microsoft to become top dog in the software industry, or was it just a case of good timing, along with a basic amount of brainpower and work?

What really set Gates apart was the boldness of his vision—"A computer on every desk, and Microsoft software in every computer"—and his natural brilliance as a businessman. While it is hard to believe now, many very intelligent people in the early 1980s thought that personal computing would not amount to much, that business applications were the real growth area. In betting their young lives on the former, Gates and Allen reaped the benefits, although luck certainly played its part. In IBM's hurry to put a personal computer onto the market, it had to use other companies' software and create a machine out of nonproprietary parts. This gave Microsoft a huge opportunity, as the ubiquity of IBM "clones" meant that software, rather than the machines themselves, became the valuable thing. And yet, it could also be said that if Gates and Allen had not had the vision in the first place, they may not have made so much of the opportunity.

As well as being a great read, *Hard Drive* highlights the benefits of working in a "star" company. In business strategy terms, this is one that doubles in size every year or so because it is the clear leader of its fast-growing category. Most of the early employees of Microsoft, once stock options were introduced, became multimillionaires or billionaires. Charles Simonyi, for instance, who oversaw the development of Microsoft Word and Excel, recently spent $25 million on a two-week holiday on the Russian space station. Thousands of other employees hit a bonanza just by working in the right company at the right time. They had to be brainy to get their foot in the door and then they worked very hard, but their experience shows that if you are not one to start a business on your own, picking the right employer is often half the task in becoming wealthy.

James Wallace & Jim Erickson

James Wallace and Jim Erickson wrote Hard Drive *while they were investigative reporters for the* Seattle Post-Intelligencer. *Wallace remains a senior journalist for the newspaper, and followed* Hard Drive *with a sequel,* Overdrive: Bill Gates and the Race to Control Cyberspace *(1997). Erickson is now a senior reporter for* Time *magazine in Hong Kong.*

1995

The E-Myth Revisited

"I don't believe your business to be the first order of business on our agenda. You are."

"Human beings are capable of performing extraordinary acts. Capable of going to the moon. Capable of creating the computer. Capable of building a bomb that can destroy us all.
The least we should be able to do is run a small business that works."

"A business that looks orderly says that while the world may not work, some things can."

In a nutshell

The key to real prosperity in business is to work on your enterprise, not in it.

In a similar vein

Peter Drucker *Innovation and Entrepreneurship* (p 80)
Guy Kawasaki *The Art of the Start* (p 174)

CHAPTER 21

Michael E. Gerber

Never before have so many people entertained the idea of starting their own business. If this applies to you, before you take the leap read this book.

Gerber's *The E-Myth* came out in 1985 and was an underground bestseller, with over a million copies sold. The initial edition became quite hard to get, but luckily Gerber brought out a new one, *The E-Myth Revisited*, containing a new Preface and revised material but with the same powerful messages.

Few people have done a better job of presenting the anatomy of a small business, including what people really do in them and what they really earn from all their efforts. Gerber learned from his consulting work that people in small businesses generally work far too much for the return they get. The "tyranny of routine" means that there is never time to take an objective overview of what they are doing. His book aimed to be a lifeline to those stuck in the quagmire.

The book proceeds partly through a running dialogue with a woman Gerber worked with called Sarah, a pie shop owner whose problems and challenges perfectly encapsulate those faced by most people going into business. Specifically, the book is a recipe for putting yourself back in control of your working hours—in short, to be able to work *on* your business, not *in* it.

Business as self-development

The surprising message of *The E-Myth Revisited* is that going into business is as much about who you are and who you want to be as a person as it is about the business itself. If you are disorganized or greedy, Gerber says, or if your information about what is happening in your business is not good, the business will become a reflection of these things. If your business is to thrive, it will engage you in a process of constant personal development. For it to change, you have to change too.

Gerber quotes Aldous Huxley: "They intoxicate themselves with work so they won't see how they really are." If you start a business with full knowledge of what doing so means to you and why you are doing it, it can be a wonderful experience. Go in blindly, and it can be—as many people discover—a nightmare.

The myth of the entrepreneur

The "e-myth," Gerber notes, is the belief that anyone who starts a small business is an entrepreneur. Yet entrepreneurs in the heroic sense of a Herculean wealth creator are actually quite rare. Most people simply want to create a job for themselves and stop working for a boss. Their thinking goes, "Why should my boss earn lots of money from what I am doing?"

The problems begin because this person may know a lot about their specialty, but nothing about business itself. Knowing their business area inside out has not prepared them to *run* a business—in fact it becomes a liability, since they become unwilling to hand over the work reins to anyone else.

As Gerber puts it:

> *Suddenly the job he knew how to do so well becomes one job he knows how to do plus a dozen others he doesn't know how to do at all.*

The new businessperson discovers that he must become three people in one:

- The Technician—the person actually doing the work itself.
- The Manager—making sure that everything is organized, pushing the Technician to ensure that goals are met.
- The Entrepreneur—the visionary or dreamer charting the overall direction of the company.

Each of these roles does battle with the others, and most people have a lopsided balance within themselves. The most common breakdown of someone who starts a small business is 10 percent entrepreneur, 20 percent manager, and 70 percent technician.

How things go wrong

The problem of the Technician is that he or she believes the answer to every problem is to work harder. When Sarah's pie shop begins to come apart at the seams, she thinks that making more and better pies will sort things out—it won't. What she needs is to step back and look at the business as a *business*. Gerber forces her to ask: Is it a system that operates effectively irrespective of who is working in it? Or is it just a place where a woman makes pies and tries to sell them? The familiar pattern of a Technician who has started a business, Gerber notes, is this: exhilaration, followed by terror, exhaustion, and despair. What they once loved most—their work—they begin to hate.

A small business in its infancy is easy to spot: You as the owner are trying to do everything. You are the only person who knows *how* to do everything, after all. But with the business growing, you have to employ someone else. This is a relief; now you don't have to think about that aspect of the business you didn't like anyway (more often than not, it is doing the accounts).

But at some point this employee decides to leave and the business is thrown into chaos again. Your answer is to do more, work harder—forget about any long-term goals, just get the product out the door! No one, you realize, can do the work like you do, so the business must stay at a size at which you can do all the work.

This point, Gerber says, when an owner does not want to move out of their comfort zone involving them being in control as the Technician, is possibly the most dangerous for a small business. Such shrinking back is a tragedy. The owner's morale dips, and eventually the business dies because it has reached its natural limits.

Take the bolder route

It does not have to be this way. Gerber tells Sarah that "the purpose of going into business is to get free of a job so you can create jobs for other people." It is not to be "free of a boss," but rather to go further in your field than you could just working for yourself—to create something great out of your life's work that makes a difference, and naturally requires more organization and resources. The key question, Michael tells Sarah, is not how small her business could be, but how big it could naturally become with the right systems and organization in place.

The first thing to do if you take the bolder route, Gerber suggests, is to crystallize where you want to go with the business and write this goal down. He is amazed how few small businesses actually have written goals, yet "any plan is better than no plan." Without such a goal or plan, should we be surprised at the lack of direction, organization, and general panic that clouds the way most enterprises are run?

A mature company, he writes, begins differently than the rest. Most great companies set out with a vision of where they want to go. Tom Watson, founder of IBM, said: "I realized that for IBM to become a great company, it had to act like a great company long before it ever became one." Watson had a template or vision and each day he tried to fashion the company after it, however far-fetched it seemed. He had a picture in his mind of how the company would look and be "when it was finally done."

The Technician's only model for his business is work, whereas for the Entrepreneur the model is the business itself; the work is secondary. This paradox is summed up in Watson's remark, "Every day at IBM was a day devoted to business development, not doing business."

This again is Gerber's message: Work on your business, not in it.

You need a system

Gerber mentions McDonald's as the perfect example of a business that "worked." The brilliance of the concept is not simply the food, but a system that can be replicated thousands of times over. Though McDonald's founder Ray Kroc loved the food, he loved even more the beauty of the system that the

McDonald brothers had originally developed: its speed, simplicity, and orderliness.

Most small businesses believe that they will grow through hiring brilliant people—managers that can take the business to a new level. In fact, Gerber suggests, this is a hit-and-miss way of doing things. What you really need is idiot-proof systems and procedures that enable merely good people to do extraordinary things—ways of operating that guarantee a customer is satisfied, not by individual people but by the system itself. This may seem like a cold way of looking at it, but anyone who has been delighted by the way a hotel or a restaurant is run will understand the distinction. If you can build a great business around ordinary people, Gerber remarks, you don't have to worry about finding extraordinary ones.

Create a world of order

You have to orchestrate, organize, and standardize your business down to the smallest details, because the only certainty in the business is that your staff will act unpredictably. With proper standards, systems, and accountability, you cut out that risk, and as a result the customer gets what they want all of the time. A business is like a machine that generates money. The more you standardize and refine the machine, the clearer its value will be.

You may say: I can't work out standards, I am a master craftsperson in what I do! But Gerber responds: What does a master craftsperson do when they have learned all there is to know? Passes it on to others. In fulfilling this duty, your skill can be multiplied many times. Orchestration through a business system leverages what you know. It is your mastery writ large.

Most people, Gerber notes, feel either a lack of purpose in their lives or a sense of isolation from others. A great business can fill both gaps, giving a sense of camaraderie and order that would otherwise be missing. It brings more life to both customers and employees, providing a "fixed point of reference"—an island of purposeful calm in an otherwise disorderly world.

Final comments

Gerber asks Sarah to imagine how her business would be run if it was the model for 5,000 exactly like it. Would the extension of her ideas and philosophy to such a grand scale mean she would have "sold out"? Or would she feel that it was the natural expression of a system she had lovingly built and that deserved to be replicated?

The success of *The E-Myth Revisited* is partly owed to the fact that it coincided with the boom in business franchising. Gerber calls franchising the "turnkey revolution," in that it allows someone to buy the right to use a business system in which all they have to do (with some capital and a reasonable amount of work) is to "turn the key" to get it going and become profitable.

Franchising rests on the understanding that "The true product of a business is the business itself." However, though you can do very well buying a franchise, you can do even better by starting some kind of business system yourself—as Sarah begins to realize.

Gerber's book can get almost mystical at times, quoting the likes of Carlos Castaneda, Robert Assagioli, and Zen writers such as Robert Pirsig. As he is a self-confessed former poem-writing hippie, this is no surprise. What is surprising is his injection of a spiritual sensibility into what is essentially a business title, and this has been a key to the book's success. It is quite an addictive read, because it is ultimately about who you are and where you want to go in life, not about business. Echoing his first principle of business achievement, Gerber notes:

Great people have a vision of their lives that they practice emulating each and every day. They go to work on their lives, not just in their lives.

The E-myth Revisited can be a bit self-promoting at times, but this can be forgiven in the context of its powerful messages. The chapter on marketing, which shows why it is so important to be clear on exactly what you are selling, is worth the price of the book alone. Another chapter contains the intriguing story of a person who, against all the odds, became a success story. Wait for the interesting twist at the end.

Michael E. Gerber

Born in 1936, the California-based Gerber once sold encyclopedias for a living. He founded his company E-Myth Worldwide in 1977, eight years before writing The E-Myth. *It assists small businesspeople through its consulting and programs. Gerber is also a widely traveled keynote speaker.*

Other books include The E-Myth Manager *(1998),* The E-Myth Contractor *(2002), and* The E-Myth Physician *(2003).*

1949

The Intelligent Investor

"[Though] business conditions may change, corporations and securities may change, and financial institutions and regulations may change, human nature remains essentially the same. Thus the important and difficult part of sound investment, which hinges upon the investor's own temperament and attitude, is not much affected by the passing years."

"Intelligent investment is more a matter of mental approach than it is of technique."

"Too many clever and experienced people are engaged simultaneously in trying to outwit one another in the market. The result, we believe, is that all their skill and efforts tend to be self-neutralizing, or to 'cancel out', so that most expert and highly informed conclusions end up being no more dependable than the toss of a coin."

In a nutshell

Don't be someone who "knows the price of everything and the value of nothing." In stock investing, consider yourself part owner of a company, not a trader.

In a similar vein

John C. Bogle *The Little Book of Common Sense Investing* (p 40)
Warren Buffett *The Essays of Warren Buffett* (edited by Lawrence Cunningham; p 52)
Peter Lynch *One Up on Wall Street* (p 186)

CHAPTER 22

Benjamin Graham

When Benjamin Graham first started working on Wall Street in 1914, most investing took the form of railroad bonds. Stocks in companies as we know them today were aimed at insiders rather than the general public, and were seen as highly risky investments compared to bonds. This impression was only boosted by the Great Crash of 1929 and the ensuing Depression.

However, Graham's focus on the value of companies, as opposed to the speculation on stocks (he has been variously called the Dean of Wall Street and the Father of Value Investing), showed it was possible for regular people to invest wisely without getting swept up in market hysteria.

In the last 20 years Graham's profile has been boosted by billionaire investor Warren Buffett, who was tutored by Graham at Columbia University and then worked at his Graham-Newman brokerage business. Buffett has described *The Intelligent Investor* as "By far the best book on investing ever written."

Writing against a background of various postwar political upheavals, Graham considered it vital to highlight investing principles that worked, irrespective of changes in society or government or great swings in the market. The book is essentially about the difference between investment and speculation, between quoted stock prices and the underlying or real value of the companies behind them. His investing approach requires a long-term horizon, the ability to tune out market "noise" in the interim, and having enough confidence in your investing choices that you won't be rattled by a catastrophe or a correction.

Be an investor, not a speculator

Graham notes that the "intelligence" the title of the book celebrates is not of the smart or shrewd type but relates more to the character of the investor; that is, not someone looking for a quick profit, but with a long-term view minded to conserve their capital, who can be firm about their investing principles in the face of an emotion-driven market.

He sticks with the distinction between investing and speculation given in his earlier book *Security Analysis* (itself a classic):

An investment operation is one in which, upon thorough analysis, promises safety of principal and a satisfactory return. Operations not meeting these requirements are speculative.

With speculation or trading, he notes, you are either right or you are wrong, the latter often disastrously so. An investor, in contrast, considers themselves a part owner in a large enterprise, looking mainly to its results and the quality of its management.

Such a thing as intelligent speculation does exist, Graham says, but it is dangerous when people who think they are investing are actually speculating. Any stock purchase that you do quickly, when you don't want to lose out on a "great opportunity," is probably speculation driven by the emotions of the market.

The intelligent investor should not get involved in trying to forecast the market's direction. This makes you a trader or speculator. The only time an investor takes account of the ups and downs in the market is when they choose to buy a stock they had their eye on anyway, and can pick it up at a low price if market sentiment is bearish. If an investor starts "swimming with the speculative tide" (particularly during a bull market when it seems easy to make money), they will lose sight of the companies they are investing in and focus only on the price of stocks.

How to find value

Graham reflects that any assessment of the long-term prospects of a company can only ever be an educated guess. If those prospects are clear enough, then they will already be reflected in the company's stock price. This is why "growth" stocks are often expensive, and why there is rarely good value to be found in the "sexy" companies that everybody likes.

Better, Graham believes, to invest in companies without dramatic predictions attached to them, "boring" companies that are overlooked and undervalued. He notes that when a company loses ground against the overall market, speculators will cast a pall of gloom over its stock and write it off as hopeless. The intelligent investor, however, will see that this is an overreaction. Surely the company is still selling things, has some market share, and may turn around?

An example Graham gives of undervaluation is Great Atlantic & Pacific Tea Company (A&P). In 1938 its stock was selling at 36 cents, a price that meant the whole enterprise was being appraised as worth less than its working capital (meaning its assets minus its liabilities). No consideration was given to all its warehouses and other assets, and the goodwill of being the biggest retailer of its time.

Graham observes that the real money to be made in the stock market is not in the buying or selling, but in having the discipline to hold and own, earning dividends and waiting for perceptions of the value of a company to align with reality. To do this obviously requires a degree of psychological strength, and indeed Graham observes: "Intelligent investment is more a matter of mental approach than it is of technique."

Look for a margin of safety

The secret of investing success, Graham ventures, can be summed up in the motto "Margin of Safety." In technical terms, this means having evidence of a company's earnings above what is required to service its interest on debt, particularly in the event of a significant sales or market decline. The intelligent investor always looks for this buffer because it means they do not need to have accurate estimates of a company's future earnings. A speculator does not usually consider the margin of safety important, but for the investor it is their touchstone.

There are two ways to invest, Graham notes: the predictive approach, or how well you think a company will do within its market given its management, products, and so on; and the protective approach, which involves looking only at the statistics of a company, such as the relationship between selling price and earnings, assets, and dividend payments. Value investors favor the second because it is based "not on optimism but on arithmetic." The first approach, in contrast, would lead you to buy on hunches rather than statistical data and reasoning.

Thanks to the way "Mr. Market" overreacts, it is possible to find a margin of safety in unexpected places. Graham mentions real-estate bonds, many of which collapsed after the crash of 1929, sometimes to very low amounts, for example 10 cents when they had been valued at a dollar. However, at these prices speculative bonds suddenly became very good value, with a margin of safety well in excess of assets.

Two types of investor

Within the Graham framework of value and safety, there is room to be either a defensive or an aggressive investor. He gives the example of a widow who is left $100,000 that she needs to support her kids, who obviously has to be defensive or conservative. However, a doctor in mid-career with thousands of dollars to sock away every year, or a young person just starting out and wanting to invest, can both be more aggressive or enterprising.

Defensive: Safety + freedom from bother

Graham's guiding rule for the conservative investor is to keep a split of roughly 50 percent of their funds in high-grade bonds (or savings accounts with an equivalent interest rate), and 50 percent in large, prominent, financially conservative companies that have a history of continuous dividend payments and whose price is not more than 25 times annual earnings (this generally excludes all growth stocks).

When the market looks dangerously high, you can reduce your exposure to common stocks to less than 50 percent, or go over 50 percent in a down market to pick up low-priced but good stocks. The formula stops the investor from getting swayed by the hysteria of the market, but at the same time gives exposure to higher potential returns. When the market goes down, Graham notes, such an investor will feel good compared to their bolder friends who have gone into stocks in a big way.

Aggressive or enterprising: Safety + more active involvement

The conventional wisdom is that if you are prepared to take higher risks you will get higher returns. Graham rejects this, saying that high returns are not necessarily related to risk, but to putting more time and effort into your investing.

For those who decide to make their own stock picks but still require a margin of safety, Graham's pointers include:

- Look for companies that have a regular dividend payment record going back 25 years or so.
- Do not invest in companies with price-to-earnings ratios of more than 10.
- When looking at a company's annual report, separate out nonrecurrent or "one-off" profits and losses from the normal operating results.
- Don't invest in an industry, invest in companies. For example, a lot of money went into air transport stocks in the postwar period and into the 1950s, but various factors meant that the industry as a whole had poor financial results.

If you do ask others to manage your funds, Graham counsels:

- Limit the investing activity you contract out to very conservative investments; or
- Make sure that you have "an unusually intimate and favorable knowledge of the person" who is going to direct your funds.

Never go with the advice of people who promise spectacular returns. Be careful also of getting advice from friends or relatives: "much bad advice is given for free."

Final comments

On the penultimate page of *The Intelligent Investor* Graham writes, "Investment is most intelligent when it is most *businesslike.*" Warren Buffett thought that this was the wisest sentence ever penned on investing. Graham meant that people in the financial world too easily forget the basic fact of investing: that it is about companies, and that buying a stock means part ownership of a specific business enterprise. Trying to make money beyond earnings related to a firm's performance was fraught with danger.

Reflecting on whether there were any rules of investment that had stood the test of time, Graham noted that most of the rules relating to particular types of securities (e.g., "A bond is a safer investment than a stock") were no longer valid, while the ones relating to human nature did not date, such as "Buy when most people (including experts) are pessimistic, and sell when they are actively optimistic." Everything changes, including companies, regulations, and the economy, but people do not, and people are what drive markets. The "Efficient Market Hypothesis" says that stock prices are always an accurate reflection of the value of a company and its probable future earnings, therefore it is not possible for anyone to "beat the market" in any sustained way by picking individual stocks. But could the phenomenal success of value investors like Warren Buffett, who base their judgments on a knowledge of human nature, really be just chance?

In the Introduction to the original 1949 edition, Graham candidly notes the risk that his book "may not stand the test of future developments," any more than a finance book written in 1914 would be relevant to investors of the 1950s. In fact, *The Intelligent Investor* is considered by many people—despite many references to companies that have now faded into history—to be quite timeless. His humility only makes you trust him more, and he has a calm style and does not talk down to the reader.

Coming up to its 60th anniversary the book has rarely been more popular, and though the commentary and examples change slightly from edition to edition, the principles remain the same; it doesn't matter which one you read.

Benjamin Graham

Born in 1894, Graham was born in London to Jewish parents (Grossbaum was their original name) who emigrated to the United States while he was still a baby. He did well in school and won a place at Columbia University in New York.

Graham started working on Wall Street in 1914 when he was 20, and later founded the famous Graham-Newman Partnership brokerage business. He also taught at Columbia's Graduate School of Business from 1928 to 1957.

Other key books are Security Analysis, *with Graham Dodd, Sidney Cottle, and Charles Tatham (1934) and* The Interpretation of Financial Statements *(1964). Graham died in 1976.*

2002

The One Minute Millionaire

"Everywhere you look, even in these economic times of uncertainty, growing numbers of people are feasting on incredible banquets of prosperity—while most of the rest settle for the crumbs that fall from the table. The journey to financial freedom starts the MINUTE you decide that you were destined for prosperity, not scarcity… It only takes a MINUTE to decide. Decide now."

In a nutshell

Everyone who becomes wealthy in the modern world knows the power of leverage: using other people's resources and technology to multiply the effect of what you do.

In a similar vein

Robert G. Allen *Multiple Streams of Income* (p 16)
David Bach *The Automatic Millionaire* (p 22)
P. T. Barnum *The Art of Money Getting* (p 28)
Thomas J. Stanley & William D. Danko *The Millionaire Next Door* (p 266)

CHAPTER 23

Mark Victor Hansen & Robert G. Allen

The format of *The One Minute Millionaire* is quite unusual. Recognizing that different people learn and are inspired in different ways, it is one half novel (the righthand pages) and one half "how to" manual (the lefthand pages).

The premise of the novel half of the book is simple: "Could you make a million if your loved ones' lives depended upon it?" Not only make a million, but achieve it quickly. The story follows a recently widowed mother who has to raise a million dollars in 90 days if she is to regain custody of her children. The learning curve she must take is steeper than the north face of Mount Everest, but her simple belief that it is possible allows her to meet the right people and develop a winning product just in time. All the principles she learns to achieve her goal are explained in the "straight" part of the book.

Despite the emphasis on getting money within a certain timeframe, in fact the title of the book is a bit of a misnomer. A more appropriate one would have been "The Enlightened Millionaire," as this is Hansen and Allen's real theme: how to create wealth in a way that has only positive effects.

The enlightened millionaire

The three principles of an enlightened millionaire are:

- Do no harm—be ethical, honest, and seek win/win outcomes.
- Do much good—improve the lives of many; by enriching others you enrich yourself.
- Operate out of stewardship—create wealth so you can give it away; financial blessings are to be shared.

Such a person understands the truth of Andrew Carnegie's dictum, "No man becomes rich unless he enriches others." How rich you become will be in proportion to what you have given out of value. To receive remarkable wealth, you must create remarkable utility for others. The enlightened millionaire is also a good steward of resources, so naturally wants eventually to give it all back to society. The creed of the enlightened millionaire is:

I make millions
I save millions
I invest millions
I give millions away.

Hansen and Allen mention maverick scientist Buckminster Fuller's idea of "precession." The work of a bee intent on getting nectar from flowers has further, precessional effects: It enables the plants to be cross-pollinated, perpetuating life and growth. In the same way, your efforts to create new value and serve people with your service or product will have many other positive effects, much of which you won't even know about. An "endarkened" millionaire, in contrast, will seek only money itself, and as a result the precessional events that result will be negative.

Focus first on the inner stuff

You are on the road to wealth as soon as you accept that you are not lacking anything to become a millionaire. Riches are not just "for others," but are yours for the taking if you believe they are. Never forget, say the authors, that *you* are your wealth.

The idea for your fortune will come from you or be adopted by you. All you need to make it reality is commitment and resources, and the resources can come from someone else. Psychologically, you have to break through to a new level of results, and do to this involves changing yourself and your perceptions. In asking yourself bigger questions, you will begin looking for bigger results. You may not realize it, but you probably have an inner resistance to becoming wealthy.

The woman in the novel half of the book has to come up with a million dollars in 90 days, and part of her challenge is to believe she is capable of it. With basic belief, it is only a matter of time and application before you create the wealth you want. Look at the times in your life when you have been really successful. Most likely, there was a congruence between what you believed about yourself and what others saw in you. Before great things happen, you must be in a mental position to accept that they will. As Hansen and Allen put it, "You must BE an Enlightened Millionaire before you DO anything."

Most of the time, when something negative happens we blame someone else. But all enlightened millionaires discover that instead of blaming they must learn from the situation. If you picture a line separating "learn" above it and "blame" below it, they live above this line. It is only in this way that you will keep moving on mentally, finding new opportunities instead of getting stuck in a rut.

Creating wealth, more often than not, is a process that can be copied. If you focus first on the process and getting it right, the rest almost takes care of itself. W. Edwards Deming, the engineer whose quality management systems transformed Japanese manufacturing, noted that if you get the first 15 percent of any system right, the other 85 percent flows easily. *The One Minute Millionaire* is designed to change the first 15 percent of your thinking, and this can transform the rest of your life. By making small changes to the way you understand wealth, the effects can be enormous.

The millionaire secret: Leverage

Have you ever wondered why a teacher makes $40,000 a year, and a professional athlete $400,000 or $4 million? Both add value (you could well argue that the teacher adds a lot more), but whereas the teacher can only teach 25 children at a time, the sportsperson provides value to a supporter base of thousands and is watched and enjoyed on television by millions. The difference between them is that the player has much greater leverage, or reach, and "If you want to create wealth, you need leverage."

Yet *The One Minute Millionaire* points out that you don't need a lot of resources to create valuable leverage. In the "zero" approach to wealth creation, you can achieve maximum leverage by utilizing other people's money, time, knowledge, ideas, and labor. Mark Victor Hansen's success is a good example of the zero approach. He and Jack Canfield have sold 60 million copies of their *Chicken Soup for the Soul* series, yet most of the content they did not even write themselves. The heart-warming stories that make up each book came from other people, but it was Hansen and Canfield that kept the copyright and therefore the huge royalties. They leveraged the power of the content by getting the books sold in huge numbers in an unusual distribution channel, supermarkets.

Millionaires are always looking to leverage things, to expand or multiply their effect and value. What is the greatest form of leverage today? The internet. Whatever you publish online can be seen by millions, all potential customers. The costs of creating an internet business can be close to zero, but the revenue can be multiplied many times over by having the whole world as your audience.

Mentors and networks

You need a team to obtain your dream. Success is not a solo project.

Another form of leverage, which can also cost nothing, is simply knowing the right people. Hansen and Allen suggest taking a millionaire out to lunch regularly and finding out all their secrets:

> *All wealthy people have systems—or "cookie cutters"—that they have developed through years of trial and error to cut real "dough" out of the market.*

By gaining a millionaire mentor, you will have learned what these valuable processes are, and on a personal level gain a shortcut to "perspective, proficiency, and patience." Having a top mentor is the quickest way to climb the millionaire mountain.

You will also begin to appreciate the leveraging power of networks. Most people think that strong, close relationships are key in business. In fact, Hansen and Allen suggest, it is the "weak ties," friends of friends or acquaintances in your field, who can make all the difference. The more you have of these, the more leads, sources of ideas, or potential champions you will have.

Reliance on the "Infinite Network," as Hansen and Allen describe spiritual faith, can be the greatest form of leverage. The power of a human being acting alone will always be limited, but if you feel you have some higher power behind you, there are no limits to achievement. They quote Buckminster Fuller again, who said: "You can rest assured that if you devote your time and attention to the highest advantage of others, the Universe will support you, always and in the nick of time."

The moment you really decide to move, providence has a way of smoothing the way. "Hidden hands" appear from apparently nowhere to help you. As Hansen and Allen put it: "God knows where the gold is. Become a partner with the Author of all Wealth."

Secrets of marketing

Though small, *The One Minute Millionaire*'s section on marketing—central to creating any kind of wealth—is necessary reading. It boils down to three points:

- In launching your service or product, court the addicts: "Addicts make the best customers. Addicts buy quickly and more often. Addicts talk to other addicts."
- Create addictive advertising and marketing. You must identify or create the unique benefit that your customers get from you that they cannot get anywhere else. Levi Strauss jeans became a must-have garment in the American gold fields in the 1870s because of their unique copper rivets that made them indestructible. Hansen and Allen ask: "What's the 'copper rivet' for your product? You must find it and flaunt it."
- Get leverage with partners. Hook up with people who already have relationships with the addicts you seek and piggyback on their database or knowledge. "Get their endorsement to introduce your product to their clients/customers for a split of the profit. Rather than competition, think cooperation."

Finally, to get and retain customers, always offer something free: a report, diagnosis, CD, or book to everyone who registers with you. Don't forget the law of prosperity: To get you must always first give.

Final comments

As Hansen and Allen are careful to note, you can become a millionaire simply by investing as little as a dollar a day, but assuming you get a return of 10 percent, a million will take you decades to amass. There are quicker ways, and this is what *The One Minute Millionaire* is about. Within the four basic areas of wealth building—investments, real estate, business, and the internet—there are unlimited possibilities. But first you must understand the importance of "generics" such as personal attitude, leverage, networks, and marketing. Both authors are brilliant marketers, and though you might not warm to Hansen's cute *Chicken Soup* book series or Allen's real-estate seminars, you can at least learn from their marketing prowess.

The One Minute Millionaire is just the sort of book that cynics of self-development sneer at, with its catchy title, short chapters, frequent references to a supporting website, and a story that would win no literary prizes. Yet the purpose of the book is to deliver "Aha!" moments, and for a person who does not know a great deal about wealth creation it provides many insights.

A frequent criticism of the book is that it focuses on creating wealth through real estate. In fact, the section specifically relating to real estate covers 40 pages within a total of 380, and if you buy a non-US edition, it will come with a caveat stating that many of the strategies will not apply in your home country. Don't let this hold you back from purchase. Even if you are already an entrepreneur, and even if you don't have to come up with a million dollars in 90 days, you will find many good tips that could transform your business or your finances.

Mark Victor Hansen & Robert G. Allen

Born in 1948, ***Hansen*** *is a motivational speaker and author. His* Chicken Soup for the Soul *series, co-authored with Jack Canfield, has sold over 130 million copies in 54 languages, and spans 105 different titles. The first title was published in 1993.*

Hansen supports a range of charitable causes, and in 2004 was inducted into the Sales & Marketing Executives International Hall of Fame. Other books include The Aladdin Factor *(with Jack Canfield, 1995) and* The Power of Focus *(with Jack Canfield and Lew Hewitt, 2000). With Robert Allen he has also written* Cracking the Millionaire Code *(2005).*

For a biography of ***Allen****, see p 21.*

2000

Natural Capitalism

"The environment is not a minor factor of production but rather is 'an envelope containing, provisioning, and sustaining the entire economy'."

"The goal of natural capitalism is to… guarantee that all forms of capital are as prudently stewarded as money is by the trustees of financial capital."

"While there may be no 'right' way to value a forest, a river, or a child, the wrong way is to give it no value at all. If there are doubts about how to value a seven-hundred-year-old tree, ask how much it would cost to make a new one. Or a new atmosphere, or a new culture."

In a nutshell

Genuine prosperity is not won at the expense of the earth.

In a similar vein

Joe Dominguez & Vicki Robin *Your Money or Your Life* (p 74)
Milton Friedman *Capitalism and Freedom* (p 110)
Paul Zane Pilzer *God Wants You to Be Rich* (p 214)

CHAPTER 24

Paul Hawken, Amory B. Lovins, & L. Hunter Lovins

Just as the foundation of all personal wealth is good health (you have no energy to make your mark if you are sick), so the foundation of global wealth is a healthy natural environment. Prosperity is inherently about wealth and wellbeing that are not won at the expense of other people or things. Real prosperity invokes the "circle of life."

Natural Capitalism popularized the idea of "natural capital," that clean air, water, and other natural assets are valuable and must be recognized by the accounting discipline, and are not free things to be looted. Yet the book is not a rant against industry and how it is destroying the world. Through copious examples it shows that being "green" can be financially smart as well as ethically right. Main author Paul Hawken was a successful businessperson before devoting most of his time to environmental issues, giving the book extra credibility. Though it could do with updating, it remains a compelling and possibly life-changing read, promising increased wealth and wellbeing on the one hand and dramatically lower use of energy and resources on the other.

In this commentary are just a sprinkling of the book's hundreds of fascinating examples and points, which can be downloaded chapter by chapter for free from a supporting website, www.natcap.org.

The capital that economists conveniently forgot

The authors note that industrial capitalism has been incredibly successful in marshaling resources and delivering great wealth. But this wealth has come at a great cost to the natural environment. They admit that the cost of raw materials continues to fall and that the actual amount of resources never becomes depleted, thanks to the development of easier ways of finding and extracting metals from the ground—and yet, these "easier" ways also come at a cost.

Underlying the industrial mentality is that nature supplies goods that can be transformed into something more valuable. But more important than the materials that nature offers are the services that it provides. For instance, a forest not only gives us wood but is a form of water storage, cleans our air, and is a buffer against weather extremes. Nature's provision of a carbon cycle involving the exchange of oxygen and carbon is irreplaceable. There is no other way to manage this other than through large amounts of green plants. The famous Biosphere 2 experiment in Arizona in the early 1990s could not even maintain enough oxygen to support the life of eight people. Planet Earth provides this every day for billions.

Conventional economics sees wealth as a cycle that begins with raw materials and ends with their distribution. What is not taken into account is the origin of the raw materials, or what happens to the products once discarded. How would our world change, the authors wonder, if these "invisibles" became integrated into accounting and economics?

Neoclassical economics has "counted only what was countable, not what really counted"; the concept of natural capitalism, in contrast, sees the environment not as "a minor factor of production" but rather as "an envelope containing, provisioning, and sustaining the entire economy." There are in fact four distinct types of capital:

- Human—what people can create.
- Financial—money and money instruments.
- Manufactured capital—infrastructure and products.
- Natural capital—the natural world from which all things come.

Each is as necessary as the others for prosperity and wellbeing.

Radical resource use

While many companies pay attention to "eco-efficiency," in reality this just means incremental improvements to existing ways of doing things. It does not alter the ever-increasing production of the wrong products, using the wrong processes, from the wrong materials, while the more fundamental factors that really affect the environment are ignored.

Amory and Hunter Lovins' previous book, *Factor Four: Doubling Wealth, Halving Resource Use* (first published in Germany where it was a bestseller), showed how companies, countries, and people could "live twice as well but use half as much material and energy." Such a revolution was not only possible, it was absolutely necessary, given that the world population would double while global natural resources available per person would decrease.

Natural Capitalism notes how the Industrial Revolution brought in technology that allowed one person to do the work that 200 were needed to do only 70 years before. The same thing could happen now, the authors say, if we embrace techniques and technologies of "radical resource productivity." It is the private sector, rather than government, that should lead this revolution, and for the most part it already has the answers; they just need to be implemented. The potential for energy efficiency in factory and manufacturing processes is enormous, and much of it involves simple retrofitting of new valves, ducts, fans, motors, insulation, heat exchangers, better compressed air maintenance, and the like. Simple fixing of leaky air ducts can save the output of ten American power plants a year. None of these things is new technology, but involves better use of what we already have.

The road to a greener world

The authors draw attention to the environmental and social effects of the automobile industry, the largest in the world. They note that up to 80 percent of the energy generated by a car engine is lost, mainly through heat loss and exhaust, with only 20 percent used to turn the wheels. Today's cars use so much energy because they are made of steel, designed more in the manner of tanks than aircraft, and are overpowered for the vast majority of their uses.

The cars of the future will be much lighter, which means far less energy will be required to move and stop them. Made of composite materials, which are much lighter than steel but stronger, they will do without weighty power steering and power brakes, and will be driven by a combination of electricity and fuel (the Toyota Prius was the first commercially successful example of this), with many fewer moving parts and without heavy clutches and transmissions. When the use of such cars becomes widespread, the authors note, it could "ultimately spell the end of today's car, oil, steel, aluminium, electricity and coal industries—and herald the birth of successor industries that are more benign."

Buildings with a future

In its chapter "Building blocks," the book takes aim at the waste incorporated in the designs of modern houses and commercial buildings. The common practice is to design and build new structures based on costings reflecting the price of putting a building up. But taking into account natural capital means having designs that incorporate costs, particularly energy use, over a long period. Sometimes these measures are more expensive to begin with (but not always), yet they provide a multitude of benefits for their owners on a commercial level and for their users because they are better to live in. Green buildings, such as the headquarters of the ING bank in the Netherlands, usually sell or lease more quickly, because they mix greater comfort with lower running costs. They have higher occupancies and can command higher rents, and the lessees report lower absenteeism rates and greater productivity.

Part of the great cost savings of green buildings is in the use of passive heating and cooling techniques that obviate the need for air conditioning systems. Many are designed with "superwindows" that allow light in but reflect heat, using heavy gas fillings like krypton. Though costing 10–15 percent more than conventional double-glazed windows, they can be four times as effective at keeping a building cool in summer and warm in winter. Mentioned are large buildings in chilly Colorado that are powered by only two small wood-burning furnaces, thanks to superinsulation and superwindows. The next generation of windows, the authors note, will use microchips to vary the heat and light automatically. Finally, use of "daylighting" (natural light from translucent panels in the roof), solar power, and the reuse of old materials can all dramatically reduce a building's "carbon footprint" in addition to the comfort and cost benefits they bring.

Government waste

The standard green-left position is that government must move in to regulate industry in order to save the natural environment. But Hawken *et al.* note that much of the time, government (in the form of subsidies and regulation that favors energy use rather than energy savings) is part of the problem, not the solution.

At the time *Natural Capitalism* was written, the US government was subsidizing the automotive industry to the tune of $464 billion per year, including road construction, and giving preferential treatment to mining, logging, and waste-disposal industries that had few incentives to change their ways. Little support was given to emerging clean technologies. The German government was subsidizing the Ruhr Valley coal industry with billions of dollars annually when it would have cost the public purse less to close the mines and pay off the workers.

The book's radical suggestion: Governments should stop taxing labor and income and instead tax pollution, waste, carbon fuels, and resource exploitation. The result would be a new order of radically better use of resources, which at the same time redirects government spending toward social ills and fixing damaged environments. Without taxes on labor, demand for it would rise (in the process minimizing social problems connected with unemployment and underemployment) while demand for precious resources would fall.

Carbon and climate

On this theme, it is interesting to read Hawken *et al.*'s views on climate change, written before the issue really rose in the public consciousness. The reader gets a sense of the fragility and thinness of the earth's atmosphere in relation to its mass, and learns that carbon dioxide makes up only 0.03 percent of the atmosphere, yet only tiny changes in its amount can have significant warming effects.

Unlike most environmentalists, the authors acknowledge the power of markets to avert a climate change catastrophe. Rather than heavy-handed regulation, they support carbon trading among corporations to reduce emissions, and note optimistically:

> *[In] the next half century, the climate problems could become as faded a memory as the energy crises of the seventies are now, because climate change is not an inevitable result of normal economic activity but an artifact of carrying out that activity in irrationally inefficient ways.*

This view—that more responsible behavior and better use of technology can restore our natural capital—sums up the whole argument of *Natural Capitalism.*

Final comments

Natural Capitalism inspires because it says that we do not need to go back and live in the forests and abandon modern comforts—in fact, part of the fulfillment of civilization will be to enjoy great technological advances that also use hugely less energy. Alternative ways of living, transporting, and working do not necessarily involve compromise.

This is a book that makes you think about prosperity in the largest sense; that is, what we leave future generations. No longer can we continue with the hubris of believing that we are separate to, or greater than, nature. As with financial capital, wise use of our natural capital will bring great returns.

Paul Hawken, Amory B. Lovins, & L. Hunter Lovins

Born in 1946, ***Hawken*** *is a leading speaker on environmental, economic, and social justice issues, and has consulted widely to corporations. In his 20s he founded Erewhon, a natural foods wholesaler, and later co-founded garden supplies company Smith & Hawken. He has been involved in the establishment of software and engineering firms Metacode, Groxis, and The Pax Group, which provides fan technology to industry.*

His 1993 book The Ecology of Commerce *introduced the concept of "comprehensive outcome" or the larger costs of a transaction beyond those immediately involved. Other titles include* The Next Economy *(1983) and* Blessed Unrest *(2007), about the growth of nonprofit bodies worldwide concerned with improving social justice and the environment. Hawken is based in Sausalito, California, where he heads the Natural Capital Institute.*

Amory B. Lovins*, born in 1947, is a longstanding advocate of "soft energy" (wind, solar, etc.) and is chairman and chief scientist of the Rocky Mountain Institute. He has an MA in physics from Oxford University.*

L. Hunter Lovins *was co-founder of the Rocky Mountain Institute and founder of Natural Capitalism Solutions. Trained as a sociologist and lawyer, she is Professor of Business at Presidio School of Management and was named a Hero of the Planet by* Time *magazine in 2000.*

2004

Ask and It is Given

"When you know that you want something, and you notice you do not have it, you assume that there is something outside of yourself that is keeping it from you, but that is never true. The only thing that ever prevents you receiving something that you desire is that your habit of thought is different from your desire."

"When emotions feel good—whether they are strong or weak—you are allowing the fulfilment of your desire.
When emotions feel bad—whether they are strong or weak—you are in a state of disallowing the fulfilment of your desire."

In a nutshell

As long as you are in a state of mind and being that is ready to receive, you can have whatever you want.

In a similar vein

Genevieve Behrend *Your Invisible Power* (p 34)
Rhonda Byrne *The Secret* (p 58)
Charles Fillmore *Prosperity* (p 98)
John Randolph Price *The Abundance Book* (p 224)

CHAPTER 25

Esther Hicks & Jerry Hicks

Most people have heard of the "law of attraction" through the film and book *The Secret* (see commentary p 58), but by the time of its release in 2006 Esther and Jerry Hicks had already spent 20 years traveling America teaching the concept. It is easy to see the influence of their writings on *The Secret* and other books of this ilk.

Why, then, are they not the bestselling writers in the field? Part of the reason must lie in their claim to be simply "channeling" information from the spiritual realm. This puts off many potential readers. Unsurprisingly, at the beginning of *Ask and It Is Given* they try to explain how they arrived at their unusual vocations.

The story begins in 1985, when Esther and Jerry visited a healer in Phoenix, Arizona. The healer was supposedly receiving spiritual communications from a spirit guide named Theo. To Esther's surprise (she had only come along at Jerry's urging), Theo told Esther that she too had a spiritual guide that wanted to make itself known. The couple were told to meditate. After some months Esther began "receiving" information from this guide, who identified itself as Abraham, representing a collective of spiritual beings. Esther found herself at her typewriter, punching out messages.

Then in her 30s, Esther had never meditated and was happy with her life. But this "absence of opinions or angst" apparently made her a good receiver of otherworldly information. The guides had made contact in order to remind people of "the Laws of the Universe that govern all things," including the transmission of desires into reality through the law of attraction. Distracted by living in "time-space-reality," she was told, humans had forgotten where we came from and how to use the laws.

The question must be asked, are the Hicks perpetrating a great hoax, or is Esther really the voice of eternal truths from the spirit world? In his foreword to *Ask and It Is Given*, spiritual self-development author Wayne Dyer (see commentary in *50 Self-Help Classics*) lends credibility by describing the book as a "publishing milestone" that contains powerful universal truths. You can decide for yourself by reading it, but the book is certainly the Hicks' most comprehensive work, containing all the basic "Abraham" teachings and, in the second half, 22 "processes" or exercises to put them into practice.

Understand the law

Simply stated, the law of attraction (a universal law that is never contradicted) is that whatever you put your attention on through thought or desire becomes reality. Whenever you are focused on what you don't have, that situation of not-having will also be your reality. You attract to yourself things or people that are the equivalent of your current state of being, or "vibration."

In the first chapter on "The power of feeling good now," Abraham notes that deciding to elevate your mood or feeling in each moment is vital for increasing your vibration, which in turn attracts things, people, and feelings of a like vibration. He says:

> *It is our powerful desire that you be pleased with where you are right now, in this moment—no matter where you are. We understand how strange these words must sound to you if you are standing in a place that seems far from where you want to be. But it is our absolute promise to you that when you understand the power of feeling good now, no matter what, you will hold the key to the achievement of any state of being, any state of health, any state of wealth, or any state of anything that you desire.*

Trying to pretend you are feeling wonderful when you are not will not work. It will not change your vibration. The idea is to choose an emotion that is slightly higher than the one you are experiencing now. The more positive you think and feel in each moment, the more open is your connection to the Source, or provider of all things and all love. The worse you feel, the more closed this connection will be.

Trust your emotions

If you are feeling depressed, being angry about someone or something is actually a "higher" feeling, since it will take you out of your depressed state. It is a relief. Once you have chosen anger as a relief from depression, you are then empowered to choose another thought or emotion higher up the scale. If you deliberately choose to be disappointed rather than feeling despair, again you have raised your vibration through choice. Once you know how to raise your emotional state deliberately, even in a small way, you are no longer powerless before your emotions.

Because your emotions indicate your vibrational frequency, they are an infallible indicator as to whether you are aligned with the Source. If you are aligned with your Source, you are on track to receive whatever you want. Your emotions are the perfect guidance system, telling you exactly how the law of attraction is working in your life.

Behind every desire is the desire to feel good, to feel joy. The objects of desire, Abraham says, are less important than the fact that you are allowing life energy to flow. When you have appreciation for things and for people and you love yourself, you are operating at a higher vibration. This changes when you begin to criticize or to find fault. The better you feel about yourself, the more you have to give others. This is not selfishness. It is only people unconnected with their true selves who are jealous, who commit violence, who are insecure.

You are born to desire and fulfill

The most common question people ask of Hicks/Abraham is: "Why is it taking me so long to get what I want?" The answer is that it is not because you don't want something enough, or because you are not worthy, or because "fate is against you." Rather, you are not in a vibrational state that matches that of your desire. "That is the only reason—ever!" Abraham states. What has prevented you from getting what you want is you—your thoughts that do not align with what you want to be and where you want to go. Whenever you ask for something it is always given, but you must mentally allow it to come, being of like mind to what you want to receive.

People feel guilty about having desires, but Abraham states that desires are the very essence of being human because they make you feel who you really are and what you intended to be when you came into this world. If you are deliberate about your thoughts and desires, then you can be more specific about the world you want to create for yourself. Life is a process of asking and receiving, and you are the creator of our own reality, whether consciously or not. You have to "feel" your thoughts and desires as you have them, being grateful that they are being fulfilled in wonderful ways—and then letting go. That is, be eager and optimistic about what is coming, while having no impatience or doubt about its coming. If you are feeling good about something you want and allowing it to come, it will.

Often, what a person thinks is a desire is not—it is a "resisted desire." If you have a wornout car, for instance, and want a new one, maybe you are resentful of the one you are currently driving. But this is no longer a desire, it is a focus on lack. Instead, you should be feeling gratitude that the universe will bring the new car soon. The key to manifesting your desires is to assume that your desire is already being experienced, that you already have it and are enjoying it. In this way, you set up a level of vibration that can only attract its material equivalent.

Abraham observes that when people discover the law of attraction and vibration, at first they become uncomfortable with their own thoughts and what they may be attracting. But the spirits note that thoughts are not like a loaded gun waiting to wreak havoc; there is always plenty of time to understand how the laws work and to begin to change your thinking, one small step at a time. There is always a time lag or buffer between having a thought and its expression in reality. Don't be afraid of uncontrolled thoughts; instead, realize that every attempt to change your thinking toward more positive, less resistant forms brings real benefits.

Final comments

Ask and It Is Given is really a work of philosophy, because it attempts to explain the link between thought and reality, and the extent to which we create or control our worlds. It says that there is no such thing as "fate" or "the gods" directing your life according to some predetermined pattern. You are a co-creator with the "Source" (God or universal law) and can shape your life exactly as you wish. It may seem like you are at the whim of fate, but this is only when you don't understand how the law of attraction works.

Some readers will find the idea of channeled messages beyond the pale, but if you can get beyond this, it could be argued that the law of attraction is really common sense. Everyone knows, for instance, that if you think about something for a long time the likelihood of it having a real effect in your life is many times greater that if you think about it briefly. It is also common sense that desires morph into beliefs, and beliefs make us who we are. When you deliberately choose your desires and beliefs, it is logical that you can begin to master your reality.

The material on the emotions is fascinating, and in a practical sense is worth the weight of stacks of psychology books. There are intriguing chapter titles such as "Trying to hinder another's freedom always costs you your freedom" and "You are only 17 seconds away from 68 seconds to fulfilment." If you enjoyed the *Conversation with God* books by Neale Donald Walsch or *A Course in Miracles* (see commentary in *50 Spiritual Classics*), which are also "channeled" works, you will like this too. Some people prefer the audio version of the book because they find the voice of "Abraham" (Esther speaking in a strange, robotic, accented voice) powerful. However, there is arguably more dignity and clarity in the written version.

Read *The Secret* after *Ask and It Is Given* and it becomes clear how much Rhonda Byrne drew from the Abraham teachings. Esther Hicks was a central figure in the original film of *The Secret*, providing a massive boost to awareness of the Abraham teachings. However, she later asked to be edited out because she felt that Byrne's organization was operating at a "different vibration." She and Jerry subsequently released their own film, *The Secret Behind the Secret*, which was strongly promoted by Oprah Winfrey.

Esther Hicks & Jerry Hicks

Esther Hicks grew up in Park City, a town outside Salt Lake City, Utah in the 1950s. Her father worked in the lumber trade. Jerry Hicks was raised in San Diego and Arkansas, mainly by his mother, before attending high school in New Orleans.

The couple met in Fresno, California in 1976 and married in 1981. Jerry was 20 years older than Esther and had been married four times. He had been a circus acrobat, touring musician, Master of Ceremonies, and comedian. Later he made money through Amway, a marketing and distrubution network, and attributes his success to reading Napoleon Hill's Think and Grow Rich. *Each has two children from previous marriages.*

Their other books include The Amazing Power of Deliberate Intent: Living the Art of Allowing *(2005) and* The Law of Attraction: The Basics of the Teachings of Abraham *(2006).*

The Abraham-Hicks organization is headquartered in San Antonio, Texas.

1965

The Master-Key to Riches

"No one has ever been known to achieve permanent success without doing more than he was paid for."

"Riches—the real riches of life—increase in exact proportion to the scope and extent of the benefit they bring to those with whom they are shared. I know this to be true for I have grown rich by sharing. I have never benefited anyone in any manner whatsoever without having received in return, from one source or another, ten times as much benefit as I have contributed to others."

In a nutshell

The basic law of prosperity is that to receive, you must first provide something of great value.

In a similar vein

Rhonda Byrne *The Secret* (p 58)
Mark Victor Hansen & Robert G. Allen *The One Minute Millionaire* (p 140)

CHAPTER 26

Napoleon Hill

When he was a 25-year-old journalist for *Success* magazine, Napoleon Hill was sent to interview the richest man in America, steel magnate Andrew Carnegie (see commentary p 64). On the spot, Carnegie offered to give Hill "the greater part of his fortune," which turned out not to be money but his accumulated wisdom on how anyone could become wealthy.

Hill took up the challenge, interviewing all the magnates of his age over a 20-year period and writing the monumental *Law of Success*. His famous *Think and Grow Rich* (1937) was essentially a condensed version of this larger work, and went on to sell over 20 million copies.

Where does *The Master-Key to Riches* fit into his written output? While *Think and Grow Rich* offers an unadulterated recipe for financial success, *The Master-Key to Riches* is a broader, more philosophical manual for wealth of every type, including happiness and life satisfaction. Given that he was in his 80s when he wrote it, it is inevitably a more well-rounded book, highlighting prosperity as opposed to simple monetary wealth.

Open the doors to riches

Stylistically, the book reads a bit like an infomercial, breathlessly inviting the reader to turn the pages to find out what the "master-key" is. In fact Hill never actually names it, but he does provide 17 principles, or "doors" through which you must pass to reach the inner chamber where you will find the source of riches. These include the following.

Definiteness of purpose

According to Hill, every kind of success begins with a definite purpose. Its advantages include inspiring the help of other people; engendering faith, which banishes doubt and fear; overcoming procrastination; and engendering a positive mental attitude. The efforts of all the great industrialists, retailers, and inventors he studied, including Woolworth, Armour, Edison, and Bell, could be summed up in this characteristic. A clear purpose "changes the biochemistry of the mind," Hill asserts, making it difficult to succumb to fear or failure.

Going the extra mile

Nature makes it hard for any living being to gain their sustenance easily. If it did not, no strong survival instinct would have developed. "Going the extra mile," which means putting in a lot of effort with no guarantee of gain, is actually the natural way for humans to be.

This was the key trait that Andrew Carnegie looked for in his workers. If they put in effort above and beyond the call of duty he would pay them handsomely. But the extra effort had to come first. Carnegie's chief manager, Charles Schwab, had been a simple day laborer in one of his steel plants. But he was known for always doing more than he was asked, and quickly rose through the ranks to earn $75,000 a year, then the highest salary paid in America. He was later given a bonus of $1 million for many more instances of going the extra mile.

Hill notes that the Carnegie philosophy may seem like a purely economic one for getting ahead. Yet it is also about ethical treatment of people; that is, going the extra mile in relationships (helping or protecting those who are not able to protect themselves), whether or not you think you will be rewarded.

Hill tells the story of an old woman who wandered into a store in New York City; her intention was clearly not to buy anything but simply to get out of the rain. A young clerk offered his assistance, bringing her a chair to sit on. When she was ready, he walked her back to the sidewalk. There was obviously no financial benefit in what he did. Some time later, the woman contacted the store asking for the services of the young man. She wanted him to travel to Scotland to help furnish a house there. This request resulted in the purchase of furniture and fittings worth hundreds of thousands of dollars. The "house" was in fact Skibo Castle, Andrew Carnegie's famously grand holiday home, and the old woman was his mother.

Hill includes several such stories to show how average workers can reap huge rewards by assisting people without complaint. Yet one should not go the extra mile simply in the hope of monetary reward; part of its worth is the enthusiasm and energy it creates. Doing more than is expected of you makes you shine, inside and out.

Applied faith

We offer no apology for our belief that no great and enduring success has ever been achieved, except by those who recognize and use the spiritual powers of the Infinite.

Hill explores the importance of faith, not in strict religious terms but as the link between your mind and the greater universal mind of "Infinite Intelligence." Faith is the engine of apparent miracles, and is vital to achieving riches in life.

Applied faith is simply the belief that "impossibilities" can become reality—from impossible thoughts come impossible things. Hill discusses the unrelenting vision of great entrepreneurs who imagined and believed in things long before they were created. This faith is worth more than any money, because it puts you in touch with the intangible riches of the universe and its power, which few people really understand.

He observes:

> *One of the strange features of [faith] is that it generally appears because of some emergency which forces men to look beyond the power of ordinary thought for the solution of their problems.*

That is, the way out of their problems seems so impossible that they have to depend on some force higher than themselves or deep within; there is no evidence that they can climb out of their hole, yet still they calmly adhere to an apparently crazy belief. This is the famous "leap of faith" that underlies so many great enterprises.

Life's riches

Hill lists "twelve riches" in life: positive mental attitude; good health; harmony in relationships; freedom from fear; hope of achievement; capacity for faith; willingness to share your blessings; having a "labor of love" or purpose; an open mind on all subjects; self-discipline; capacity to understand people; economic security.

He notes what may seem like a strange aspect of wealth and prosperity: readiness to receive. He talks of a "priceless asset" that, if you are aware of how it works, can deliver you whatever you want. This is your "vibration center," which continually broadcasts your state of mind to the rest of the universe and also subconsciously takes in messages from it. You have two selves, a negative and a positive. When the negative self is in control, you attract like minds to you and negative situations; when the positive is in control, the opposite happens. Hill wrote: "A positive mental attitude (PMA) is the starting point of all riches, whether they be riches of a material nature or intangible riches."

Surely there are plenty of negative, mean people who have become rich? Yes, but they did not have the broader, intangible life riches, which Hill notes include love, friendship, camaraderie, domestic harmony, enjoyment of one's work, health, freedom from fear, hope for the future, and the appreciation of nature. If your aim is to be both rich and happy, Hill says, you must make a positive mental attitude a basic habit of living.

Law of compensation

Hill discusses what he calls the "great Cosmic plan" of compensation, according to which it is impossible to provide a service to others without receiving a corresponding return. Whether received now, in the future, or in unexpected form, the law is infallible. To achieve any kind of riches, to "get," you must first give. As life proves the truth of this rule again and again, why so many people try to ignore it is a mystery.

Riches are a two-way street: Your riches will in large part rest on the knowledge or help of others. (For instance, Hill's own success as a writer and speaker rested on the wisdom of Andrew Carnegie and the hundreds of other businesspeople from whom he learned the secrets of success.) In return, the universal laws oblige you to help others and pass your knowledge on. You are a vehicle for the endless circle of giving and receiving. Great riches go to those who provide things of the most value, and they in turn must pass the riches on.

Final comments

This is one of those old motivational books that are easy to dismiss at first glance. It lacks a real ending and seems slightly disjointed, but Napoleon Hill is not considered a great figure in the success movement for nothing. His books deserve concentration and thinking about, and if you read them carefully you will be rewarded.

Hill is interesting because his concepts of "vibration" and "broadcasting" could come right out of the pages of a New Age prosperity manual, yet the ideas came from the secret strategies of America's most successful businessmen of his time. If you doubt the validity of all the "mind stuff" when it comes to prosperity, the fact that it is central to the work of this major wealth-creation writer may make you think again. Hill did not, by any means, invent the laws of attraction or compensation, but rather has been important in highlighting them to a larger public who might not have stomached them from someone less straitlaced.

Napoleon Hill

Hill was born in 1883 in a one-room cabin in Wise County, Virginia. His mother died while he was only 10. He was considered one of the roughest boys in the county, but his new stepmother encouraged him to become literate. At 15 he began providing articles for local newspapers.

Hill had worked for President Woodrow Wilson as a public relations adviser, and returned to the White House under Roosevelt to help write the famous "fireside chats" broadcast over radio to Americans during the Depression. He was also personal adviser to Manuel Quezon before the latter became the first president of the Philippines.

With W. Clement Stone, Hill started the magazine Success Unlimited, *and wrote the bestseller* Success through a Positive Mental Attitude *(1960). His last full work was* Grow Rich with Peace of Mind *(1967).*

Hill died in 1970, and the Napoleon Hill Foundation carries on his work.

1957

Be My Guest

"To accomplish big things I am convinced you must first dream big dreams. True, it must be in line with progress, human and divine, or you are wasting your prayer. It has to be backed by work and faith, or it has no hands and feet. Maybe there's even an element of luck mixed in. But I am sure now that, without this master plan, you have nothing."

"I was twenty-three years old. I had been working for eleven years. So far I had earned a partnership in a store in the town in which I was born. But it was my father's store. A.H. Hilton & Son. A.H. Hilton & Shadow? a small voice within me was questioning. Wasn't it time I formulated a dream of my own? I had an idea..."

In a nutshell

Having a dream and thinking big are the basic elements of all great enterprises and fortunes.

In a similar vein

Richard Branson *Losing My Virginity* (p 46)
Anita Roddick *Business as Unusual* (p 238)
Howard Schultz *Pour Your Heart into It* (p 248)
Donald Trump *The Art of the Deal* (p 272)

CHAPTER 27

Conrad Hilton

These days Conrad Hilton is a historical figure, obscure to most people compared to his celebrity great-granddaughter Paris. Yet it is so easy to forget that our prosperity often rests on the hard work and vision of our parents or grandparents.

Given that his name is synonymous with the great wave of American postwar business success, Hilton's autobiography is less celebrated than it should be. Most people come across it in their bedside drawer during a stay at a Hilton hotel. Yet it is one of the more engrossing of the hundreds of "how I did it" self-told business stories, to be enjoyed alongside titles such as Sam Walton's *Made in America*. And unlike most books of this type, Hilton actually wrote it himself.

Be My Guest is a fascinating window into the life of a frontier American family around the turn of the twentieth century, and is a gripping story of the creation of one of the world's biggest businesses and brands. It is also a superb motivational work on why it is important to think big.

Young Conrad

Conrad Hilton was born on Christmas Day 1887. His father Gus was a Norwegian immigrant who made his living selling supplies to men working in the backwoods of New Mexico. From his store in the small town of San Antonio (not the Texas city), he eventually made enough money for the family to leave behind the dusty South West frontier. They moved to Long Beach, California, where it was hoped Mrs. Hilton could enjoy an easier life.

But with a financial crash in 1907, Gus Hilton was caught holding a lot of stock no one would buy. The family reluctantly moved back to New Mexico and took a hard look at their assets. These included a very large adobe house next to a main railway line; Mrs Hilton's great cooking; and with several kids, plenty of helping hands. The Hiltons decided to turn their house into a hotel. With room and all meals only \$2.50 a day, the business did well.

By the time he was 23, Conrad had been working for his father for 11 years. He was finally made a business partner, but was eager to do something on his own. Not particularly interested in trading or hotels, he ran for the state legislature in Sante Fe, but his dream was to own a chain of banks. At 26, he had raised enough money to start a very small one of his own.

The First World War intervened, however, and in 1917 he enlisted. He spent most of his service in France, but while on active duty back in the US received news that his father had died in a car accident. Returning to New Mexico, his home town now seemed like "a toy town of adobe and wood surrounded by emptiness."

Hilton took stock. He had savings of $5,011 (about $50,000 in today's money) and "big ideas," but was not sure what to do. A friend of his father's gave him some advice: "If you want to launch big ships, you have to go where the water is deep." He first went to Albuquerque and continued to pursue his dream of owning a chain of banks, then another friend of his father's instructed him to go to Texas, saying, "There you will make your fortune." So in 1920, now 33, Hilton moved to Cisco, where he looked around to buy a small bank. Again his efforts came to nothing and one day, exhausted, he entered a small, very crowded hotel to find a room for the night.

It dawned on him that this bustling, rundown hotel, the Mobley, might be a better proposition than owning a bank. He got talking to the owner, who despite his good turnover and margins was desperate to sell. This was a town crazed by the possibility of oil riches, and the owner wanted to make his fortune in oil. The Mobley was the first of several "old dowagers" that Hilton bought, decrepit properties yet with good accounts and room for potential.

Hilton's dream now shifted to owning a chain of hotels around Texas. He bought one, the Waldorf (not the famous Waldorf-Astoria) in downtown Dallas. Included in the manager's library was a set of books by seminal inspirational author Elbert Hubbard, *Little Journeys to the Homes of the Great*. Though already ambitious, Hilton's idea of what might be possible grew through the stories of financiers and entrepreneurs such as Meyer Rothschild, Andrew Carnegie, Stephen Girard, and Peter Cooper, plus great statesmen, artists, scientists, and philosophers.

Times good and bad

Hilton ran his shabby collection of hotels for several years, but began to want something more: his own "Hilton" hotel. The Hilton Hotel, Dallas, was a much bigger project than anything he had done before. He had to race against time to raise a million dollars, and in 1924 he broke ground on the site. After running out of money twice, in August 1925 the hotel finally opened.

With his confidence high, Hilton got married and had two sons, Nick and Barron. By the time of his 41st birthday the chain had nine hotels, including the new El Paso Hilton. Opened in the fall of 1929 and built at great expense, it seemed like the crown of a growing empire. Yet as Hilton ruefully records, "Nineteen days later the stock market crashed."

Looking back, Hilton marvels at how he got through the torturous years of the Depression. Many times it seemed as if he was about to go bankrupt, but then "something happened" (a family friend or business acquaintance would step in at the last minute to provide an injection of funds) that would enable him to keep going.

Reflecting on his Catholic faith, he comments that in these years it seemed that it was "the only gilt-edged security" he owned. Yet the time, energy, and constant travel required to keep things afloat also meant time away from his wife and family, and it cost him his marriage.

The need for a dream

In the depths of the Depression, deep in debt with a court judgment against him and his clothes at the pawnbroker, Hilton had clipped out a picture of the newly completed Waldorf-Astoria Hotel in New York. Later, when he had enough cash to buy a desk again, he put that picture under the glass top. At that time owning the hotel seemed like a ridiculous fantasy, yet it was a recognition to himself that you had to have things to aim for.

He recalls that his mother's tip for success in life could be boiled down to one word: "Pray." His father's philosophy could be reduced to another: "Work." By the time he and his siblings had grown up, they had heard the "pray and work" mantra hundreds of times, yet his brother Barron had noted, "There must be some other ingredient that goes in but I can't put my finger on it."

Writing the book at age 70, Hilton recalls sitting in the ballroom of the Waldorf-Astoria, which he now owned, and wondering whether there was anything to be added to his parents' wisdom. It was only then that it came to him: "You had to dream!"

Final comments

Despite later becoming known as the founder of an international hotel chain, Hilton was almost 50 before he bought a hotel outside Texas. Yet what seemed like slowness at the time had its benefits. By buying and operating all these other hotels before the Hilton franchise was properly established, it allowed him to truly master his industry and avoid risking the Hilton name.

His story also provides inspiration for anyone who does not yet know what they want to do but are hungry for a big opportunity. It suggests keeping our eyes and ears open, as the next chance meeting, purchase, or trip may be the turning point in our lives, just as Hilton's discovery of the Mobley hotel was to him. The moral of the book is that it does not matter if you have not yet found your life's mission or achieved your dream of riches, as long as you are in a state of readiness to seize it when it comes.

1973

The Lazy Man's Way to Riches

"Never again will you look at a particularly successful person and sigh, 'How lucky he is.' Because you will know that 'luck' or 'fate' has absolutely nothing to do with success or failure. What we call 'luck' is, in fact, a direct result of the correct or incorrect application of natural laws anyone can use effectively if he knows how."

"Most people are too busy earning a living to make any money."

In a nutshell

Mental conditioning is the foundation of wealth; once your goals are programmed in, success comes easily.

In a similar vein

Robert G. Allen *Multiple Streams of Income* (p 16)
Michael E. Gerber *The E-Myth Revisited* (p 128)
Robert Kiyosaki *Cashflow Quadrant* (p 180)

CHAPTER 28

Joe Karbo

Joe Karbo was renting a ramshackle house in a bad neighborhood along with his wife and eight children. He was $50,000 in debt and had had to refinance his car. In such a predicament, he notes, he was willing to try anything, "even if it seemed foolish and ridiculously easy."

A friend told him about a system of mental conditioning that had amazing results when tried out on corporate executives. With nothing to lose, Karbo began implementing its principles. First, he wrote out his goals, which included "I own a $75,000 house on the water," "My bills are paid," and "I earn $100,000 a year." Using the system these became his reality remarkably quickly, and he resolved to write a simple book describing what he had discovered.

Self-published, *The Lazy Man's Way to Riches* claimed to give readers "everything in the world you really want," and went on to sell over three million copies, assisted by Karbo's now-famous advertisements and sales letters. These gave some people to think it was all a lot of hype, but did the book contain something of real value?

A scientific success system

Karbo spent 12 years running an advertising agency for the television industry. He did well, but lost a bundle when he tried to produce his own TV show. The failure, he says, was "the best thing that ever happened to me. It made me desperate enough to try anything—and I found Dyna/Psyc."

Dyna/Psyc was his made-up term (dynamic + psychology/mind) for the goal-setting system he discovered. He defines it as:

> *the programmed study and practice of achieving success by the planned application of important but little understood natural laws.*

These laws are like electricity, a neutral force that can be used or misused, but through conscious development of the force you can usher in tremendous changes to your life.

The first element in the system is to identify exactly what you want.

State your destination

You don't go the airport, Karbo comments, and buy a ticket to "somewhere." You have an exact place you need to get to.

He makes you ask youself: "What do I want?" When you have to answer this in the specific it can be daunting, for while it is one thing to say to yourself "That would be nice to have" or "I wish I could...," it is quite another to sit down and write out what you want in life. This is surprising, since it has been shown that people who do have written goals tend to live up to them. Those who don't, drift.

As well as listing specific things you both need and want, Karbo asks you to put in black and white desired personal attributes—who you would like to be as well as what you would like to have. These lists are then turned into concrete goals and "Super Suggestions" using a checklist.

The strange thing about goals is that once they are written down, they immediately begin to seem more realistic. In fact, Karbo warns you to make sure your goals are high enough. This is your chance not to ask for an extra $5,000 on your salary but to reach toward what would really make your life amazing. Either way, he notes, "Without clear, well-defined goals, success is impossible."

Get there

An interesting effect of this process is you find that some things you thought you really wanted, in fact you don't. Working through your goals in this way tends to isolate and highlight what really matters to you.

Most people work too hard and have no real goals, never knowing that if they have very clear aims things will fall into place for them with less effort. This is the essence of the "lazy way." But you still have to do some work. You have to RSVP—read, study, visualize, perform—and with some time and effort you can reap huge dividends.

The goals you create are turned into a page of "Daily Declarations" that you ideally read out loud first thing in the morning and before you go to bed, visualizing each goal as if it were reality. The way the goals are written is vital. Karbo stresses that they must be in the present tense and specific (e.g., "I have a silver Lexus LS400").

What you read out may not seem possible right now, but through repetition you will condition yourself into acceptance remarkably quickly. Karbo describes the unconscious as the "idiot mind," accepting without question whatever you state as fact. Your life then begins to reflect what you believe and expect.

Form a new self-picture

Most people suffer from an inadequate self-image, Karbo observes, and yet the way you see yourself is probably the single greatest determinant of your failure or success in life. Fear is ingrained into people from a very early age, and helps to create the person you are. But the conscious mind, because fear is unpleasant, tends to subsume fears into the subconscious mind. The result is that fear is "driven underground," but it becomes even more powerful because the subconscious mind is not logical or critical, accepting whatever falls into it. Thus, fears you develop in your childhood shape your actions decades later—unless you do something to change this conditioning. A vital part of the Dyna/Psyc system is to create new beliefs about yourself as confident, effective, and energetic. Karbo shows you how to do this.

People conform to expectations about themselves. Karbo once worked at an advertising agency where he had a Ford car dealership as a client. Its manager told him that each salesperson earned about the same amount in commissions from month to month, and that what they earned from year to year did not vary much either. What they earned invariably matched their expectations. The lesson: Expectations drive results, but expectations can easily be changed.

How to make decisions

Karbo includes an extremely useful chapter on getting your unconscious mind to help you make important decisions. The process, he says, works in a seemingly magical way, and has been used by many of the great minds in history. It involves three steps:

1 Write down the problem as concisely as you can on a piece of paper.
2 Try to obtain an answer by listing in one column the reasons for taking a particular action, and in another the reasons against. Often, just doing these two steps will solve the problem with no further effort.
3 If you don't arrive at a satisfactory answer, ask your "unconscious computer" to solve it for you. Give it a definite timeframe, e.g., "By 4 o'clock tomorrow I will know exactly what to do about..." If it's a really big issue, give the computer more time. Then, just forget about the problem altogether.

How do you know when you have the answer? You will just "know"—it will pop into your head while driving or gardening or when you wake up. But Karbo gives a word of warning: When you get the answer, act on it! Otherwise, you will find that your unconscious computer is less willing to help next time.

Create a living

The first half of *The Lazy Man's Way to Riches* covers the themes above. Then it takes a surprising direction. In the second part, Karbo relates his hard-won secrets for running a successful direct-response marketing company and how to write great advertisements. For the reader it seems like a strange transition to make, until you remember the title of the book. His "lazy way" relates not just to conditioning your mind for success, but providing the reader with a practical way to make money that does not involve a regular job tied to a set wage and location. He promotes direct-response marketing as a career because "it's one of the last areas where a little guy can get a start, live where he pleases, work where he wants."

A fair amount of the material in these chapters is dated, as it was written over 20 years before the advent of the internet. Today's equivalent to going into traditional mail-order or direct-response sales is to start an online store. And yet, much of what Karbo says in relation to starting your own business and getting people to buy your products is timeless, and copywriters still pay homage to the power of his thinking on what attracts people to your product and what doesn't. He promises the reader:

If you'll follow the principles I've outlined in this book, you're sure to come up with an Idea. At the very least your idea will double or triple your present income. Even if your idea is nothing more than how to do what you're doing right now—better.

In essence, his message is that to do well in business you have to solve problems for people. If you have found something annoying or difficult, the chances are that others have too, and you can make a lot of money by saving people time and effort.

Final comments

As a strange combination of a self-development/goal-setting manual and an instruction book for how to run a mail-order business and write magnetic advertisements, *The Lazy Man's Way to Riches* is now a classic in two domains: prosperity and self-development, but also marketing and copywriting.

It was a self-published work sold through advertisements (it was never listed in *Books in Print*); the book looks very amateurish and can easily be dismissed as a marketing scam. It is said that Karbo wrote it only after he had received $50,000 in orders. If true, what a good way to write a book! And yet, wherever it came from, and despite its laid-back, conversational style, many have found the Dyna/Psyc system very powerful in helping them achieve their goals, financial or otherwise.

There are hundreds of books on goal setting, but it is the clarity of Karbo's system that seems to make it work. His assertion that "Without clear, well-defined goals, success is impossible" is hard to prove. Everyone surely knows successful people who have not had written goals, yet they have likely been a success *despite* not having goals, not because of that. Dyna/Psyc shows us that through clear goals you create certainty in your mind, and it is conviction that moves mountains.

Joe Karbo

Born in 1925, Karbo grew up in California. After high school, he served for almost three years in the US armed services as a Third Class Pharmacist Mate. On discharge in 1945 he got married, and with his wife Betty had the first of their children. He had intended to enrol at the University of California but instead had to look for a job. After rejecting one making rollerskates, he instead began buying unwanted cardboard boxes from department stores and reselling them to small businesses.

Karbo spent 12 years running an advertising agency in the television industry, but went into debt after a foray into television production. At 40 he was advised to declare bankruptcy, but decided to pay back all his debts. Ten years later he was a millionaire, partly from sales of his books and also from a vitamin mail-order company. He died in 1980.

2004

The Art of the Start

"The best reason to start an organization is to make meaning—to create a product or service that makes the world a better place. So your first task is to decide how you can make meaning."

"BE SPECIFIC. The more precisely you can describe your customer, the better. Many entrepreneurs are afraid of being 'niched' to death and then not achieving ubiquity. However, most successful companies started off targeting specific markets and grew (often unexpectedly) to great size by addressing other segments. Few started off with grandiose goals and achieved them."

In a nutshell

Before anything else, the fundamental purpose in starting any new enterprise is to *create meaning*.
Start off catering to a small market, and if what you are doing is worthwhile, other opportunities will emerge.

In a similar vein

Richard Branson *Losing My Virginity* (p 46)
Peter Drucker *Innovation and Entrepreneurship* (p 80)
Michael E. Gerber *The E-Myth Revisited* (p 128)
Anita Roddick *Business as Unusual* (p 238)
Howard Schultz *Pour Your Heart into It* (p 248)

CHAPTER 29

Guy Kawasaki

There are hundreds of books on starting a business or organization. Most provide reams of quality advice covering hundreds of pages. But when he sat down to write *The Art of the Start*, Guy Kawasaki—software company founder, venture capitalist, and former chief "evangelist" (promoter) for Apple Computer—made the assumption that anyone wanting to start a new enterprise does not want to get bogged down in theory, they want to change the world. His aim was to "cut the crap," providing only really useful information. One of his first insights is that being an entrepreneur is more a state of mind than a job title, and he covers the psychological and spiritual side of being an entrepreneur as well as revealing vital practical strategies.

He wrote the book, he notes, not just for Silicon Valley types, but for anyone wanting to create a great organization. This includes people within existing companies who want to bring great new products or services to market, and even "saints" wanting to start schools, churches, and not-for-profit bodies. Organizations may or may not be set up in order to make money, but what they must all have is a meaningful reason for being.

Meaning and mantra

The best reason for starting anything new, Kawasaki says, is to make meaning. "Meaning" can include simply trying to make the world a better place, but can also involve righting a wrong or saving something good from ending.

When Kawasaki joined Apple, the company got its meaning from the mission to replace IBM's typewriters with its Macintosh computers. Later, it was driven by the wish to overtake Microsoft and its Windows operating system. His point is that you need to have a reason for being that will make you want to go to work in the morning, a great challenge separate to money or perks.

The world is full of boring corporate mission statements, but who remembers them or believes in them? Much better, Kawasaki says, to have a mantra (a "sacred verbal formula" or incantation that involves power and emotion) that encapsulates the meaning of your organization. It will be short enough for everyone to know it and believe in it, and it doesn't even have to be written down. Coca-Cola's mission statement, for instance, is "The Coca-Cola company exists to benefit and refresh everyone it touches." But its mantra if it had one, Kawasaki says, would be a simple and powerful "Refresh the world." There is a difference between mantras (which are really for employees) and taglines, which are for customers. Nike's tagline is "Just do it," but its mantra is "Authentic athletic performance."

Kawasaki provides many tips for recruiting and choosing the right people for your organization, but the main one is to hire people who believe in your meaning or vision, even if they lack qualifications or experience. Through these "soul mates" great organizations are built, not—as myth suggests—through a single individual. Many companies have a driving force or a figurehead, but dig a bit deeper and you discover that these people had business soul mates who made the dream a reality.

What you do, how you do it

The Art of the Start points out that good business models (often overlooked in the dot-com world) are fundamental to success. You can have endless innovation in other areas, but your business model (or how you reliably make your money) must be down to earth. Chances are, yours will be a variation on one that already exists. You should be able to sum it up in ten words or less. Kawasaki's unusual tip is to first run your business model concept by a woman. He has found that they are much more realistic and savvy about the real economic chances of an idea.

You may be afraid of creating too small a niche for your product, but he points out that all large, successful companies initially developed from very specific products aimed at small markets. These segments grew, revealing other, usually unexpected markets. Even Microsoft started off with a "sliver" of a market (a particular programming language, BASIC, for a particular operating system), which expanded and revealed further potential customers and products. This is the real way to success, he says, not having grandiose goals.

He suggests weaving a MAT for your organization—milestones, assumptions, and tasks. You need to have clear goals you want to reach, you need to know the assumptions that are part of your business model, and you need to know what tasks have to be fulfilled to create a great organization.

Pitches and plans

In the era of the elevator pitch and groveling to possible financiers, Kawasaki makes a radical suggestion: Don't focus on pitches and plans, actually start making and selling your product first. Get customers almost before you start your business.

Heading a chapter on business plans, he quotes Dwight Eisenhower: "In preparing for battle, I have found that plans are useless, but planning is indispensable." Against the conventional wisdom, Kawasaki notes that business plans for start-up enterprises have limited use, since they are all based on unknowns. You cannot predict the future of something that has no track record. It is implementation and execution that matter. Although business plans can be a good exercise for the people involved to clarify aims, and investors do require them, in fact a plan is unlikely to sway an investor one way or another. They will probably have already made up their mind earlier, and the plan just provides confirmation of their position.

Whenever you do give a pitch or presentation, he writes, imagine a little man sitting on your shoulder who, every time you say something, asks: "So what?" This will prevent you from assuming that what you are saying is self-evident, awe-inspiring, or even interesting. Instead, whenever you make a general statement, back it up with an example. People want to know how something works in practice.

Bootstrapping

The alternative to receiving a cushion of money from venture capitalists or other investors for your enterprise is "bootstrapping"—starting with very little and keeping costs skeletal.

The primary consideration for a bootstrapped business, Kawasaki writes, is not establishing market share, growth, or paper profits, but cash flow. You should also piggyback on already successful products or services, thus reducing your risk. At least in the early stages, you need to have regular cash coming in even at the expense of longer-term, more profitable sales. This means getting your product to the market as soon as possible, even if it is not perfect. If you would let your own parents use your product in its current state, Kawasaki says, then ship it. Even if you only sell it to a limited market or area, you are getting cash revenues coming in plus real-world feedback. This allows you to put out a better version sooner. The downside is that you risk your reputation. However, it is better to have a reputation to risk than no business at all.

Such things make your enterprise into a lean machine focused on results and execution. If you start with a lot of venture capital behind you, he says, it can be like steroids: They can give you an initial boost, but they can also kill you. Fund your business from cash, and it will be a strong one from the beginning.

Rules of marketing

To sell a lot of whatever you are making, the product itself has to be effective, simple, and focused. In the words of innovation legend Peter Drucker, "It should do only one thing, otherwise it confuses. If it is not simple, it won't work."

In launching something new, the key word is "contagion." That is, once people hear about it or use it, they can't stop telling others about it and this creates "buzz." But to reach your largest potential market, you must lower the barriers to entry (make your product cheaper or easier to use) so that more people use it and know about it. These people create excitement, which attracts the press who will write about you, providing free, credible advertising.

People make the mistake of taking their company too seriously. Kawasaki advises you to "achieve humanness" in your marketing. This could include featuring users of your product in your marketing materials, making fun of yourself in your advertising, targeting the young, or diverting some of your resources to the needy. He also counsels you to "Make friends before you need them—and even before they can help you." In his role at Apple, he assisted journalists from sources no one had ever heard of, not just *The New York Times* or *Forbes*. Later, many of these journalists had moved to larger media organizations, and they remembered Kawasaki's help.

He also gives these tips on naming your enterprise:

- The name should start with a letter early in the alphabet, so you are always at the top of any list.
- Don't have numbers in the name.
- Have a name with verb potential (e.g., "Xerox it," "Google her").
- Avoid trendiness (e.g., only lower-case letters).

The art of being a mensch

Mensch is a Yiddish word meaning someone who does what's right and helps people. If you want to build a great company, Kawasaki says, you must have high moral and ethical standards to set the example for others. For instance, observe the spirit of agreements and always pay for what you receive, whether you are charged for it or not.

The right thing is not always the easiest thing to do, but you have to create good karma. Helping people who have no way of returning the favor is a means of thanking the universe for the many gifts you have received, including family and friends, good health, and economic success.

Final comments

Wealth and prosperity always begin with an idea, but ideas alone are not worth much. As Kawasaki points out, the art of getting an enterprise off to a good start combines both the practical and the psychological. Not many books of this type exhort the reader to focus on "creating meaning" and "being a mensch" while at the same time making sure you have a reliable business model and good cash flow. Yet to overlook either side of this equation will ensure the business dies or is less than it might have been. To prosper in the long term, you must have both meaning and nobility of intention, *and* business smarts about the practical things. This holistic view is what makes *The Art of the Start* an especially worthwhile read.

Despite the book's strong technology industry focus, most of its lessons can be applied to the establishment of anything new, and indeed its subtitle makes the claim: "The time-tested, battle-hardened guide for anyone starting anything." This includes having children, no less, and Kawasaki notes in his dedication, "A child is the ultimate startup. I have three. This makes me rich." Just as the decision to have a child should not be taken casually, requiring years of your loving attention and hard work, so starting a business should not be entered into without sufficient motivation. This is why making meaning is of primary importance. If you have a "why" (a powerful reason to to do what you are doing), you will be able to cope with, and see beyond, any kind of "how" (obstacles, difficulties) that life throws your way.

Guy Kawasaki

Kawasaki was born in 1954 in Honolulu, Hawaii. His mother was a housewife and his father variously a fireman, real-estate broker, government official, and politician. After leaving school Kawasaki went to Stanford University, graduating in 1976 with a psychology major. He attended law school briefly before doing an MBA at the University of California, Los Angeles. While still a student he began working in the jewelry business for Nova Stylings. His success in sales, plus a growing interest in software, led to his hiring at Apple.

Kawasaki is a founder and director of Garage Technology Ventures, a venture capital firm, and the offbeat news website Truemors.com. He has also established and sold on software companies, including Fog City Software.

A noted speaker, his other books include The Macintosh Way *(1990),* Selling the Dream *(1991),* How to Drive Your Competition Crazy *(1995), and* Rules for Revolutionaries *(1999).*

1998

Cashflow Quadrant

"The primary reason most people have money problems is they were never schooled in the science of cash flow management. They were taught how to read, write, drive cars and swim, but they were not taught how to manage their cash flow. Without this training they wind up having money problems, then work harder believing that more money will solve the problem. As my rich dad often said, 'More money will not solve the problem, if cash flow management is the problem.'"

"The idea of 'study hard and find a safe, secure job' is an idea born in the Industrial Age. We're not in that age anymore... Many think that the 'I' quadrant is not their responsibility. They continue to think that the government or big business or the labor union or their mutual fund or their family will take care of them when their working days are over. For their sake, I hope they're right."

In a nutshell

The mindset and income patterns of the rich are totally different to those of the poor and middle class.

In a similar vein

Robert G. Allen *Multiple Streams of Income* (p 16)
T. Harv Eker *Secrets of the Millionaire Mind* (p 86)
Michael E. Gerber *The E-Myth Revisited* (p 128)
Joe Karbo *The Lazy Man's Way to Riches* (p 168)
Andrew McLean & Gary W. Eldred *Investing in Real Estate* (p 190)
William Nickerson *How I Turned $1,000 into Three Million in Real Estate—in My Spare Time* (p 200)
Thomas J. Stanley & William D. Danko *The Millionaire Next Door* (p 266)

CHAPTER 30

Robert Kiyosaki

Given the huge difference it makes to our lives, it is astounding that we are given little or no education on money matters at school. The result: millions of financially illiterate people, living from pay check to pay check, at the mercy of others who are financially intelligent.

The lack of actual knowledge is compounded by psychological issues to do with money: We find it difficult to be logical about something that goes to the very core of our survival. In the place of logic is fear, including not wanting to know the true state of our spending and income patterns.

There are now plenty of authors and speakers who make a living trying to fill in the knowledge gaps and deal with people's emotional money issues. Perhaps the most famous of them is Robert Kiyosaki, whose *Rich Dad, Poor Dad* sold millions (see commentary in *50 Success Classics*).

Kiyosaki grew up in Hawaii, where his father was an educator. Disliking the idea of becoming a wage-earning teacher himself, he instead pursued a business career. The irony, not lost on him, is that he later became a passionate teacher through his writings and financial seminars. His ideas, however came not from his real dad but his "rich dad," a wealthy capitalist mentor.

His argument in this book is that everyone lives out of one of four financial quadrants, which describe both a mindset and a way of making money. Continuing the *Rich Dad, Poor Dad* message, *Cashflow Quadrant* is an equally good read that may have you rethinking your ideas about financial security.

The quadrants

The four quadrants are represented by the letters E, S, B, and I.

E The Employee, someone who works for the system	B The Business Owner, who owns a part of the system
S The Self-employed, whose activities effectively *are* the system	I The Investor, who gets wealthy in a hands-off way by seeking a return on money he/she has put into the system

Kiyosaki explains the quadrants this way: When an "E" needs money, they automatically look for a job. Their key word is "security" and they believe a waged position provides this. An "S" person, on the other hand, will do something to make money on their own. Their key words are "perfectionism" and "control"; they have to make sure things are done right, which means doing it their way. Thanks to this, their operations remain small.

In contrast, a "B" person will start or buy a system that generates money, and an "I" will put money into a system that will produce more money without them having to be directly involved.

What is your cash-flow pattern?

Kiyosaki identifies the basic cash-flow patterns of the poor, the middle class, and the rich. For both the poor and the middle class, most of what they earn comes from a job, and as soon as they receive it the money goes out again for expenses and debts. All that varies is the amount they earn. This is the cash-flow pattern of the "E" person. Most of the income of the rich, in contrast, comes from assets. All liabilities are paid for as they arise through the cash generated by the assets.

The middle-class cash-flow pattern is considered normal in our society. Outwardly it makes you look like you are doing well (you have cars and a house and go on holidays), but in fact you live from month to month. If you stopped working, for how long could you survive? Most people, even those with a high salary, work at the financial "red line." Their money goes out of their bank account as quickly as it comes in. The golden rule of personal finance, Kiyosaki notes, is "pay yourself first," but most people continually work to earn money, while others, including their boss and the government, live off their labors. As Kiyosaki's rich dad said to him, "People who cannot control their cashflow work for those who can."

The middle-class cash-flow pattern was the norm for the industrial age, but in the information age, Kiyosaki comments, it is madness to rely on a wage for nearly all your income. To win back your time and get in control of your financial destiny, money has to come from cash-generating assets. He observes: "In the Information Age, the people who work physically the hardest will be paid the least." Yet most people still believe in the "hard work and spend" mode of life.

But I own my house!

Your response to this discussion is probably: "Yes, but I do own an asset, my house." Is your house really an asset, though? Rich Dad defined an asset as something that "puts money into my pocket," but when most people buy a house they take out a long mortgage, which is effectively a hole into which they will pour money for the next 20 or 30 years (the word "mortgage" is a French one meaning "agreement until death").

Your house *is* an asset, Kiyosaki notes, but whose asset? For the bank that loaned you the money it is indeed a wonderful asset, generating cash in the form of interest for years to come. Not only that, it is virtually risk free: If the "owner" of the house stops paying the mortgage payments the bank can move in, sell the house, and get its money back.

Your house is not an asset unless you own it outright and are about to sell it, but then you have to buy somewhere else to live anyway. Otherwise, it is a liability. The familiar pattern is, if your income goes up, to buy a bigger house and take on more debt. You look richer, but nothing has changed. You are still putting all your money into something that is making money for someone else.

Be financially literate

People on the left side of the quadrant tend to blame others for their plight, when the real reason for their situation is lack of knowledge about money. They base their financial lives on opinions such as "your house is an asset" or "you need money to make money," without ever really looking at the facts.

People on the right side of the quadrant, in contrast, have become successful by trusting facts. They think in numbers, not words. If you simply want to work for others all your life, you don't need to be accurate or knowledgeable about numbers. Most people put money into what looks good to them visually or emotionally, but the smart investor, Rich Dad said, creates their own picture of an investment from the numbers alone.

Wealthy people put much more time into their investing and as a result get better returns. They are adept at finding financial problems caused by people who have less knowledge than them, then taking the problem out of their hands with potentially great rewards.

The educated, Kiyosaki notes, tend to sneer at the power and freedom of the rich. If you have an advanced degree, you have a sense of entitlement. But capitalism favors those with *financial* intelligence. His rich dad made him read books on economic history, including biographies of Rockefeller, J. P. Morgan, and Henry Ford, and he also read about the great economists and economic trends.

His conclusion: Wealth, over time, flows from people on the left side of the quadrant to those on the right. When legislation changes or markets crash, those on the right wait ready to seize assets—as Kiyosaki himself did in 1986, when there was a property crash in the US and he bought real estate cheaply.

Make the transition

Kiyosaki himself was "paralyzed with fear" when he handed in his resignation note for his full-time job at Xerox, having nothing certain to go on to. But he was determined to leave the "E" quadrant and move into the "B."

Kiyosaki's rich dad told him, "Money is a drug." People become addicted to paid employment. They are happy when they get paid, and are miserable and anxious when they don't. The person with a "B" or "I" mindset, on the other hand—the mindset of the rich—can remain confident and upbeat even when they have little, knowing that things will change. They are intent on creating business systems that generate money. When Kiyosaki and his wife could only afford to live in their car, and then a basement (while they developed a seminar business), friends and relatives wondered why they were not out trying to get a job. They were indeed sorely tempted to go back to paid employment, but reminded themselves that it was an addiction they had to rid themselves of if they really wanted to be rich.

Change who you are first

When an "E" person tries to become a "B," often there will be a violent internal reaction, since the move seems to go against their very survival. As Rich Dad put it, "The part of you that still seeks security is in a war with that part of you that wants freedom." It is easy to forget what you set out to do, what you are aiming for, when the fearful emotions crowd in. At this point, he said, you have to remember the passion you had for change: "Passion builds businesses, not fear."

The shift from one quadrant to another is mentally a big step. Kiyosaki's advice is to take small first steps rather than attempting it in one big go. Above all, you have to think long term and have a vision. It is not about getting rich quick. People come to Kiyosaki asking him what to do in their situation. He doesn't tell them what to do, only what they need to become as a person to attain long-term financial independence. Before they can "have," they have to "be."

Many people believe that trying to copy how rich people live will make them rich. It won't—quite the opposite. Much more important is to *think* like rich people do. Change yourself first, and the lifestyle will eventually follow.

Financial IQ is mostly emotional IQ

The primary difference between the rich and everyone else is their different attitude to failure. Kiyosaki's rich dad told him:

> *The reason there are few self-made rich people is because few people can tolerate disappointment. Instead of learning to face disappointment, they spend their lives avoiding it.*

If you can learn to expect disappointment, yet move on regardless toward your goals, your success—even though it won't seem like it at the time—is virtually assured. People try new business ideas, are excited at the beginning, then soon give up, blaming the idea. What has actually happened, Kiyosaki says, is that disappointment won, and won too easily. The mentality of the business owner and investor is different: They know that success takes time and are prepared for the ups and downs. He observes: "Financial IQ is 90 percent Emotional IQ and only 10 percent technical information about finance or money." People on the right side of the quadrant have fears too, but they actively try to master them in pursuit of a dream.

Final comments

Kiyosaki is controversial. Some people complain there is not enough hard information in his books on how to move from an employee to a business-minded person. Yet providing this information was never his intention. His writings are aimed at creating a new mindset in the reader, and *Cashflow Quadrant* includes many caveats about hard work and not rushing into anything too quickly. The key, he repeatedly says, is education, which can cost little but bring you millions.

The other point of controversy is Rich Dad, who despite being the source of wisdom in the book may not have really existed. He may be Richard Kimi, a Hawaiian hotel owner whose son Michael is mentioned several times in the book. Another candidate is Marshall Thurber, a student of visionary scientist Buckminster Fuller, whose courses on self-development and real estate Kiyosaki took in the 1980s. Maybe Rich Dad is a composite of both.

If you can forgive minor annoyances including typographical errors and plugs for network marketing, this is a fascinating book, a valuable financial education that may inspire you to think more about which quadrant you wish to exist in. As Kiyosaki notes, it is fine to remain a wage earner as long as you are receiving money from investments as well, but to be only a wage earner is, in today's world, a risky path.

Robert Kiyosaki

Born in 1947, Robert Toru Kiyosaki grew up in Hawaii, where his father was the chief of education for the state. After college in New York he worked for Standard Oil in tanker shipping, as a salesman for Xerox, and in his mid-20s joined the Marines, going to Vietnam as an officer and a helicopter pilot. He also began to buy and sell apartments and invest in stocks, and in 1977 successfully introduced nylon and velcro "surfer wallets" to the United States.

His Cashflow Technologies firm, based in Phoenix, Arizona, sells business educational products around the world and he is a popular seminar speaker. Other books include Rich Dad's Guide to Investing *(2000),* Rich Dad's Prophecy *(2002), and* Retire Young, Retire Rich *(2002). The Rich Dad series has been translated into 46 languages and has sold over 20 million copies.*

1989

One Up on Wall Street

"Twenty years in this business convinces me that any normal person using the customary three percent of the brain can pick stocks just as well, if not better, than the average Wall Street expert."

"It's best to define your objectives and clarify your attitudes beforehand, because if you are undecided and lack conviction, then you are a potential market victim, who abandons all hope and reason at the worst moment and sells out at a loss. It is personal preparation, as much as knowledge and research, that distinguishes the successful stockpicker from the chronic loser."

In a nutshell

Alert investors who focus on the fundamentals and do not get swayed by market sentiments can outperform the professionals.

In a similar vein

John C. Bogle *The Little Book of Common Sense Investing* (p 40)
Warren Buffett *The Essays of Warren Buffett* (edited by Lawrence Cunningham; p 52)
Benjamin Graham *The Intelligent Investor* (p 134)

CHAPTER 31

Peter Lynch

When *One Up on Wall Street* was published in 1989, Peter Lynch was the vice-chairman of Fidelity Management & Research Company and the portfolio manager of Fidelity Magellan Fund. Under his stewardship, the obscure Magellan Fund grew from a tiny $20 million in 1977 to $14 billion in 1990, making it the best performing in the world with an annualized rate of return of 29.2 percent.

Despite his stellar success as a fund manager, Lynch wanted to write a book that would "offer encouragement and basic information to the individual investor" who did not necessarily want to cede control of their money to someone else. He was taken by surprise when it became a bestseller. *One Up on Wall Street* has since gone into 30 reprints and has sold more than a million copies. Published in the gloom following the stock-market crash of 1987, the book goads investors to consider stock investments as a serious option—as long as every share is hand picked with care and consideration.

Informal and very readable, the humor and light mood of the book make it easier for its serious lessons to hit home. Even given the flights and fashions of the stock market its advice is relatively timeless, and its coverage of all aspects of stock investing makes it a perfect primer for people about to enter the market. Indeed, a common reader reaction to the book is to wish that they'd read it years ago—before they got their fingers burnt.

Individuals can outperform the market

It is easy to believe that stock-market investing is a complicated and risky activity best left to geniuses and experts. Lynch's main message therefore comes as a surprise: Believe in yourself. While it is not his intention to wean people off investing in mutual funds, having seen every type of mistake and folly in the industry he sees no reason that an individual cannot outperform the professionals at their own game. "Tenbagger" is a term he uses often, to mean stocks that return ten times the money you originally invested. Such opportunities abound; taking advantage of them is just a matter of having your antennae out to spot them.

Lynch advises entering the stock market only if you meet three criteria: You should have first invested in a house; you should not be in need of any urgent funds; and you should have the mental qualities to succeed in the market. He warns against getting caught up in any theories that attempt to predict market trends, and to give up buying "hot tips." The only winning strategy is identifying the correct stock to purchase, and he repeatedly stresses the importance of understanding the company you are investing in.

The book has three sections. "Preparing to invest" is an orientation session that takes the reader through the differences between bonds, shares, and other securities, and attempts to allay some of the fears of beginner investors. "Picking winners" is a guide to finding the good companies, knowing which ones to avoid, and how to glean important facts from annual reports. Technical terms such as p/e ratio, book value, and cash flow are elaborated on. And "The long-term view" shows how to design a portfolio that can maximize gains and minimize risks, and suggests the best times to buy and sell.

Do the legwork

Lynch chides investors "who spend weekends searching for the best deals on airfares to London, but buy 500 shares of KLM without having spent five minutes learning about the company." His advice: Put as much effort into picking your stocks as you do into buying your groceries.

He usefully divides companies into categories: slow growers (buy for their dividends); stalwarts (which won't go out of business); fast growers (need a lot of research, but very rewarding); cyclicals (need a close watch, but can be rewarding); asset plays (companies with undervalued or hidden assets in their balance sheet); turnarounds (those that seem about to turn a corner). Lynch remarks: "Although it is easy to forget, a share of stock is not a lottery ticket. It's part ownership of a business."

He advises the reader to get comfortable looking at company annual reports and doing some number crunching, discussing factors such as the p/e (price/earnings) ratio (low for slow growers and high for fast growers), the cash position, the debt factor, dividend record, book value, and so on. If at all possible, he suggests, visit the company you want to invest in. First-hand experience combined with annual report analysis is unbeatable.

Avoid market fashion

Echoing Benjamin Graham and Warren Buffett, Lynch remarks, "I don't believe in predicting markets. I believe in buying great companies." He proposes a list of thirteen attributes to look for, some of them surprising. Start getting interested, he says, if a company sounds dull (for example Automatic Data Processing); does something dull (like Crown, Cork and Seal, which makes cans and bottle caps); does something disagreeable (such as Safety Kleen, which washes the grease from gas stations); is a spin-off (of a company with sound fundamentals); is not owned by institutions or followed by analysts; has something depressing about it (for example SCI, which manages burials).

Also look for companies that are in a niche that means people have to keep buying their products, or if the company is buying back its own shares.

In terms of companies to avoid, Lynch advises you to steer clear of the hottest stocks that everyone is talking about, ones that are diversifying into areas unconnected to their core business, and those who supply most of their wares to one customer.

Trust the fundamentals

For small portfolios, Lynch suggests, hold between three to ten stocks. Diversifying into unknown companies just for the sake of diversity would be foolish. Once you have established the portfolio, trust the work you have done and do not buy and sell based only on market sentiments, unless there is a strong reason to believe that the company is doing badly.

Final comments

Lynch convincingly argues that the stock market should be seen neither as a gambling den nor a safe investment haven. If approached with the proper attitude and a well-thought-out strategy, and if your investments are based on thorough research and understanding of the company, then it is a rewarding place to be.

Although little of what Lynch says in *One Up on Wall Street* has not been said before, his insights are presented in an enjoyable and memorable way, and of course are backed by a remarkable track record. The twist of the book, and part of the reason for its popularity, is that a famous fund manager is warning the reader about his own industry, saying it is not necessary to be part of managed funds to secure your financial future. In fact, anyone with half a brain can manage quite well on their own if they are diligent, careful, and consider their stock purchases as investments rather than speculative plays.

Peter Lynch

Lynch was born in 1944 to parents who had a strong distrust of the stock market. One of seven children, he lost his father at the age of 7 and took part-time jobs to supplement the family income, including becoming a golf caddie to businessmen and stockbrokers at his local country club in Massachusetts. He bought his first stock while still in college, Flying Tiger Airlines, an investment that paid for his education. After serving for two years in the US Army, he began working at Fidelity as an intern and was later hired as an analyst.

Other books include the bestselling Beating the Street *(1995) and* Learn to Earn *(1996). Lynch now spends most of his time disbursing funds from his Lynch Foundation.*

Co-author John Rothchild has written for Time, Fortune, *and the* New York Times Book Review. *He is also the author of* A Fool and His Money *and* Going for Broke.

2005

Investing in Real Estate

"You can speculate in stocks. You can even speculate in real estate. You can buy lottery tickets. You can shoot craps in Las Vegas. Maybe any or all of these will pay off for you. But the odds are stacked against you. In contrast, selectively acquire just four or five rental properties (residential or commercial), and you will build an income for life—a monthly cash flow that will generously finance the quality of life you would like to enjoy."

"For future income that you can live well on for as long as you live, no investment comes close to matching the amount and certainty of income provided by rental properties. Inflation does not eat away your rental income because... rents tend to increase over time."

In a nutshell

Buying rental properties is one of the lowest-risk and best-performing forms of investment.

In a similar vein

Benjamin Graham *The Intelligent Investor* (p 134)
Robert Kiyosaki *Cashflow Quadrant* (p 180)
William Nickerson *How I Turned $1,000 into Three Million in Real Estate—in My Spare Time* (p 200)
Donald Trump *The Art of the Deal* (p 272)

CHAPTER 32

Andrew McLean & Gary W. Eldred

In *The Intelligent Investor*, stock guru Benjamin Graham made his well-known distinction between investing and speculating, noting that the two activities were worlds apart. *Investing in Real Estate* remarks on the same distinction, but tells readers to stay out of stock investing altogether. McLean and Eldred maintain that property is easily the better form of investment, and provide a compelling case (with plenty of examples) to support their view, stating that, all round, property is a "safer, surer path to wealth and income."

The book was written for an American audience, and if you do not live in the US some of the terms and strategies will not apply to you. The essence of real-estate intelligence is, after all, local knowledge. However, *Investing in Real Estate* is considered a modern bible in the field, and provides a wealth of ideas that could keep you up into the night thinking about the possibilities for entering the market where you live. It may also bring about a sea change in your investing priorities.

Property vs. stock investing

McLean and Eldred examine the widely accepted view in the investing world that stocks give the best returns in the long run. Where did this idea come from? It is partly based on fact, but when you look more closely, in terms of assets that actually put money in your pocket it is plain wrong. Given their commissions and fund management fees it is a belief that legions of financial advisers wish to perpetuate, but the effect has been too many people putting too much money into the stock markets, creating "irrational exuberance" or bubbles. Some people will do well out of stocks, the authors admit, but they are the lucky ones. Most are disappointed.

Consider, instead, the many benefits of investing in real estate. McLean and Eldred give an example of how it is difficult *not* to make money with property assets. Say you buy a property for $250,000, putting $50,000 down and with a mortgage over 20 years. During this period the property generates no surplus cash to you, with all the rental income going to pay off the mortgage. At the end of 20 years when the mortgage is paid off, you sell the property for the same price you paid for it: $250,000. It is highly unlikely the property would not have appreciated, but even assuming it has not, thanks to the power of leveraged money you are still left with an asset worth five times your original stake. And this is the worst-case scenario. You will make a lot more if the property has appreciated, if you renovated it well, or if you got it for a good price in the first place. Admittedly with inflation $250,000 in 20 years' time will not be worth what it is now in buying power, but it is unusual for capital appreciation not to keep up with or surpass the rate of inflation. Over 20 years, the $250,000 original value of the property could double or treble.

Yet property has an even more enticing benefit: regular cash-flow returns. McLean and Eldred observe, "Investors never buy assets, *per se*. They buy flows of future income." And once you have paid off a mortgage on a property, you have a permanent cash-generating asset—a "cash cow."

In contrast, cash returns on stock investments (dividends) are purposefully kept low, which means that most people whose retirement income is tied to dividends will have to eat into their nest egg to keep living comfortably. They must also deal with stock-market volatility, which historically is a lot greater than property price movements.

As safe as houses

Ups and downs do occur in the real-estate market, but the fact is that people have to rent even in recessions, and while property prices or rents may be static for a time, you still do not have to worry about "bubbles" to the extent you do with the stock market, when prices can fall 50 percent or more virtually overnight. The price of a property may also drop, but almost never precipitously, and you can still keep earning rental income. The important point about real-estate investing, in contrast to stocks, is safety of capital.

In contrast, stocks provide too little return for the amount of risk involved. You may protest that you are buying stocks mainly for the increase in their values, but history demonstrates that investing in real estate provides both good cash returns *and* very good capital appreciation.

Many people buy bonds to have a guaranteed future income. Indeed, bonds often pay more income than stocks, but the amount is still a lot less than rental income and tends not to keep pace with inflation. Rental income nearly always does.

What about vacancy rates and difficulty in rent collection? Most people still hang on to equity investing because of an erroneous belief in the perils of being a landlord—people ringing you in the middle of the night to come and fix a blocked toilet, for example. But McLean and Eldred note that despite being owners of many rental properties, they have never had to do this. Problems crop up less often than you may think, and you can pay other people to sort them out from your rental income. In a well-managed, well-located property such issues will be minimal.

One final reason to invest in property over stocks: Property is less prone to sudden impulses. "You can't buy, own or sell real estate with the click of a mouse," McLean and Eldred note. It does take more thought, creativity, and time on your part as opposed to just handing your money over to a mutual fund, but this also means much greater control over your investment. Paradoxically, greater control can mean less worry and at the same time greater rewards.

High-leverage financing

McLean and Eldred write warily about the "nothing down" merchants who promise people that they can get wealthy from real estate without using any of their own money. It is possible, they admit, but is it good practice?

Buying property with no deposit is a form of creative financing that, if it always worked, would have seen millions more people become successful property investors. In fact, most of these people are looking for a quick and painless way to get out of their debt or other money problems. They want to buy property without any of their own money for a reason: They tend not to have any in the first place. At any rate, *Investing in Real Estate* points out, "nothing down" financing is increasingly difficult to get. Most banks and lenders—quite reasonably—require a deposit. Your having one tells them that the person they are lending to has financial sense and discipline.

To become a genuine property investor, the book advises, first follow the example of Stanley and Danko's "millionaires next door" (see commentary p 266) and live well within your means, saving all the time so that you have capital to invest when the right opportunity comes along. Many "nothing down" property buyers are in real estate to make a quick killing, but when investing in any asset (be it wine, old masters, stocks, or property), McLean and Eldred warn, never depend on the rate of appreciation to make it pay off. Instead, focus on what the asset is costing you *now* to own. If it produces a negative cash flow (e.g., the rent from a property does not meet the repayment amount for the mortgage) it is an "alligator" that will eat up your reserves fast. It is likely to be a poor investment in the first place.

If you do go into high-leverage financing, make sure that your original purchase price is a bargain; you can easily improve the property to raise the rent; and the loan you take out is low interest. These factors will give you much more of a cushion if the property is vacant for a while, if you face unexpected costs, or if interest rates go up.

If you don't have a lot of money to invest, buy a home with owner-occupied mortgage financing, which generally requires a much smaller deposit. To get the finance you have to live in the property for at least a year, but after that you can rent it out. Though you paid little of your own money to obtain it, now it becomes an investment property. It is possible to do this several times quite legally, and it can deliver you a portfolio of assets in quite a short space of time.

Where is property headed?

A section on "Why rents can only increase" contains the following demographic facts:

- The US population will grow by 40 million people over the next 20 years. (A similar rate of growth can be expected in many other countries.)
- Household size will decrease, from 2.3 people to only 2.0, meaning there will be a need for more housing units per head of population.
- Incomes are likely to keep rising, with people owning more second homes.

These factors mean that demand for rental properties will outstrip supply. Surely new homes being built will simply meet demand? No, because there is a lack of suitable land where people want to live; developers have to go through a lot of red tape to build new properties; and infrastructure is not good enough to service the new homes. The result is that builders are continually playing "catch-up."

In an extra chapter on future trends and developments in the latest edition of the book, Eldred refers to Richard Florida's *The Rise of the Creative Class*, which identified US cities that are likely to experience long-term growth thanks to the smart, creative people who want to live in them. Florida suggested that people no longer go where the jobs are; the jobs go where these "creatives" like living.

What does this mean for the real-estate investor? Do not just look at the traditional indicators for how well an area or city is doing, but find out if there are cafés, cinemas, and bookstores that are opening there, and whether there are many festivals or activities that attract people. "In other words, look for areas that are developing a certain cachet." This factor will inevitably see prices rise. Chances are, if you or your friends want to live somewhere, others will too. Which of these desirable places still seem a bit of a secret? Buy into them now and you will probably do well. They are "right place, right time" investments.

Final comments

Investing in Real Estate claims that as people discover the benefits of property investing the rates of return will fall. Instead of 10 percent, for instance, you may only get 5 percent. But this is still a better return than most stock investments. You may feel you have missed the boat in terms of the property market, since prices are so high and have gone up so much in the last ten years. However, McLean and Eldred note an even worse time to buy: "five years from now, ten years from now, or any other time in the foreseeable future."

In the early 1990s two Harvard economists published a paper predicting that by 2005 property prices in America would be 40 percent lower. Eldred argued just the opposite—and was proved right. At present, prices have stabilized or have fallen in most parts of the United States, creating the widespread belief that property is overvalued. *Investing in Real Estate*, however, predicts that prices will appreciate between now and 2020 as much as they did between 1990 and 2005.

With the recent downturn in property prices, you may think this may not happen. However, recall the book's message that it is difficult to go badly wrong in real-estate *investing*; that is, buying for the long term and riding out the shakier times. The idea of "value investing" as laid down by stock wizards Graham and Buffett is equally applicable to buying real estate. If you are careful it will set you up for real prosperity, not just on paper but as cash flowing to you every month for the rest of your life.

Get *Investing in Real Estate* for its comprehensive treatment of virtually every property-related subject, including arranging finance; finding great properties; maximizing cash flows; profiting from foreclosures; "flipping" (buying and selling a property quickly at a profit); negotiating contracts; writing rental agreements; and paying less tax. Many references are supplied for further reading, including recommended websites.

Andrew McLean & Gary W. Eldred

Only the first edition of Investing in Real Estate *is the product of both authors. All later revisions and added sections are by Gary Eldred.*

***Eldred** made his first real-estate investment at the age of 21, and has combined an academic career in land economics and property investing with success as an actual investor in office buildings, apartments, and shopping centers. He has held faculty positions at Stanford University, University of Illinois, University of British Columbia, the American University of Sharjah in Dubai, and Trump University.*

In addition to three college textbooks, Eldred's books include The Complete Guide to Second Homes for Vacations, Retirement, and Investment *(1999),* Make Money with Condominiums and Townhouses *(2003),* The 106 Common Mistakes Homebuyers Make (and How to Avoid Them) *(4th edn, 2005), and* Trump University Real Estate 101 *(with Donald Trump, 2006).*

***McLean**'s other titles include* Making a Fortune Quickly in Fix-Up Properties *(1997),* The Home Buyer's Advisor *(2004), and* Making Money in Foreclosures *(2006).*

1988

How to Get Out of Debt, Stay Out of Debt, and Live Prosperously

"Paul is already free. A forty-year-old Chicago real estate salesman, he was down $36,000 and on the verge of bankruptcy when he began this program. Now, five years later, he has repaid his creditors in full and increased his income from $40,000 to $70,000...
Vivian, sixty, works in high fashion in New York, is not free yet. She still owes $80,000. On the other hand, she owed $240,000 when she first began four years ago.
There are countless more. With this program, if you choose, you too can do what they have done."

"The missiles won't be launched. Blood isn't running in the streets. You owe some money, that's all. You're not going to be shot at dawn. There is no debtors prison."

In a nutshell

Your debts may seem insurmountable, but there is a well-worn, reliable path that can rescue you from despair.

In a similar vein

Joe Dominguez & Vicki Robin *Your Money or Your Life* (p 74)
Catherine Ponder *Open Your Mind to Prosperity* (p 218)
Dave Ramsey *Financial Peace Revisited* (p 228)

CHAPTER 33

Jerrold Mundis

When he began to practice the principles in *How to Get Out of Debt, Stay Out of Debt, and Live Prosperously*, Jerrold Mundis was $50,000 in debt and had a guaranteed income of only $350 a month. An illness, a divorce, and the unreliable nature of freelance writing were among the things he blamed for getting into his financial mess. It was only later, having been through the "Back to the Black" program at Debtors Anonymous, that he realized a change in circumstances was rarely the cause of problem debts.

For a book about personal finance, and particularly the fearful subject of debt, *How to Get Out of Debt* is surprisingly engrossing and enjoyable. Mundis is a seasoned novelist applying his skills to a different subject, but what makes the book a great read is the fact that he lays his own soul and finances bare. If *he* was capable of climbing out of debt, anyone could.

Even though Debtors Anonymous does not endorse the book in any way, many of the strategies and concepts the organization uses are incorporated in it, and they have been tried and tested on thousands of people. Though written for an American audience, the principles are universal.

What is debt and when does it become a problem?

Mundis defines debt as anything you have used or are obliged to pay but have not yet paid for: credit card balances, store card balances, personal loans, taxes, rent, phone bills, loans from friends, child support, tuition fees, and so on—basically, anything you owe that is not backed by collateral. Home loans are not really debt, in that they are secured against the house. If you stop making the mortgage payments, the house reverts to the bank and you owe nothing.

The first misconception about mounting debt, Mundis notes, is that it only happens to less well-off people. In fact, consumer debt (which has steadily risen since the book's initial release) is a problem across all social and income sectors, whether you are a carpenter, teacher, doctor, or executive.

While people's level of debt may differ greatly, in each case it brings the same feelings: sick-to-the-stomach desperation, poisoning the life of the debtor and in the worst-case scenarios leading to clinical depression or suicide attempts.

Of course, none of this relates to *you*. You have debts, sure, but they have not taken over your life... yet. Debts often grow by stealth over many years, Mundis observes from experience, until a tipping point is reached when you are driven to extreme measures.

The warning signs

Mundis goes through the warning signs of a debt problem. They include:

- You are constantly juggling payment demands, still dealing with last month's bills when the new ones arrive.
- You regularly miss payment-due demands and find yourself in arrears.
- You stop opening your mail because of the fear of what it contains.
- You stop wanting to know how much is left in your bank account, always fearing the worst.
- You are ignorant of the terms of your various loans and card agreements; all you know is what your limit is and how much you can spend before it is reached.
- You rarely pay off more than the minimum due on your credit cards, and when you max out on one card, you turn to the other one/s.
- Where once you paid cash for most things, now you use store cards.
- When you buy things on credit, you opt for the longest payback terms available.
- You use your credit card for cash advances, and often borrow small amounts from friends to get you through to the next paycheck.
- You are delighted when a credit card company increases your limit or offers to give you a new card, as it makes you feel like a person of "worth, accomplishment and responsibility."
- You get a sense of accomplishment out of just meeting basic expenses for food, shelter, and clothing.
- You have little or no savings or investments, no back-up if you get unemployed or ill.
- You have little idea of your monthly costs and outgoings or how they match up to what you earn.

Admit you have a problem

One of the planks of the Debtors Anonymous program (echoing the creed of Alcoholics Anonymous) is: "Just for today, one day, do not incur any new debt." As Mundis discovered, people often get into a debt spiral as the result of compulsive, emotion-driven thinking. Terrified of running out of money, you take out a larger loan to cover basic living expenses, but the more debt you have, the more you have to pay out to service it. With less and less discretionary income, your quality of life goes down. The dread and desperation associated with your finances grow. While some people do go into debt because of unusual circumstances, for most it flows from compulsive thinking.

As with any recovery program, the first step is to admit you have a problem "and that it's caused a lot of pain and trouble in your life." People dread this moment, believing it will make them feel weak, useless, a bad person. In fact, the opposite usually happens. When you write out a list of your debts and add them up, there is typically a feeling of release. You are no longer hiding, and with a figure in black and white you can begin to take some action. What is more, you realize that your debts are not "you," and that they can be managed and reduced. Your situation is temporary, and in time you will return to a rightful prosperity, a state fully deserved for having courageously faced up to your debts—and it does take guts.

"But I'm a special case"

The Debtors Anonymous approach, as you would expect, focuses on the self before anything. The root cause of your debt is dysfunctional attitudes you have built up about money, attitudes that no sudden windfall or pay rise is going to change. One of these beliefs is: "When the going gets tough, the tough get shopping." When you use shopping as a substitute for love or to cure anxiety or as a reward, you are on your way to a debt problem.

Many people justify going into debt in the belief that soon a Big Fix of money will come along to wipe out their debts. They will make a killing on the stock market, get their inheritance, win a court case, get a raise, win the account, find an oil well. Yet when debtors do suddenly earn more, they just get higher debt levels and the spiral continues.

Remembering a large check he received for writing a popular novel that was quickly eaten up by existing obligations, Mundis ruefully observes:

The Big Fix rarely arrives. If it does, it doesn't fix anything at all. The money is either already owed or it just buys a little more time. Sooner or later you end up in the same place again.

Another mistake people make is that they think they are a special case. Their debts relate to the particular nature of their role or job as clergyman, actor, small business owner, ski instructor, father of five, writer, medical intern, unskilled laborer, and so on. Others blame their indebtedness on the costs of being young, being old, having a medical problem, divorce, or getting paid irregularly.

The fact is, Mundis writes, no one ever forced you to go into debt, and no one is forcing you to take on more. The day you take a firm line on not borrowing any more—whatever your circumstances—is the start of your recovery.

Climb out

Getting out of debt usually does not mean working yourself into the ground while living on nothing, but rather changing your attitudes to money and altering (but not drastically changing) your daily habits. As Mundis remarks, "This isn't about eating cat food and working harder."

Even if you are significantly in debt, always remember that today, you have food to eat and a roof over your head. You are not going to starve and no one will take away your children. There is always more time than you think to deal with your situation, and many more options for solving it than you thought. It is easy to get caught up in an emotional maelstrom when you are in debt, doing fewer things you enjoy, seeing fewer people. You can start to believe that you are worthless, that things are hopeless.

But echoing cognitive psychologists, Mundis stresses that "feelings are not facts." The way people feel about a situation is often wrong, particularly if you have poured your fear and anguish into it. He reminds the reader:

> *Your creditors do not own you. You owe them money, not your life.*

The first step to getting free of debt is having a Spending Record, a tool described as "nearly as good as the wheel." *How to Get Out of Debt* shows you how to draw one up and maintain it, so that you will never again be one of those people who wonders what happened to the $50 you took from the bank yesterday. Without a record of all the money you spend, Mundis warns, it is almost impossible to get out of debt. Since most debtors have—on purpose—a very foggy appreciation of their finances, knowing exactly what you are spending your money on will help you become a different sort of person: not a penny pincher, simply someone who is in control of their finances.

One of the first things you do in devising your spending record is allocate money for yourself: haircuts, flowers, seeing a movie, buying a book. Just because you are in debt does not mean you have to stop living and suffer, and these small expenses signal to you that you are on your way back to prosperity, that you are not the sum of your debts.

Final comments

How to Get Out of Debt has plenty of good advice on topics including the dangers of consolidation loans, why a bad credit rating is not as bad as you think, the importance of having a fund for contingencies, particularly if you are self-employed, and why there is now no reason for anyone to have a credit card.

The last part of the book takes a surprising turn. Having mostly discussed the nuts and bolts of indebtedness, Mundis moves on to the more spiritual issues of prosperity and abundance, underlining how getting free of debt is first and foremost an "inside job" that requires a change to the way you see the world, from a perception of "there is never enough" to "there is always enough—and more." It is your duty as a human being to get back to your prosperous nature.

Among other concepts he discusses is the vacuum principle. This says that if you want more money or particular things, you first have to pay what you owe or give freely. Mundis recounts a period during his recovery from debt when he decided to pay his bills as soon as they came in, even though it would leave him with little to live on for the following few months. He had to take a leap of faith that the money that went out would be replaced. Duly, over the next months he received money from unexpected sources that kept him afloat.

How and why does this work? Mundis admits that he doesn't know, only that it seems to be infallible, almost as if God goes out on a limb to help people who are determined to be free of debt.

Whether you accept this or not, *How to Get Out of Debt* remains one of the best books on the subject, particularly if you get the revised and updated 2003 edition. If you are solvent or well-off it is still worth reading, if only to become well versed in the thinking and strategies that can help a relative or friend regain their prosperity.

Jerrold Mundis

Born in Chicago in 1941, Mundis grew up in Wisconsin in a family of modest means. He enrolled at Beloit College in Wisconsin before moving to New York, where he graduated from New York University.

He was an editor at the New York Times *and has been a contributor to many American magazines and newspapers. He gives seminars and talks on personal money management, and runs a consultancy to help writers improve their work and output.*

Mundis' 17 novels include Gerhardt's Children *(2000) and* The Dogs *(2001), and his non-fiction books include* Break Writer's Block Now! *(1991),* Earn What You Deserve: How to Stop Underearning and Start Thriving *(1995), and* Making Peace with Money *(1999). His work has been translated into 12 languages. He has two grown sons and lives in New York City.*

1969

How I Turned $1,000 into Three Million in Real Estate–in My Spare Time

"After working twelve more years for the company, and operating rental property as a sideline, we had pyramided our estate to a half-million dollars... I retired at forty-two to concentrate on managing my property, with considerable time out for gardening our sunny acre in the San Ramon Valley, swimming in our back-yard pool, hunting, fishing, and traveling."

"Though maximum success demands consistent effort, the realty road to riches requires neither superhuman endeavor nor superintelligence. The chief attributes of successful realty investing are imagination, enterprise and persistence."

In a nutshell

Over a 20-year period, it is difficult not to get rich from real estate if you follow a simple formula.

In a similar vein

Robert G. Allen *Multiple Streams of Income* (p 16)
Mark Victor Hansen & Robert G. Allen *The One Minute Millionaire* (p 140)
Robert Kiyosaki *Cashflow Quadrant* (p 180)
Andrew McLean & Gary W. Eldred *Investing in Real Estate* (p 190)
Donald Trump *The Art of the Deal* (p 266)

CHAPTER 34

William Nickerson

It is amusing to read the first paragraph of *How I Turned $1,000 into Three Million in Real Estate*, in which Nickerson notes that, a decade after the first edition came out, people were asking him whether it was still possible to make money from real estate. The year was 1969.

If you had bought real estate virtually anywhere in the developed world in 1969 and hung onto it, you would now be well off. People always think they have missed the boat when it comes to property, yet time inexorably increases its value; it is the simplest way to accumulate wealth.

When Nickerson was writing in 1969, there were 90,000 millionaires in America. Today, some estimates go as high as 9 million (measured in terms of wealth outside the family home). We have experienced an explosion in personal wealth, and a good deal of it has come through real-estate investing.

However, despite the outrageous title, this book is actually (by today's "creative financing" standards) quite a common-sense property-investing guide. Nickerson assumes the reader will make a 25 percent deposit on their first purchase (an amount that has taken them some years to save), and then does not promise riches until a full 20 years have passed.

The original 1959 edition was titled *How I Turned $1,000 into a Million in Real Estate—in My Spare Time*. Reflecting inflation and Nickerson's growing fortune, the 1969 edition became "Three Million," and by the third edition (1980) his original $1,000 had become "Five Million." All three are now out of print, but the lucrative market for secondhand copies is some indication of the book's enduring value.

Good reasons to buy

When Nickerson was 25 and working at a telephone company, he and his wife Lucille took three years to save $1,000 for a deposit on their first home. The house was sold a couple of years later to buy two apartments. He continued in his job for another 12 years, in his spare time buying larger and larger properties. At 42—almost by accident, he notes—he had built up an estate to the value of half a million dollars (a lot of money in the early 1950s). Seeing no reason to continue working for a salary, he retired.

After friends began asking Nickerson the secret to his success, he decided to write a book that packed in everything he had learned plus the wisdom of other investors. The result was a "real estate bible" that is still highly sought after by the canny property investor.

Nickerson never intended to become wealthy from real estate, just to have a regular but modest income from a rental property when he retired at 65. But he soon discovered the "pyramiding power" of borrowing money to buy rental properties, and without any particular striving soon built up a valuable portfolio. Both he and his wife had come of age in the Great Depression, when the "smart" consensus (including that of his economics teacher) was that all the great opportunities for wealth had passed; the most the average person could hope for was to have a modest pension and stay off welfare.

But with his steady salary as surety and his accumulated savings, in the Depression Nickerson ignored his banker's advice and bought flats. He was warned that rents would not cover his mortgage, but because he picked up properties for such low prices, his repayments were more than covered. When the Second World War began, bankers again counseled against buying, this time on the basis that rent controls would hold down income. In fact, the controls only reduced competition and meant that properties did not have to be expensively maintained.

While there are many lessons to take from Nickerson's story, the first is this: There are always "good reasons" not to buy, but always more and better reasons *to* buy.

How to make a million

There are ten parts to *How I Turned $1,000 into Three Million*, but Part One is the most important, in which Nickerson reveals his formula for making a million. The formula is based on the purchase price of a house of—wait for it—$10,000. These days, of course, this amount would hardly buy a car, but remember Nickerson was writing decades ago. In your mind you may change the figure to $100,000 or $200,000, however what matters is the mathematics. This is the formula in essence:

- Save enough money for a 25 percent downpayment on a property, borrowing the remaining 75 percent, giving you a total of $10,000. (Nickerson notes that you can probably get away with only a 10 percent downpayment, but while experienced buyers like himself can often obtain 100 percent financing on a property, he wrote his book for the regular, inexperienced property buyer who normally has to lay down a decent deposit.)
- Buy a rental property that is in need of renovation. At some point within the next two years, use some of your savings, plus any net rental income gains, to paint and renovate the property (while still renting it out).

- ❖ Two years later, sell the improved property for $14,000. Repay the $7,500 loan, and after the cost of selling the property, you now have equity of $5,800. Thanks to the use of borrowed money, this $5,800 has given you a return of around 67 percent on what you personally invested, or 33 percent annualized.
- ❖ Take your $5,800 equity and borrow three times the amount again. With the $23,200, you buy an apartment block of four units that requires renovation. Over the next two years you put in $1,200, combined with any net rental income, to do up the property while still renting out the units.
- ❖ Sell the property after two years for $30,500, and again you make a 25 percent gross profit. After paying back the loan and sales costs you are left with a profit of $4,575, and now have equity of $11,575.
- ❖ Again, take this money and borrow three times as much, to buy an eight-unit property worth $46,000. After the usual renovation, you sell it two years later for $59,000, leaving you now with equity of over $21,000.

This process, if repeated over a period of 20 years, results in the following:

After 8 years	$39,363
After 10 years	$70,548
After 12 years	$124,884
After 14 years	$219,972
After 16 years	$386,376
After 18 years	$677,583
After 20 years	$1,187,195

Thus, after 20 years you are an asset millionaire, enjoying a very handsome annual rental income based on a reasonable 6 percent return.

Notice that your equity grows exponentially, in the same way that savings, if compounded over time, produce surprising returns. This occurs without putting any more time into your realty efforts, and indeed Nickerson affirms that the above can be achieved operating on a part-time basis.

The formula, Nickerson notes, is based on a conservative return on investment and reasonable interest rates. With some property turnovers you will do better than a 25 percent return, and with others you may make only a little money or break even. But whatever your return year to year, do not diverge from these four principles:

1 Don't borrow more than you can safely repay from rental returns.
2 Only buy properties that need renovation.
3 Only make improvements that increase the property's value.
4 Keep selling at a profit and reinvesting your profits.

The rest of the book provides a wealth of detail about how to enact these principles in practice, including finding good properties and dealing with problem renters.

The myth of real-estate risk

Nickerson notes that all ventures have some risk attached to them, but investing in rent-producing property using borrowed funds is surprisingly low in risk. In borrowing, you are simply making use of other people's unproductive savings for productive ends, and he describes the "pyramiding power of borrowed money" as the "secret force of capitalism," used by every great industrialist. Yet the returns from real estate are greatly more reliable compared to business. While a majority of businesses fail within the first few years, the chances of you actually having a foreclosure go through on a property you own are statistically very small. Even if prices do not go up and you make no profit, you will have lost nothing.

At present foreclosure rates have skyrocketed, but if you obey Nickerson's law to borrow only what you can safely repay, this won't happen to you. He wonders why people are willing to put their savings into a business with no certainty of success, possessing only optimism and skills. Real-estate investments, although they require research and effort, do not rest on hope, and banks and tax agencies take the same view. They do not view property ownership as a small business but as a form of investment, the difference being that real estate is valuable aside from the character or skills of the owner, whereas success through a business is very much reliant on these. Also, whereas most businesses require the close involvement of the owner to ensure their success, real estate requires only limited oversight and involvement to earn good returns.

Of course there is some risk with property, but it is usually overstated by the fearful. Some people insure themselves to the hilt so as to gain "security," yet in doing so they lose out on the potential of capital returns. Insurance companies, Nickerson wryly observes, invest much of their profits in real estate.

Final comments

In assessing Nickerson's success, we should remember that his wealth originated in an original savings nest egg. Some real-estate writers now promote "nothing down" deals even for first-time buyers, but nothing beats the discipline and satisfaction of saving for that first downpayment, whether it is for your own home or to buy a rental property. As Nickerson notes, the hardest money you accumulate is often for this initial amount, but henceforth that money can work for you and its diligence can be astounding.

In the book Nickerson correctly forecasts that the rising US population would require millions more units of housing, and that a good proportion of this would be rented. He writes:

When you invest in housing you buy a prime necessity of existence... Salability may fluctuate with inflation and recession. But your real estate will always retain an intrinsic value which economic forces cannot destroy.

Although fortune favors the early starters, given this basic truth it is never too late to begin building your property fortune. Today, the average lifespan continues to increase and you may have a very long retirement. Even if you are in your 50s you may, as Nickerson did, live another 40 years, and all this living will require money. Given you may not want to work long hours as you get older or risk your savings in buying or building a business, property investing is the least risky solution.

Friends complained to Nickerson that if he put his formula into a book it would ruin their chances of making a million. He responded that population and income growth, plus the deterioration of housing stock over time, meant that there were always plenty of opportunities to do well from his formula.

William Nickerson

Born in 1908, Nickerson came from a poor family, as did his wife. They both attended Fresno State College in California and graduated in 1931. He retired from his telephone company job around 1950 to enjoy the couple's acreage near Alamo, California. He died in 2000.

Nickerson's two other books are How to Make a Fortune Today—Starting from Scratch *(1975) and* Nickerson's No-Risk Way to Real Estate Fortunes *(1986).*

2007

Women and Money

"I can't put it any more simply or emphatically: How we behave toward our money, how we treat our money, speaks volumes about how we perceive and value ourselves. If we aren't powerful with money, we aren't powerful period."

"For the sake of all the mothers who came before you and for the sake of the daughters who will come after you, I'm calling you to move out of the past and into the future, armed with knowledge and confidence. That means leaving behind old attitudes, old excuses, and tired alibis for not becoming as fully competent and able in the area of personal finance as you are in every other role you inhabit in your life."

In a nutshell

To ensure their financial freedom, women need to have new respect for their relationship to money and defy cultural conditioning.

In a similar vein

David Bach *The Automatic Millionaire* (p 22)
Dave Ramsey *Financial Peace Revisited* (p 228)
Sanaya Roman & Duane Packer *Creating Money* (p 242)

CHAPTER 35

Suze Orman

When she was in her early 20s, Suze (pronounced Suzie) Orman dropped out of college to go traveling with friends. Borrowing some money from her brother, she bought a van so she could sleep in the back, and left Chicago with the aim of reaching California.

After working for a couple of months in a timber operation she found herself waitressing at a bakery café in Berkeley near San Francisco. Six years later she was still there, living on a waitress's wage of $400 a month. At 29, however, she decided she wanted to open a restaurant. She had no capital, but a kindly customer at the café lent her $20,000 to get it started. He advised parking the money in a Merrill Lynch fund until she was ready to use it, which she duly did.

Unfortunately, knowing nothing about financial matters, Orman allowed her broker to put the cash into highly risky investments. She earned great returns for a while... before losing it all. Unable to pay the money back, she realized she would have to start earning more and wondered if she could make it as a broker herself. Seeing an advertisement for trainees at "the enemy," Merrill Lynch, she decided to apply. To her great surprise (she believes it was simply to fill a female quota) she got the job. She did well, and later successfully sued her own employer to get the money back that she had lost.

What is the point of Orman relating her own story? She does it to show her own almost total ignorance about financial matters for the first three decades of her life. As a waitress she did not consider herself a high achiever, and she also felt shame at having dropped out of college. However, in time she became one of America's most recognized authorities on personal finance, with a thriving financial planning business, eight books to her name, and a popular television show. Her point is that lack of financial knowledge can trip up, or trap, any woman. However, if you are willing to educate yourself and take bold steps, your circumstances can be transformed.

Why *women* and money?

At the beginning of *Women and Money*, Orman notes that it had previously never occurred to her to write about women's relationship with personal finances, since she fervently believed that money management had nothing to do with one's gender. But she was shocked to discover that women close to her, who were otherwise smart, confident, and capable, were actually "clueless" when it came to managing their own money. Partly out of shame, they had succeeded in keeping their real situation to themselves.

Orman highlights the "huge disconnect" between women's pride in how far they have come economically and at work in the past 30 years, and the harsh facts of most women's financial situation. Most pour so much energy into the needs of others, doing a juggling act of children, partner, parents, friends, and work, that little time or energy is devoted to money management. They develop a psychological black hole in regard to saving and investing for themselves. She notes:

It doesn't matter if I am in a room full of business executives or stay-at-home moms, I find the core problem to be universal: When it comes to making decisions with money, you refuse to own your own power, to act in your best interest... Your inner nurturer reigns supreme; you do for everyone before you do for yourself.

It is not so much the *amount* women are earning but how they are managing their finances that is the issue. When Orman started her financial career at Merrill Lynch, her boss directed all the women customers to her. She found that virtually all did not like the job of managing their money, whether they had made it themselves or obtained it through a divorce or inheritance. Most women deal with money issues only when they are forced to. The reasons for this, she believes, are societal and cultural. Women learn from their own mothers how to handle money, and perpetuate these ways whether consciously or not. Women are very focused on relationships, but their relationship with money is often neglected or dysfunctional. A new respect for that relationship is vital if they are to enjoy security, both psychological and financial.

Money and love

The vast majority of women who call in to my television show have problems not with money per se, *but with relationships. The money problem is usually a symptom or a consequence of the relationship problem.*

Many women depend financially on their husband or partner, which often takes away their courage to "speak their truth." Stay-at-home mums are usually afraid to ask their husbands for more money because they are not "earning it." But as Orman points out, you are doing at least half the work in keeping the household going, so that money is yours together, not his.

Many women also find it difficult to say "No," wanting to be seen as givers. But if doing so means that you have to use credit card debt to buy things for people, or deplete your own savings to bail others out, or be a cosignee on loans, this will have an impact emotionally as well as financially.

When your husband has a midlife crisis and wants to risk the equity in your home on a start-up business, you need to be strong enough to say no.

When you have to support your parents to such an extent that you can't pay your own bills, you have at some point to say no. When your brother asks for a significant loan to help him out of a tight spot, one of many he has been in, you have to draw the line somewhere. Saying no in all such cases may risk the relationship, but it is better to have self-respect than be dragged down by other people's negligence or unreliability with money. As Orman notes from the experience of those who have been there, when you make financial decisions with a view to saving a relationship, it never works.

Many women still love their partners, but they no longer *like* them due to their financial irresponsibility and unreasonable demands. The more you and your partner talk about your finances and come clean on their true state, the sooner you can have a relationship based on truth. Remember: "It takes more power to say no out of love than to say yes out of weakness." You must do what is right, not what is easy.

When it comes to children, be honest with them if you don't have the money to buy them a $150 pair of jeans. They might not appreciate it now, but you will earn their respect more by being a parent who is solvent and looks to the future. Many women feel terrible if they do not have the means to pay for their kids' college education, but Orman asserts that if you have to make a choice between your financial security in retirement and their tuition fees, *you* should be your priority. Help your kids to research early on all the possibilities for aid and scholarships, and have them try working in part-time jobs to get used to paying their way.

Money and happiness

Orman makes the startling assertion that "nothing more directly affects your happiness than money." She imagines the reactions of her readers to this: that happiness comes from the things money can *never* buy. However, she points out that your actual quality of life, once you have a basic level of love, health, and respect, is highly influenced by how much money you have. You can't really live life to the full or reach your potential if you remain poor.

Millions of women stay in relationships where there is no love simply because they could not financially make it on their own, or cannot imagine being in control of their own affairs. But Orman asks readers to see things another way: If you can identify what you truly value, then you will take steps to protect it and enlarge it in your life.

Whatever you cherish, make this your motivation to fix up your finances. Orman consulted for a songwriter who was so focused on "being creative" that even though she was earning good money, she neglected her financial affairs. Orman led her to understand that being a good financial manager would mean that she could actually focus more on her work.

Order your life

One of Orman's "eight qualities of a wealthy woman" is cleanliness, or the need for order and organization in your affairs. She writes:

> *When you don't know where your money is, when you have no filing system for your important documents, when you dive into your pocketbook to pull out crumpled bills, when your car looks like a garbage can, when your closets are filled with junk and clutter—I'm sorry, but you can't possibly be a wealthy woman.*

She suggests giving to charity clothes you have not worn in the last year, and throwing out any unused beauty products. You must have a good system to organize your documents, because only in doing so can you make good financial decisions. If your affairs remain a mess, "Wealth will elude you."

Say your name

Because only women change their surname on marriage, there is an unconscious assumption that women's names are not as important as men's. Yet without the ability to say your name confidently and look people in the eye when you say it, you lack power.

When Orman speaks at women's organizations, often those involved in setting up the event are asked to stand up in the audience so everyone can applaud them. Most stand up and sit down again quicker than the blink of an eye, squirming back into their seats. Why is the average woman so afraid to take credit for things and to enjoy her name being spoken?

Orman notes how the editor on her previous books, Julie Grau, was invited to start up a new book imprint within a large publishing house with her colleague Cindy Spiegel. This would be a big advance both personally and professionally, yet when the issue came up they dismissed suggestions to name it after themselves. Compared to men, who *love* having anything in their name, this was a typical female reaction. In the end they did call it Spiegel & Grau and were glad they did—they had learned the power of saying their name.

Final comments

Why do many women still struggle with money? In terms of the span of history, Orman notes that the time over which women have been expected to be income producers and in control of their money is a tiny blip, a new experience. But she asks every reader to rewrite this story, to "see yourself as an agent of change in your own life and on a global scale." She notes the facts that women generally live longer than their partners, and that others are marrying later or not at all, not to mention the continuing high rate of divorce.

This means that the number of years over which the average woman is solely responsible for her finances is growing. No longer can women "leave it up to the men."

A significant part of the book is Orman's five-month "Save yourself plan" aimed at getting every reader on the financial straight and narrow, and covering everything from savings to credit cards, to credit scores, and wills and insurance.

While this "nuts and bolts" advice will need to be updated in the future, other aspects of the book, such as her "8 qualities of a wealthy woman" and the need to "say your name," will not date.

Orman has written three or four books that might be considered modern classics, but *Women and Money* is destined to be her biggest title, since it combines all the good points of her previous writings but zooms in on a topic of vital interest to at least half the population.

Suze Orman

Orman was born in 1951 in Chicago. Her father ran a takeout chicken shack where she worked part-time and the family were not well off. After graduating from school she enrolled in a social work degree at the University of Illinois-Champaign. Though she dropped out of the course to travel, she was later awarded the degree.

Orman worked at the Buttercup Bakery in Berkeley until 1980. From 1980 to 1983 she worked as a stockbroker at Merrill Lynch, then as a vice-president of investments at Prudential Bache Securities. In 1987 she started Suze Orman Financial Group, which she ran until 1997. The retirement seminars she was giving evolved into her first book, You've Earned It, Don't Lose It *(1994), which sold 750,000 copies. Subsequent bestsellers include* The 9 Steps to Financial Freedom *(1997),* The Courage to Be Rich *(1999),* The Road to Wealth *(2001), and* The Money Book for the Young, Fabulous and Broke *(2005).*

Her two televisions shows are The Suze Orman Show *on the cable television channel CNBC and* Suze Orman's Financial Freedom *on QVC. She also has a financial advice column in Oprah Winfrey's O magazine.*
In 2007 Orman "came out," revealing her long-term relationship with partner Kathy Travis.

1995

God Wants You to Be Rich

"The incorrect supposition that we live in a world of scarce resources has done more than preclude most individuals from achieving economic success. Over the centuries, this zero-sum-game view of the world has been responsible for wars, revolutions, political strategies, and human suffering of unfathomable proportions."

"Since 1750 the gross world output has increased more than seventeen hundred times, while world population has increased only six times."

In a nutshell

The world was designed as a super-abundant place, with technology as the engine that delivers the greatest benefits to the greatest number.

In a similar vein

Milton Friedman *Capitalism and Freedom* (p 110)
Thomas Friedman *The World Is Flat* (p 116)
Paul Hawken, Amory B. Lovins, & L. Hunter Lovins *Natural Capitalism* (p 146)
Catherine Ponder *Open Your Mind to Prosperity* (p 218)
Sanaya Roman & Duane Packer *Creating Money* (p 242)
Adam Smith *The Wealth of Nations* (p 260)

CHAPTER 36

Paul Zane Pilzer

For hundreds of years people believed that the earth was at the center of the universe. This assumption meant that calendars were always out of whack, despite their importance for regulating agriculture. Only with Copernicus's model of the sun at the center of the universe, and the planets revolving around it, did everything begin to make sense.

Pilzer begins *God Wants You to Be Rich* with this piece of information to reveal an analogy. For the last 200 years, he writes, we have been laboring under a similar mistake in relation to economics, which traditionally has been defined as "the study of how people choose to employ scarce resources." In this view, a society's wealth is fundamentally determined by its supply of physical things such as land, oil, and minerals, and economic life is a zero-sum game in which people or countries win by taking resources away from others. This worldview, naturally, has led to wars and endless suffering.

In contrast, Pilzer and his fellow "cornucopian" economists believe that physical resources are not limited at all. In fact, they have demonstrated statistically that the price of all raw materials decreases over time thanks to their abundance, and that the threat of shortages is alone enough for human beings to find different materials or make better use of existing ones.

Subtitled *A Theology of Economics*, Pilzer's book asks: Surely we were not put on the earth to compete and benefit at the expense of each other? If God is loving and abundant, would not the universe have been designed in such a way that there is more than enough to go around for everyone?

The blessings of technology

Given its aim to find the most equitable distribution of scarce resources, it is no wonder, Pilzer notes, that economics was given the title of the "dismal science." But economics takes little account of two factors that are in fact central to its understanding: *people*, who have limitless creativity to create new products and services that make life better; and *technology*, enabling us to produce things with greater ease and at lower cost.

For many, "technology" is a word that means millions of people thrown out of their jobs. Pilzer admits that the majority of unemployment comes as the result of new technology making redundant existing products or ways of making them. Yet this tells only part of the story. For instance, in 1930 30 million America farmers were growing only just enough food for a nation of 100 million. Yet thanks to huge advances in farm productivity, by 1980 only 3 million farmers were producing food to feed 300 million people. What happened to all the farmers' sons and daughters? They left the farms and got work in new industries. The nation was not worse off, as it had more people to employ in emerging sectors that were creating a great deal of wealth. It can be painful when individual workers lose their jobs, but society as a whole benefits.

Pilzer observes: "the greatest economic opportunities of tomorrow, almost by definition, are in sectors of our economy that may not even exist today." New technologies, by reducing the cost of what it takes to make something, create demand that was not there before. There is no limit to demand for cheaper, newer, or better products, and therefore no limit to the creation of new fortunes and wealth. As long as this is allowed to continue, we will have low unemployment.

Industrial competition forces ever advancing technological replacement to produce the best, cheapest products for the consumer, a process the economist Joseph Schumpeter called "creative destruction." Pilzer describes this process as "the grease that [keeps] the wheels of prosperity in motion."

We won't run out of anything, particularly not ingenuity

The whaling industry was vital to the world economy for hundreds of years. Whale oil was used for lighting and heating, and other parts of the whale made candles, lubricants, and even women's corsets. However, by the mid-nineteenth century whale stocks began to decline rapidly, and in 1859 the world's first "energy crisis" occurred because of the lack of availability of whale oil. In the United States, center of the whaling world, terrible things were predicted. In the very same year, though, the first successful oil well was drilled in Pennsylvania, bringing with it the petroleum age. Another source of energy had been found "just in time."

Throughout history many have predicted the end of prosperity because of a coming shortage of a particular resource, and unfortunately it is the dire predictions that get the most notice. Yet the world has generally been very successful at accommodating a greatly increased population. Life expectancy has shot up in most places, billions have been lifted out of poverty, and many more have become rich. Against the tide of doom-mongering, Pilzer provides this fact: Since 1750 the world population has increased sixfold, but in the same period world output, or wealth, has increased more than *1,700* times.

Why God wants us to be rich

The cornucopian view, Pilzer admits, has had difficulty finding traction beyond the already wealthy. The reason is that despite the logic of the economics of abundance, people still live according to deep-rooted theological beliefs about wealth. Today, most Christians, Muslims, and Jews still believe that God does not want them to be rich, and it is easy to understand why: If you live in a world of scarcity, then to get wealthy you have to take resources from other people, which must be a bad thing in the eyes of God.

Yet the essence of God is constant new creation, Pilzer argues. Things are always being formed out of what did not exist before. Therefore, if you believe that the nature of God is abundance, you can begin to believe in the possibility of unlimited wealth on earth.

Final comments

God Wants You to Be Rich was written in the shadow of a deep recession in which millions of jobs were lost through the decline of old industries. The book stood out against an avalanche of dire warnings about the economy and the future of humanity. However, given the massive increase of global wealth in the last 20 years, its rosy belief in untrammeled prosperity thanks to the limitless ingenuity of people and the spread of new technology has proved accurate.

On the other hand, how does Pilzer's cornucopian economics stand up in the age of climate change? Surely a theory that celebrates limitless resources is now redundant? The doom-laden predictions for the world's climate are based on the way we currently use energy, and what we use. But energy sources have changed throughout history (generally from dirtier to cleaner) and always will. New demand is already strong for products that do as little environmental damage as possible, and as "green" awareness grows, this demand will only get stronger. Do not believe everything you read in the newspapers, is this book's message. We live in a world of plenty, and virtually every problem is solvable if we put our minds to it.

Paul Zane Pilzer

Born in 1954, Pilzer spent his college years at Lehigh University before receiving an MBA from the Wharton School at the University of Pennsylvania. He was employed by Citibank and three years later became its youngest vice-president. At 24 he was made an adjunct professor at New York University. During his 20s he started several businesses, and was worth $10 million before he turned 30. He has founded or taken public several software and healthcare companies, and been an economic adviser in two US presidential administrations.

Other books include The Wellness Revolution: How to Make a Fortune in the Next Trillion Dollar Industry *(2002), and* The Next Millionaires *(2005). He lives in Utah with his family.*

1971

Open Your Mind to Prosperity

"Cleansing or purification is the first step in prosperity. Without releasing mentally, emotionally, and in our visible world, there can be no permanent, satisfying prosperity... Along with cleaning out the closets, clean up and clean out your life. The skeletons in the closet have got to go, if you wish to be truly prospered."

"Once the work is done on the mental plane, you can be assured your pictured good will manifest on the outer plane just as soon as the time, people and events have arranged themselves accordingly."

"You are not trying to make God give you anything. You are only opening your mind to receive the abundance God has promised you from the beginning."

In a nutshell

If you transform your beliefs about spirituality and wealth, you can welcome great wellbeing and prosperity into your life.

In a similar vein

Rhonda Byrne *The Secret* (p 58)
Charles Fillmore *Prosperity* (p 98)
Esther Hicks & Jerry Hicks *Ask and It Is Given* (p 152)
Sanaya Roman & Duane Packer *Creating Money* (p 242)

CHAPTER 37

Catherine Ponder

Catherine Ponder grew up in a part of the American South where children often went without lunch and had no shoes to wear. She would give away her lunch money, food, and the clothing off her back to poorer classmates. When she was older, she wanted to wage a "war on poverty," but came to the view that it was better to understand the sources of prosperity and teach people about them. This was the beginning of her career as a leading teacher of the prosperity mindset.

While her first book, *The Dynamic Laws of Prosperity* (see the commentary in *50 Success Classics*), introduced all the general principles of prosperity consciousness, its sequel *Open Your Mind to Prosperity* provides a more direct, simple, and powerful formula for prosperity that is easily followed.

Don't feel guilty

Ponder began giving talks and classes on prosperity in the late 1950s, as a newly ordained Unity church minister. At this time she was far from rich herself. Living in a one-room dwelling, she was embarrassed about teaching the subject, yet at the same time she also felt that opening her mind to the universe's abundance would be her ticket to something better. Three years later she moved into a nice new home, but says she would have done so earlier if she knew then what she later formularized in this book.

Many of Ponder's early pupils felt guilty about even studying the subject, believing that seeking prosperity was sinful, even when they were struggling through a deep recession. But as soon as they were told that prosperity was "spiritually right," backed by Ponder's many examples from the Bible, suddenly the floodgates of good fortune were opened.

Ponder describes the Bible as "the greatest prosperity textbook ever written." Among the Hebrew leaders, she notes, Abraham, Isaac, Jacob, and Joseph were well-off men, even millionaires. *Genesis* tells us that Abraham, for instance, "was very rich in cattle, in silver, and in gold." The word "gold" appears more than 400 times in the Bible, and among the three or four thousand promises it makes, many are literal promises of prosperity. Jesus produced many prosperity miracles, including multiplying the loaves and fishes, and turning water into wine at a feast in Canaan.

The real source of prosperity

Many will say that Jesus only used the symbolism of money in his parables to demonstrate spiritual riches, but Ponder insists that Jesus saw prosperity and spirituality as one and the same. All good things come when we are aligned with God, she told her students, and it is only attachment to possessions that is sinful. The ultimate prosperity secret is that *God is the source of your supply*. As Moses told the Hebrews (*Deuteronomy* 8:18), "You shall remember the Lord your God, for it is he who gives you power to get wealth." When you focus on other people and circumstances as the source of your prosperity, you tend to lose it.

Ponder asks: Is affirming a nonphysical entity (God) as the source of your prosperity really practical? She includes examples of people who over the years have contacted her, amazed at just how perfectly this belief works. For instance, a struggling doctor who affirmed that his supply did not depend on his patients or economic conditions was able to build a smart new clinic within a few months. Ponder amusingly relates how both the typists of her first book resigned because the lessons they were typing out had such positive effects. The first typist left because, after she followed the book's lessons, her husband's sales career took off to such an extent that she no longer had to work. The second typist's husband had been unemployed, but suddenly was appointed to his dream job in engineering, requiring them to move to another state. Ponder's housekeeper, to whom she had explained the prosperity laws, also resigned to follow her dream of becoming a dressmaker. She was very successful.

Yet this openness does not just mean openness to receiving money. Prosperity, in Ponder's mind, is peace of mind, harmony with others, and physical health. Many people who have attended her classes are surprised to find dramatic improvements in these areas in their lives, in addition to demonstrations of financial plenty.

Furthermore, if use of the techniques sounds a bit selfish to you, Ponder notes that they can be used equally well to prosper others. Picturing a loved one's good, or affirming it through the spoken word, can have tremendous effects.

First purify yourself

The practice of purification before receiving something good is an ancient prosperity secret. The principle involves cleansing your mind of clutter and negative emotions. In forming a vacuum, you allow good things to rush in.

You can begin by clearing out the clutter in your home, car, and place of work. Many people are reluctant to throw out expensive things, even if they are no longer being used, just because they are expensive. But if you want valuable things to come into your life, you should get rid of what you don't want no matter its perceived value.

Ponder points out that the universe is perfectly ordered, therefore the person who makes their own affairs more orderly is attuned to universal richness. God tends to hold back on largesse until you have taken steps to make your present affairs orderly. Once you do, three things happen: people and situations lose their chaotic nature; others not right for your development drift out of your life; the people and events necessary for your fulfillment are attracted into your life.

One important way to cleanse your mind is to forgive. When you are resentful "you are bound to that person or condition by an emotional link that is stronger than steel," Ponder notes. "The practice of forgiveness is the only way to dissolve that link and be free." It can feel like you "lose" if you forgive someone. But Ponder observes that if something is truly yours by "divine right" you can never lose it, and by releasing a person or an emotion you make room for the manifestation of good in ways you cannot imagine.

Three steps to prosperity

Prosperity is created mentally in three steps: writing down your desires; creating pictures of your good; and the spoken word.

Write it down

Your desires are given to you by God, but for them to manifest they first need to take form as the written word. Once you get definite about what you want and write it down, the universe or God can be definite in delivering you what you want.

Create pictures

"Instead of fighting problems," Ponder instructs, "*picture* your way out of them." The best way to do this is to create a "wheel of fortune," pasting images of everything you want to appear in your life to a board. If you look at this and enjoy it every day, these images will be absorbed into your subconscious mind and begin to help shape your reality.

You do not have to create an elaborate wheel of fortune to manifest your desires; even doing it in a casual way can work. When Ponder was a little girl she longed for and pictured in her mind a gemstone ring in the shape of a heart, as she was born on Valentine's Day. She never asked for it, as her family was not well off. Decades later, a woman who had studied her books telephoned her from across the country. She had just inherited a large estate and wanted to give Ponder something from it. Despite the many more valuable things she had to offer, the woman felt moved, for some reason, to give an amethyst ring. As amethyst was her birthstone, Ponder was delighted. But the woman said, "Yes, but you might not want this one. It's different. It's in the shape of a heart." The incident confirmed to Ponder that, no matter the time or distance involved, picturing your good is amazingly powerful.

Magic of the spoken word

It is not enough simply to read about prosperity. It is through the words you speak that it actually comes to you. Speaking daily affirmations such as "I am surrounded by divine substance and this divine substance now manifests for me in rich appropriate form" can have quick results. (A man Ponder knew, after speaking these exact words, doubled his salary within six weeks.)

Why exactly are prosperity affirmations so powerful? The ancients knew that particular arrangements of words produce vibrations that resonate with the Infinite Intelligence that pervades the universe. Statements broadcast into the universe attract a certain reality, and in time are expressed as fact.

Ponder's message: Do not struggle needlessly when the prospering power of words is available to you. Use it. If you are Christian-minded, frequently say the Lord's Prayer, for this is essentially a set of powerful affirmations that can change your life.

Trust the divine plan

If you are not sure exactly what you want, there is another way to bring about your good: affirming that there is a divine plan for your life that is falling perfectly into place. Doing this is a kind of shortcut that "takes away all sense of confusion, uncertainty, and mistakes" from your life.

But be prepared for changes, Ponder warns, as the speed at which your divine plan comes into being can be breathtaking. On the other hand, if nothing much seems to change, it does not mean the plan is not falling into place. It is, but according to divine timing. Flowers bloom when they are ready, and not before.

The magic number of increase

The book's chapter on tithing is quite inspirational. One man confided to Ponder that although he loved her books, whatever she wrote on this subject he quietly avoided. People want to receive but don't want to give, yet tithing is a healing act.

Why give 10 percent of what you earn? Ancient people knew that the number 10 had a magical power of increase—the word "tithe" means a tenth—and that giving a small amount of what comes to us ensures more will follow.

Tithing is about "putting God first financially." While many give in an almost mechanical way out of a sense of duty, in fact the prospering power of tithing only comes when you give lovingly, willingly, and gratefully. You should tithe to whatever body or organization gives you and others spiritual inspiration, that helps to "lift up humanity."

Final comments

The commentary above relates to half the book at most. Other prosperity laws that Ponder reveals, including the "love concept" and the "wisdom concept," can be tremendously powerful if you are willing to use them, and the amazing final chapter on "Prosperity through divine restoration" should lift up any reader.

People love Ponder's writings not just for what she says, but for how she says it. Her examples seem to come from another era. For instance, "Decked out in a fashionable pants suit, an attractive Southern Californian businesswoman once said to the author…" goes the first line of the book. The warm and enjoyable style of her writing, often in the third person, is perhaps typical of a gracious Southern woman.

Yet this image can be misleading, since Ponder was a true entrepreneur of ideas who drew from a range of sources—the Bible, New Thought philosophers, esoteric teachings, and so on—to create easily digestible books that significantly expanded the average person's knowledge and awareness of the prosperity laws.

Though strongly influenced by Charles Fillmore's *Prosperity*, Ponder's book is a complete, standalone manual on the subject, and you may turn a pencil blunt with all your underlining.

All her books provide a sense of peace. Troubles are put into perspective, and the heart lifts on reading stories of people who experienced a prosperity miracle when they had known only hard times. Yet Ponder's writings are not escapist, providing the tools to take your life to a new level if you are willing to open your mind to the spiritual side of prosperity.

Ponder herself was a widowed single mother working as a secretary when she embarked on her prosperity journey. Where are you now, and where might you be if you practiced the laws she highlights?

Catherine Ponder

Born in Hartsville, South Carolina in 1927, after her school years Ponder attended Worth Business College, and in 1956 received a degree in Education from the Unity Ministerial School. She was ordained by the nondenominational Unity church in 1958, and in that year gave her first prosperity class. She served as a minister in Birmingham, Alabama (1958–61), Austin, Texas (1961–69), and San Antonio (1969–73), and in 1973 became minister of the Palm Desert Unity church in California, a role she fills today. She has lectured widely around the United States.

Other books include The Dynamic Laws of Prosperity *(1962),* The Prosperity Secrets of the Ages *(1967),* The Millionaires of Genesis *(1976),* The Millionaire Joshua *(1978),* Open Your Mind to Receive *(1983),* The Dynamic Laws of Prayer *(1987), and her memoir,* Prosperity Love Story: From Rags to Enrichment *(2003).*

1987

The Abundance Book

"Money is an effect. When you concentrate on the effect, you are forgetting the cause, and when you forget the cause, the effect begins to diminish. When you focus your attention on getting money, you are actually shutting off your supply. You must begin at this very moment to cease believing that money is your substance, your supply, your support, your security, or your safety. Money is not—but God is!"

"If you look to your job, your employer, your spouse or your investments as the source of your supply, you are cutting off the real Source."

"You are the offspring of the Infinite Abundance of the Universe."

In a nutshell

Life is in part a test to see if we can learn the laws of abundance, specifically the law of "all-sufficiency."

In a similar vein

Rhonda Byrne *The Secret* (p 58)
Charles Fillmore *Prosperity* (p 98)
Napoleon Hill *The Master-Key to Riches* (p 158)
Catherine Ponder *Open Your Mind to Prosperity* (p 218)
Lynne Twist *The Soul of Money* (p 278)

CHAPTER 38

John Randolph Price

The first thing that strikes you about *The Abundance Book* is its size. Small enough to fit into your pocket, it runs to fewer than 80 pages. Price's intention was to give readers access to uplifting prosperity ideas any time of the day, and the book condenses many of the great concepts in prosperity writing. It also provides some intriguing background as to the origins of the field.

Many people get the book for one reason only: the "40 day prosperity plan" presented in Part II. There isn't space to give the details here, but the plan is based on the notion that it takes the human mind 40 days to turn an idea into accepted truth.

Here we focus on the rest of the book, including Price's explanation of the age-old principle of "all-sufficiency," and his distinction between wealth symbols ("the effects") and the deeper spiritual reality of abundance behind them.

Secrets of the manifesting power

Where did the ideas behind prosperity consciousness originate? In Part 1 of *The Abundance Book*, Price discusses the concept of "all-sufficiency," which he says underlies all the early systems of religion and philosophy.

The ancient mystery schools of Asia, Egypt, Persia, and Greece taught that through understanding the self you could understand God. Meditation was the means for discovering your power to "transmute discord into harmony, ignorance into wisdom, fear into love, and lack into abundance." By going deeper into the self, paradoxically you would discover universal laws of manifestation in the real world. By becoming an embodiment of love and peace—Price uses the term "harmlessness"—you could break through all limitations.

This knowledge of "harmony and fulfillment" can be found in the sacred books and teachings of the Hebrew Kabbalah, the Hindu and Buddhist mystics, the Christian Gnostics, and even early versions of the Bible. Common to all of these is the idea of the unity between God and humans, that each person has within them the divine essence. The gnostic gospel of Thomas, uncovered as a scroll in Egypt in 1945, states that self-knowledge opens the door to knowledge of God—and by implication, to "divine" powers.

The later Christian church, however, opposed all ideas of personal power and the indwelling spirit in man, replacing it with church power and dogma.

As the Dark Ages began, the techniques relating to prosperity consciousness and manifestation were pushed underground.

Fortunately, the Rosicrucians and Freemasons kept the knowledge alive, and by the nineteenth century it had emerged again with the Transcendental movement of Emerson and Thoreau, the Theosophists led by Madame Blavatsky, Mary Baker Eddy's Christian Science, the New Thought movement of Charles Fillmore and Ernest Holmes, Rudolf Steiner and his Anthroposophical Society, and Paramhansa Yogananda's Self-Realization Fellowship.

Seek first the Kingdom

According to Price, money is just an "outer symbol of the inner supply." However, if you chase after the symbol alone, the inner supply dries up.

Most people think that their job, their employer, their investment portfolio, or their spouse is the source of their money, but in the focus on these "externals" they forget the real source that brings them into being in the first place. Actual money does not make you secure; what does is a thorough knowledge of God and the universe's power to provide.

Yet it is wrong to think that you can get more money if you become more spiritual. This mystical approach to attaining wealth, Price says, will not work. Instead, your intention should be to truly understand and appreciate the spiritual cause of abundance. Seek this knowing first, and what you need will then come to you. The "spiritual way to abundance," he notes, "is 'rigged' in favor of those with purity of motive."

Every soul must pass the test

Many people still think that it is unspiritual to seek wealth, but in fact the closer you get to God, the more difficult it is to turn away wealth. This is because spiritual understanding automatically reveals to us the laws of manifestation. Mother Teresa, for example, thought only of the work she needed to do, and trusted that the money she needed to keep doing it would come. With the strength of her faith, it always did.

You, too, can live with a similar certainty about this continuous supply of love and material things. Every person comes to a point, Price says, when they are compelled to believe that money will come even if there seems no evidence of it. If you don't make this leap of faith, as long as you live you will continue to feel that there is never enough. Price emphasizes:

> *Every soul must learn this lesson, and until it does, it will be given opportunity after opportunity in the form of apparent lack and limitation.*

If you pass the test, you won't have to do it again. Your knowledge of the inexhaustible flow of prosperity will be with you forever, a priceless asset.

You earn what you are

The book provides a novel way of understanding money: as an acronym. MONEY stands for "My Own Natural Energy Yield." By this Price means that what you attract is the direct result of your inner condition.

The universe demands that you express your true essence through meditation, visualization of your desires, joyous loving and gratitude, and right action. These things all create energy and attract the like energy of money. The more you exist in a state of love, the closer you get to the true reality of the universe. In this state, it is natural that more love and abundance will flow to you. Practicing "harmlessness" in your thoughts and words will end all limitations in your life. In contrast, if you constantly criticize, abuse, or hate, these things "darken the soul... and remove [you] from the Way of Wholeness."

Yet Price is not all ethereal about abundance. Quoting from one of his previous books, *The Manifestation Process*, he observes that if you are out of money, find some way to earn some. The universe wants to show you abundance, but you have to meet it halfway, as a "co-creator."

Final comments

It would be easy to dismiss *The Abundance Book* because of its brevity and packaging as a pocket volume. In fact, thanks to his lifelong quest for knowledge in the spiritual prosperity field, Price has the ability to convey timeless truths in a few pages. Some will feel his writings are too spaced out or New Agey, but keep an open mind and you will get much out of them.

The warning implicit in the book is that we should never try to get money out of someone or something as if our prosperity depended on it. God provides many sources of income, and through faith and trust these will become clear. Even if you do not think of yourself as religious, there is a part of everyone (Price calls it the "Master Self") that recognizes the laws and eternal truths of the universe. Life is in part a test to see whether you can recognize the infallible law of abundance, even when you could easily choose to believe in scarcity.

John Randolph Price

Before becoming a lecturer and author, Price held senior positions in the advertising industry in Chicago and Houston. He has a BSc in Radio and Television from the University of Houston. In 1981 he left the corporate world to form the Quartus Foundation for Spiritual Research with his wife Jan. Based in Boerne, Texas, Quartus publishes a journal and conducts seminars.

Other books include The Superbeings *(1987),* The Success Book *(1998),* The Jesus Code *(2000),* The Alchemist's Handbook *(2000), and* Removing the Masks that Bind Us *(2000).*

2003

Financial Peace Revisited

"There are those who believe that finance is merely an exact mathematical science. That is the way it is taught in the universities. In fact, finance is an exact mathematical science—until a human touches it. Personal finance is who you are. The personal, philosophical, and emotional problems and strengths that you have will be reflected in your use of money."

In a nutshell

More than money itself, what most people need is peace of mind. If you don't take control of your finances, they will control you (no matter how much you earn).

In a similar vein

James Allen *The Path of Prosperity* (p 10)
David Bach *The Automatic Millionaire* (p 22)
Joe Dominguez & Vicki Robin *Your Money or Your Life* (p 74)
Jerrold Mundis *How to Get Out of Debt, Stay Out of Debt, and Live Prosperously* (p 196)
Suze Orman *Women and Money* (p 208)

CHAPTER 39

Dave Ramsey

In the mid-1980s, Dave Ramsey was a "young hotshot" in real estate in Nashville, Tennessee, specializing in the home foreclosure market. By the time he was 26 he had built a company that owned property worth $4 million. He and his wife went on great vacations, drove expensive cars, and wore designer clothes. Bankers liked him and gave him plenty of credit. Ramsey had a degree in finance, so he knew what he was doing.

However, a couple of years later the economy turned cold, and banks began to tighten credit and call in loans. Ramsey was given a three-month period to pay back $1.2 million. He scraped the money together, but in doing so his business was almost destroyed. Left only with his home and his clothes, he would cry in the shower every morning and think about suicide, figuring his million-dollar life insurance policy would at least look after his family. His "unraveling" took three and a half years, ending in bankruptcy.

As he rebuilt his business and managed to keep his marriage intact, business associates and friends (who were going through their own problems) came to him for advice, and he also began giving counseling at his church. People wanted materials to help them, and he formulated a "Financial Peace" plan that became a book. Most of the early copies he gave away, but after he landed a spot on a local radio show Ramsey's message gained a larger audience. The show was later syndicated nationally and a revised book became a bestseller.

With additional comments from his wife Sharon, new chapters, and updated statistics, *Financial Peace Revisited* is now firmly in the canon of personal finance classics, helping many people to become solvent.

Alarming facts

The early part of the book reveals the following:

- The typical American household has debts of around $40,000, and 71 percent of householders said debt was creating an unhappy home life.
- A large proportion of marriage failures are attributed to money problems.
- Mortgage debt has more than doubled over the last 15 years.
- Since 1980, foreclosures have increased 200 percent [and this was before the mortgage market meltdown in the US].

- The typical bankrupt is not "a guy under a bridge" but a middle-class baby boomer who has "lived too high on the hog."
- Consumer debt has tripled since 1980. With a billion credit cards in circulation in the US alone, you are now considered a bit weird if you don't have one.
- 37 percent of people have made a cash advance on one credit card in order to make a payment on another.
- More than two-thirds of people "live from pay check to pay check."

In short, Ramsey notes, our great-grandparents would be shocked at our financial irresponsibility. We are focused too much on being consumers and not enough on being producers. We don't own "stuff," he says, the "stuff" owns us.

Dangerous debt

Debt has become a way of life for most people, and the idea of having no debt at all is radical. But Ramsey tries to convince you that it is possible to become debt free within a few years.

He devotes quite a few pages to the evils of credit cards. A gold, platinum, or black card may make you feel good about yourself, he notes, but makes its issuer rich. Try to pay for most things by cash or at least a debit card. You will spend less.

He warns never to get a car loan or lease, because you are usually locked into a repayment program that covers five years and will have to keep paying it even if you hit hard times. Instead, save some money and buy a cheaper car, spending only $100 a month on the repayments instead of $300. Put the $200 you don't spend every month directly into a savings account, which at good interest will enable you to buy a brand new car every seven years, and still have thousands left over to invest.

If you must borrow money, Ramsey pleads that you do it over as short a term as possible, and for things that increase in value. Most people need to take on debt to buy a home, but he advises you to pay off your mortgage as soon as you can. His example is a loan of $80,000 on a property at 10 percent interest. You could pay it off over 30 years, making 360 payments of $702 a month (total $252,720), or instead pay $860 a month over 15 years (total $154,800). The 15-year loan would save you a huge $97,920. If you are already tied into a long mortgage, you may be able to make extra payments every year off the principal, also making dramatic savings.

Ramsey is well known for promoting the "debt snowball" technique of debt reduction. In essence, you pay off the smallest debt first (no matter how much interest you are paying on the larger ones), then apply the money you would normally have paid off each month to your normal payment on your next biggest debt. When this debt is paid off, you move on to the next one. Something amazing happens: The amount you can pay off a debt each month begins to get bigger and bigger, like a snowball, helping you to pay off obligations quicker than you thought. The technique has helped many people demolish their debt mountain in two or three years.

Salvation in saving

To many people, saving is as novel a concept as taking all debt out of your life. Ramsey notes three reasons to save: to create an emergency fund; to have cash to buy things so you don't have to buy them on credit; and to build wealth in the long term.

An emergency fund is a pool of cash in a savings account (accessible immediately, but still earning interest) to cover three to six months' normal living expenses. If you earn $36,000 a year, for instance, you will need to have $9,000–18,000 invested. Sharon Ramsey notes to male readers that such a fund (aside from the purpose for which it is designed) is also an investment in your marriage. Men are generally happier with higher levels of risk, but women (quite rightly) value a certain margin of safety.

When, having created an emergency fund and paid off your debts, you have extra money to invest, Ramsey advises to follow the KISS rule: Keep It Simple, Stupid. People like to prove they are geniuses by knowing about complicated investments, but you should forget the "exotic bird partnerships with tax sheltered 200 percent returns," he warns. If you are not absolutely clear how you will earn your money, don't invest, and if you sink money into real estate outside your home, make sure you have back-up savings to cover vacant months and all the other expenses.

Ramsey once wined and dined some wealthy men in order to obtain from them the secrets of their success. He was told that "the quickest way to get rich quick is *not* to get rich quick." That is, the discipline of saving, and not trying to chase after elaborate tax-minimization schemes, will make you wealthy in the long run.

Just spend less... and plan your spending

Ramsey notes, "We can always spend more than we can make." If you are not wealthy, do not try to have a wealthy lifestyle.

When, for instance, you think about buying an expensive watch (his cost $19.95), think what the value of that money will be to your family in ten years if you earn interest on it. Make larger purchasing decisions slowly. All sales techniques are designed to make you buy on the spot. Buy slow and you will invariably save money and get exactly what you want.

Around 90 percent of families do not have a written record of income and expenses. Any business operating this way would go broke quickly. If you hate the idea of a budget, Ramsey suggests calling it a "cash flow plan." Having a written plan means you have to "gather, organize, categorize, and analyze information about your money situation." You have to become master of your data and information. Commit to doing it for 90 days, Ramsey says, and it will put you on the road to financial peace. It doesn't take much time, but its effects can deliver freedom. You can finally take that vacation—without putting it on a credit card.

Money and marriage

Though he never set out to work on people's marriages, Ramsey found that when a couple strives toward financial mastery together, it can have wonderful effects on their relationship.

Usually in a relationship one person is the tightwad and budgeter, and the other is the spender. Opposites attract. But marriage is not a "joint venture" with separate accounts, bills, and debts—the aim is *unity*. To have financial peace you need to know what you are both spending money on, and though doing a spending plan may be difficult at first, ultimately it will bring you closer together. The book notes that 97 percent of women have said they want more communication in their marriage, and Sharon Ramsey professes, "We have healed many of the wounds in our marriage by working on our budget together."

Her husband stresses "never underestimate the power of your spouse's counsel." He was once told by his wife that he had made a wrong decision on buying a dilapidated house. On the way home from the site, he explained all the ways in which she was wrong. A $25,000 loss later, he appreciated her intuitive wisdom.

Love your work

Finally, Ramsey notes that people who love their work create a "circle of excellence" that inevitably brings them a higher income compared to people who do not. But if you are not happy in your current work, don't quit today. Fulfill your current position to the utmost (slacking off is thieving from the company you work for), take aptitude testing as a starter, then explore career change possibilities.

When you do find the work you love, Ramsey says, *work hard*. Enjoyment combined with effort will ensure your prosperity.

Final comments

Thanks to our culture's celebration of money, if we have financial problems we prefer to keep them to ourselves. Could there be anything more embarrassing than your credit card being rejected while paying for a meal, or more shaming than having your house taken away or your car repossessed? The majority of people are not in control of their finances and live day to day in a state of fear. Yet it could all be so different with some self-education and self-discipline.

Finance is only an impersonal subject, Ramsey notes, "until a human touches it." That is, issues with money are usually not about the money itself but the person. Too little or too much will just magnify personal deficiencies; or it will show up the good character that was already there. Therefore, in relation to your financial life, working on yourself is always worthwhile.

Financial Peace Revisited provides wise counsel on a range of issues, including your credit rating, retirement planning, teaching your children financial sense, tax-effective saving for their education, and how to find bargains and negotiate. Though the revised version was published at the height of a decade or more of apparently endless prosperity, the book now seems more prescient than ever, with a doubling of house foreclosures in recent times and record levels of personal debt. Despite its serious subject, Ramsey manages to inject quite a bit of humor into the book, and whether your finances are in good shape or not it is an enjoyable read.

Ramsey is a Christian and is not afraid to say so. But this does not make his a "Christian book." He simply says that being spiritually grounded, spending some time every day on meditation and prayer, will do as much as anything to put you on the road to financial health. And don't forget to give money away. Ramsey quotes Methodist founder John Wesley: "Make all you can, save all you can, give all you can." Giving money away makes good financial sense, since it reminds us what is important in life and that we do not exist in isolation.

Dave Ramsey

Born in 1960 in Antioch, Tennessee, and raised in Nashville, Ramsey has a BSc in finance and real estate from the University of Tennessee.

In 1994 he established Financial Peace University, a training program for live audiences, which is now mainly a video education series run for schoolchildren in 46 American states. The Dave Ramsey Show *is broadcast every week across America, allowing listeners to call in with their problems.*

Financial Peace *was first published in 1992 and has sold over 750,000 copies. Other books include* More Than Enough *(2002),* The Total Money Makeover *(2007), and a children's finance series.*

1966

Capitalism

"No political-economic system in history has ever proved its value so eloquently or has benefited mankind so greatly as capitalism—and none has ever been attacked so savagely, viciously, and blindly. The flood of misinformation, misrepresentation, distortion, and outright falsehood about capitalism is such that the young people of today have no idea (and virtually no way of discovering any idea) of its actual nature."

"What they have to discover, what all the efforts of capitalism's enemies are frantically aimed at hiding, is the fact that capitalism is not merely the 'practical', but the only moral *system in history."*

In a nutshell

In capitalism, wealth is created by free, individual minds with no coercion involved. This makes it a moral system of political economy.

In a similar vein

Milton Friedman *Capitalism and Freedom* (p 110)
Thomas Friedman *The World Is Flat* (p 116)
Paul Zane Pilzer *God Wants You to Be Rich* (p 214)
Adam Smith *The Wealth of Nations* (p 260)

CHAPTER 40

Ayn Rand

Ayn Rand is author of the famous 1,400-page philosophical novel *Atlas Shrugged* (1957), which glorifies individual freedom and the ability to create wealth unhampered by government (see the commentary in *50 Success Classics*). *Capitalism: The Unknown Ideal* is essentially a nonfiction version, laying out Rand's Objectivist philosophy of the importance of personal motives above any kind of collectivist or tribal outlook. The power of the book rests on Rand's surprising contention that capitalism is a system morally superior to any other, built on personal freedom and delivering astounding wealth—and yet that it remains the most misunderstood system of political economy.

She wrote the book because she was confounded by the fact that young people blamed every societal ill on capitalism, which was hardly surprising since they had not lived under any other system. Socialism and communism, at the time she was writing, had legions of promoters and defenders, but capitalist ideals seemed to be trampled on everywhere and held up as evil. An American immigrant who had witnessed the economic misery and attacks on individual dignity that defined communist Russia, Rand had at an early age resolved to be capitalism's defender.

The 24 essays in the book originally appeared in Rand's *The Objectivist Newsletter*. While most are by her, there are two by then acolyte Alan Greenspan, who became chairman of the US Federal Reserve Board, and a couple by Nathaniel Branden, whom self-development readers will know as the author of *The Psychology of Self-Esteem* (see commentary in *50 Self-Help Classics*).

The first essay "What Is Capitalism?" incorporates most of her thinking. Its main points are discussed below.

Beware "the common good"

Rand rounds on what is usually considered a source of impeccably objective information, the *Encyclopaedia Britannica*. She had discovered its entry on capitalism, which described it as simply another way in which a society organizes itself to produce a "social surplus," and contained no mention of wealth being created by individual minds. Rather, wealth is described as an impersonal aggregate produced by the efficient allocation of resources.

This infuriated Rand, as in her view there is no such thing as a social surplus. All wealth is created by *somebody* and therefore belongs to them. In modern society, it is very clear who has contributed what. To see wealth as some social good produced by the tribe was "morally obscene." In her words:

When "the common good" of a society is regarded as something apart from and superior to the individual good of its members, it means that the good of some men takes precedence over the good of others, with those others consigned to the status of sacrificial animals.

When the good of the majority overrides individual rights, Rand observes, you may as well have no rights at all, since what you are left with, taken to its logical conclusion, is regimes like the former Soviet Union, where "the greater good of all" means misery for almost every individual. In Russia people were told to bear many hardships in the service of achieving some vision of a prosperous, industrialized state. Tough conditions were only temporary; soon they would overtake the capitalist West. But while they waited for tractors and generators, the government was spending fortunes on atomic power and putting men into space. In a socialist or communist society, Rand notes, everything gained comes at the expense of something else.

This does not happen in a capitalist system. America grew rich not by public sacrifices to some "common good," but by people's freedom to use their brains in pursuing their own fortunes. No one had to starve for America to become industrialized. In fact, the freedom of innovators to do their thing led to "better jobs, higher wages, and cheaper goods with every new machine they invented, with every scientific or technological advance."

Give free reign to the thinkers

Civilization has been built on the thought of individuals, the "intransigent innovators" as Rand calls them. She describes the creation of new things as "the application of reason to the problem of survival." Prosperity requires such people to have absolute freedom to think, and not to be held back by those who do not, who are simply blind followers. The most truly successful cultures in an economic sense have always been the freest politically.

Property rights are so important to a capitalist system because thinking people need to be able to dispose of the products of their efforts freely in order to support their life. They must not be accountable to the tribe, the state, the society, or the collective. When people make money in a free market, Rand comments, "They did not take it from those who had not created it." The law must support their sovereign nature.

The free world's economic progress came about precisely because no one was forced into doing anything by some method of central planning. Rather, the great achievements occurred through voluntary thought and action, not only in pursuit of financial fortunes but motivated by individual values. Capitalism cannot only be seen as a practical system that works to deliver the greatest economic output for all, but as the most moral system to achieve this end.

Final comments

Most of the "anticapitalists" of today actually know little about the system into which they were born. They have eyes only for some actors within it (such as large companies) and their apparent greed, while being blind to the fantastic freedoms and prosperity they have inherited. Free markets, they believe, will mean a "race to the bottom" of greater and greater exploitation of workers. Such arguments fail to notice that the sweatshop workers in developing countries who make goods sold in the rich world have usually arrived there by choice, leaving behind back-breaking lives of rural poverty. Their wages may be a pittance, but they represent the beginnings of a way out; their conditions look bad, but are little different to those endured by our grandparents or great-grandparents when their countries were industrializing.

The usual accusation leveled at Rand and her followers is of extremism. A more intelligent view is that she was a supreme rationalist who valued personal freedom to the highest degree. Capitalism for her was not just a system for people to get richer, but was the only system in which people were free to act according to their best interests. Today, because we take our comfortable lives for granted, we take capitalism for granted as well.

Ayn Rand

Rand was born Alissa Rosenbaum in 1905 in St Petersburg, Russia. Her father had owned a business that was taken over by the state after the Bolshevik Revolution erupted. She graduated from the University of Petrograd (Leningrad) in 1924, before beginning a screenwriting course. The following year she traveled to Chicago ostensibly to visit a cousin, never returning. After six months she moved to Hollywood to become a screenwriter, changing her name to Ayn Rand. "Ayn" was the first name of a Finnish writer, "Rand" the model of her Remington typewriter. On her second day in Los Angeles she famously met Cecil B. de Mille, who offered her work as an extra on a film where her future husband, Frank O'Connor, was on the set.

Rand never broke in to screenwriting, but in 1935 her play Woman on Trial *began on Broadway as* Night of January 16th. *Her novels* We the Living *(1936) and* Anthem *(1938) were well received critically but were not bestsellers. Rand's fortunes changed with the success of* The Fountainhead *(1943), a 700-page story of a modernist architect who battles to realize his vision.* Atlas Shrugged *was also an instant bestseller. In 1958 Rand and Nathaniel Branden (who was her lover for several years) opened the institute in New York that would spread Objectivist philosophy. She died in 1982.*

2000

Business as Unusual

"I have never believed that business was in a separate compartment from civilising the world. That's why I have always been an activist, an agitator and an entrepreneur rather than a conventional business leader. On the other hand, I did manage to found and build up a company which is said to be one of the top 30 worldwide brands. It now has over 2,000 stores in 51 countries serving some eight million customers a day, so I must have done something right."

"I am not interested in business as usual. It is business as unusual *that excites me."*

In a nutshell

When starting a business, do the opposite of the established industry. Make your business a powerful force for social change.

In a similar vein

Richard Branson *Losing My Virginity* (p 46)
Lynne Twist *The Soul of Money* (p 278)
Muhammad Yunus *Banker to the Poor* (p 286)

CHAPTER 41

Anita Roddick

Though she was regarded as one of the leading entrepreneurs of our time, Anita Roddick was never obsessed with business or money itself. The Body Shop chain that she founded grew to over 2,000 stores in 55 countries, and its socially conscious ways have had a significant influence on the political side of retailing, particularly the hygiene and cosmetics industry.

In *Business as Unusual*, the closest thing she wrote to an autobiography, Roddick spends as much time talking about issues of conscience as she does relating what actually happened in her years developing the company. Though haphazardly organized, in its pages aspiring entrepreneurs will learn how uniqueness can be a powerful business tool, and how "doing the right thing" can have many positive long-term effects for a company, not only internally but for all its customers and suppliers.

A heritage of difference

Roddick's Italian mother and American father ran a successful café in working-class Littlehampton on the south coast of England. There Roddick learned about having "a sense of theatre" in running a business, and the importance of the owners' personalities. Her mother, a Catholic, nevertheless disliked priests and taught her children to challenge all types of authority. She told them: "Be special. Be anything but mediocre."

Anita trained to be a teacher and enjoyed her work, but then hit the "hippy trail," traveling around the world for two years. On her return, her mother had lined her up with a young Scot named Gordon Roddick, who was trying to earn money writing children's stories. Four days later Anita moved in with him.

The couple opened a bed-and-breakfast hotel, which did well, then a restaurant, which flopped. They changed the décor to an American-style hamburger place and it boomed. After three years of running both, Gordon went off on an adventure to ride on horseback from Buenos Aires to New York, while Anita decided to open a shop with normal 9 to 5 hours so she could spend more time with their children. She settled on skincare, reading everything she could find on the subject.

At this point she had no intention of starting a large business, noting:

> *It wasn't about business, it was simply about creating a livelihood—my own livelihood. It was about being a mistress of my own time and space.*

In March 1976, the first branch of The Body Shop opened in Brighton. Roddick had paid an artist £25 for the logo and painted the premises dark green, not to make an environmental statement but because "it was the only colour that would cover up all the damp patches on the walls." Everything, she writes, was done to save money, including using plastic hospital bottles for soap and shampoo that customers could get refilled. But there was also a philosophical difference, which meant being honest to customers about the products and what they could achieve. Considering herself a child of the 1960s, anything "corporate" was anathema to Roddick. She had no organizational charts or five-year plans, she recalls, just some core values and a desire to expand.

Principled profit

Roddick wanted to have a shop that was the total opposite of what the cosmetics industry provided, "to stand for more than a mere bubble-bath." Yet it took some years before she realized that the company could be a platform for her and Gordon's political beliefs.

The Body Shop's unique advantage has been the story behind each of the products it sells. Today people routinely buy things based on what they know about the company that made them, but The Body Shop's emergence perfectly chimed with a growth in consumer awareness of issues such as animal testing for cosmetics and fair prices for suppliers from the developing world.

Above all, Roddick wanted to create a community of like-minded people. Yes, managers had to know something about shampoos and moisturizers and running a shop, but more important was sharing a view that The Body Shop could be a microcosm of a kinder, more connected world, with the buying decisions of people in the UK or America positively affecting communities thousands of miles away.

This social conscience led to some rather unorthodox business decisions. When the growth of the company required it to begin making its own soap, Roddick chose one of the most deprived parts of Britain, Glasgow's Easterhouse, to build a factory, knowing it would provide secure employment for many. It was "a moral business decision that worked," she says.

Roddick the entrepreneur

Listing the attributes of an entrepreneur, including "craziness" and "pathological optimism," Roddick emphasizes that he or she must be a great storyteller: The story behind your business and its products will set it apart.

She asserts that she was always more concerned with building a better, more values-driven company than creating a bigger one, and that ideas rather than money were her motivation. But she also loved buying and selling and connecting with customers, and beyond her social concerns she was obviously a very savvy retailer.

Business as Unusual makes fascinating reading on the expansion of the company into the US and the challenges it met. It attracted a lot of copycat chains that did not have to follow its own strict ethical standards; it also had problems supplying the full range of products, since about half the raw materials then available had been tested on animals. The Body Shop came under pressure to go the way of other cosmetics companies, and Roddick even had to fight against the company's own top managers who wanted to focus more on the bottom line at the expense of its unique culture. She later regretted letting in outsiders and consultants to fix problems, as they could never be in tune with the company's ethos. She offers a warning to fellow entrepreneurs:

Don't let people fiddle and play! Don't let anyone touch or change the DNA of your company unless it is to polish the differences and sing those differences out from every rooftop.

Final comments

Many people consider it the greatest irony that in 2006 The Body Shop was taken over by the biggest cosmetics company in the world, L'Oréal. From the £652 million purchase price, Anita and Gordon Roddick received £130 million through their 18 percent stake. Since L'Oréal still engages in animal testing, the change hurt and surprised many Body Shop loyalists. However, Roddick pointed out that The Body Shop's testing and other socially aware policies were "ring fenced" under the sale.

Until her untimely death in 2007 from a brain hemorrhage, Roddick remained a sort of conscience for the company, and its employees (many of whom were grief stricken) are likely to fight to keep her principles alive. Gordon Roddick remains a trustee of The Body Shop charitable foundation, which the couple started in 1990.

You may not have supported all of Roddick's causes, but you have to admire her gall in trying to create a "responsibility revolution" that made business a voice for the poor and powerless instead of their exploiter. These days having a social conscience is almost *de rigueur* for large companies that want to be seen in a good light, but The Body Shop was doing this years ago and it was not just a marketing ploy.

In wanting to use her business as an instrument to change the world, Roddick followed the great Quaker businessmen of the nineteenth century, for whom wealth was only true wealth when it benefited everyone involved. The best enterprise, this outlook holds, is a purposeful community that also happens to make money.

1988

Creating Money

"Money is energy, and energy exists in all realms. The spiritual laws of money are universal energy laws that create abundance: the principles of ebb and flow, unlimited thinking, giving and receiving, appreciation, honoring your worth, clear agreements, magnetism, and more."

"Whatever you think having more money will give you—aliveness, peace, self-esteem—is the quality you need to develop to become more magnetic to money and abundance. View money and things not as something you create to fill a lack, but as tools to help you more fully express yourself and realize your potential."

In a nutshell

If you know the universe to be an abundant place, you won't fear not having the resources to pursue your purpose or mission in life.

In a similar vein

T. Harv Eker *Secrets of the Millionaire Mind* (p 86)
Charles Fillmore *Prosperity* (p 98)
Esther Hicks & Jerry Hicks *Ask and It Is Given* (p 152)
Napoleon Hill *The Master-Key to Riches* (p 158)
Marsha Sinetar *Do What You Love, the Money Will Follow* (p 254)
Lynne Twist *The Soul of Money* (p 278)
Max Weber *The Protestant Ethic and the Spirit of Capitalism* (p 282)

CHAPTER 42

Sanaya Roman & Duane Packer

When you see a book with the title *Creating Money* you may wonder if its subject is the operations of a government mint. Unless you are a worker in the mint—or a counterfeiter—you do not create money, but rather *earn* it. It is something separate to you, to be won over to your side as the result of hard work.

Roman and Packer's book, an important modern prosperity title, provided an alternative view. Money could be "manifested" once you learned the spiritual laws that governed its flow. Things you wanted could be "magnetized" toward you through the practice of certain exercises.

Their aim was to give the reader "a sense of confidence and trust in the universe," and remind you that abundance is not about quantities of things, but rather whether those things fulfill you. You are in alignment with the spiritual laws of money if you:

- Do the life's work you were born to do, which is always something that helps others and fulfills your talents and interests simultaneously.
- Engage in cooperation rather than competition, looking for everyone to win in all situations.
- Invest, spend, or make money in a way that causes no harm and is good for the planet.

Yet wisely, *Creating Money* notes that there are two sets of laws regarding money: the spiritual; and the *man-made*, which relate to financial management, planning, taxes, cash flow, and so on. You can achieve abundance simply by following the spiritual laws of money, the authors claim, but it is good also to be in harmony with society's rules for creating and maintaining wealth. You can accommodate, know, and respect both.

Money is energy

If you pick up *Creating Money* thinking it is a straight "mental prosperity" title, you may be turned off by Roman and Packer's claim that it was "channeled." *They* did not write it, they say, but were given the words by spirit guides (Orin and DaBen), who they say had been in contact with them for many years.

Roman was struggling to make ends meet, and asked her guide to provide some answers to her situation. It was suggested she give classes on the principles of abundance and manifesting, which she began to do based on the "received" wisdom of the guides. These classes eventually turned into the book *Creating Money*.

Roman wondered: What did spiritual guides, who did not live in the real world, know about money? The answer came: "Money is energy, and energy exists in all realms." When human beings learn that money is a form of energy, they can begin to appreciate that it is not something to get, but is all around waiting to be attracted, tapped, or channeled.

Keep up the flow

The saying "money makes the world go around" is true, say Roman and Packer. Money is in a constant state of flow and circulation, and the more it flows the better. The quicker a store turns over its inventory, the healthier it is; the more money pumping through a nation, the wealthier it gets. Every time you resent the payment of a bill, you are stopping the flow. Consider, instead, giving a mental blessing to the institution you are making a payment to, wishing it prosperity. The more you happily spend and give, the quicker and more powerfully the flow comes back to you. When you are poor, you feel that you are outside the stream of money; to get back into its current you must again starting giving or spending.

When shopping, *Creating Money* suggests, it is better to buy one good thing of quality that you will enjoy rather than stuff of greater quantity whose mediocrity you will resent. Buying a good thing gives your subconscious mind the message that you deserve it. It is important to be joyful and appreciative in how you spend your money, as joy is the catalyst for having more money to spend in the future. Whatever you earn, be thankful for how much it is and you will find it goes further. Be resentful, and more will never be enough.

What is the essence of what you want?

Many people believe that money itself will make them happy, when really it is a particular state of mind that they want. You believe that money will make you feel secure, when there are many ways to engender a feeling of security without the need for a weighty bank account. Some think that money will bring them peace, but things such as meditation, stillness, and forgiveness are in fact better routes to peace than money. Others believe money will make them feel powerful and give them self-respect, when these may more easily come from doing work they love.

When you desire something material, spend time contemplating the essence of that thing. Do you want a new car because your existing one is unreliable? If it is reliable transportation you want, maybe catching the train would fulfill this need. Many people buy a house because they love the look of it, but soon find that it does not really suit their requirements. If they had first thought about the essence of what they wanted, they would have been led to a house that truly suited them.

"By becoming clear on the essence you want," Roman and Packer say, "you increase the range of possible forms and ways in which these forms can come to you." Paradoxically, clarity about your desires increases the range and quality of options for fulfilling them.

Magnetize your desires

Creating Money contains a chapter on "Magnetizing what you want," followed by one on "Following your inner guidance."

You "magnetize" something to you by visualizing it in a state of stillness. By being still, you gain access to a much greater range and depth of information, way beyond your own mind. Your thoughts and pictures concerning what you want "go out into the universe." Your higher self is the conduit to larger thought fields and naturally works out the best way of realizing your desires, often including "chance" meetings with people who can help you on your path. This is why it is so important, once you have established your purpose and goals, to trust your intuition and go with spontaneous hunches.

You should take action that puts you in the right direction. If you want a particular car, for instance, get the brochures and learn everything you can about the car, or create a special bank account for its purchase. This will "signal the universe" that you intend to get it, that you are serious about it. Always remember that the universe responds to *intent* rather than hope or wishing.

If you don't seem to get what you want using the techniques of magnetizing, Roman and Packer warn, it may be that your higher self considers that this thing is not in your best interests just at this moment. When you are dealing with spiritual money laws you are involving forces greater and wiser than yourself, so allow for natural timing. As the saying goes, "God's delays are not God's denials."

Transform your thoughts about money

It is possible that you are not prosperous at the moment because of your beliefs about whether you "deserve" to be well off. By affirming that you are entitled to abundance as much as anyone else, no matter what your past financial history, this change in perception may be all you need to attract a higher standard of living. Sometimes, you simply need to *allow* success.

Your debts do not determine your value; it may be that you have simply not "monetized" what you are worth. This is certainly the case for students who have loans to pay for their education. Their worth is in the knowledge, skills, and time they can offer, which inevitably is expressed in its financial equivalent.

Don't be too perturbed if you have been living for many years at bare survival level. It is probable, Roman and Packer say, that this was meant to be in order for you to learn certain life lessons. One of these lessons may be that there always seems to be enough, despite all the obvious financial pressures. Such a lesson is worth more than money alone, because it guarantees your prosperity no matter how much money you actually have. You gain the knowledge that the universe is intrinsically abundant.

Because money is a form of energy, it ebbs and flows. Don't worry when it is in an ebb phase, as the laws of nature dictate that money will flow again. When you can appreciate what you already have when the tide is out, it is likely to come back in more quickly. "Focus on the abundance you have," Roman and Packer write, "rather than all the bills." If you are not receiving enough money from your usual sources, ask the universe for it to come from other, unexpected places.

Find your life's work

Most people do not pursue the work that makes them feel most alive because of the fear that it won't bring in enough money. But *Creating Money* asserts, "Finding and creating your life's work will bring you more abundance than any other single action you can take." By becoming more individual, you will attract true wealth. And don't worry about the state of the economy, as if it is a reason holding you back. Instead, believe that you yourself can alter the economy through what you create.

Some people believe it is "spiritual" to charge less for what they do, yet the way the universe works is that we exchange things of value with others based on their special gifts or products. If you are following your true purpose in life then you are unique, and uniqueness attracts a premium.

If you are a free agent or small business owner, the chapter on "Honoring your value and worth" should make you wary of lowering your costs too much to make sales. It is more important to charge an appropriate price for what you do, and you will end up having good, reliable customers who respect you. Roman and Packer observe, "Honor your integrity, and you will be repaid many times over with increased prosperity."

Final comments

Creating Money was a seminal work preceding the new wave of "money and spirit" books that emerged in the 1990s. Though now 20 years old it has hardly dated because its ideas, including living out your life purpose and only doing things that do not harm the planet, are actually very in tune with our times.

If you have read the odd prosperity book in the past but gave up on them after a while, *Creating Money* is a good title to reinspire you. Though you may think the idea of "channeled wisdom" odd, overall the book contains a lot of common sense, is comprehensive and easy to read, and is full of useful exercises. If nothing else, it should disabuse you of the belief that money and things are hard to create, because if you are aware of the spiritual laws of money, and if what you desire will help serve a greater purpose, you will only see evidence of plenty. Doing their bit for world peace and sustainability, Roman and Packer note:

> *Most war and strife come from a belief in scarcity. People who believe in scarcity also try to squeeze more and more out of nature, wasting the planet's resources. If you want to contribute to planetary peace, you can start by believing in abundance for yourself and others.*

Trusting that there is plenty to go around for everyone may seem like a big leap of faith. It may be hard to simply "trust the universe" when you need money or resources, but in being very clear about the essence of your needs you can find myriad ways to satisfy them.

Sanaya Roman & Duane Packer

***Roman** is a graduate of the University of California, Berkeley, where she studied mathematics and sociology.*

***Packer** has a PhD in geology and geophysics, and traveled the word as a geologist before devoting his time to healing work based on an ability to see energy fields around the body.*

Both are based in Oregon and conduct seminars. Their other book is Opening to Channel: How to Connect with Your Guide *(1993).*

1997

Pour Your Heart into It

"I believe in destiny. In Yiddish, they call it bashert. *At that moment, flying 35,000 feet above the earth, I could feel the tug of Starbucks. There was something magic about it, a passion and authenticity I had never experienced in business."*

"It's also about how a company can be built in a different way. It's about a company completely unlike the ones my father worked for. It's living proof that a company can lead with its heart and nurture its soul and still make money."

"If you want to build a great enterprise, you have to have the courage to dream great dreams. If you dream small dreams, you may succeed in building something small. For many people, that is enough. But if you want to achieve widespread impact and lasting value, be bold."

In a nutshell

Nothing great is ever achieved without people making frightening leaps of faith.
Huge enterprises can be built by giving people a small moment of joy in their day.

In a similar vein

Richard Branson *Losing My Virginity* (p 46)
Conrad Hilton *Be My Guest* (p 164)
Anita Roddick *Business as Unusual* (p 238)

CHAPTER 43

Howard Schultz

Starbucks has become like the McDonald's of the beverage world, seemingly everywhere. It would therefore be easy to dismiss the company as yet another American corporate symbol bent on profit and world domination. The true story is more complex and interesting, however.

To begin with, Starbucks existed as a ground coffee merchant for a decade before it began serving coffee as a drink. Its founders were genuine coffee lovers who were more interested in educating people about the joys of real coffee than they were in making money.

Not dissimilar to the way Ray Kroc discovered the McDonald brothers and their remarkable restaurant in a small town in California, Howard Schultz, then a marketer of kitchen goods and housewares, had an epiphany when he first visited the original Starbucks stores in Seattle in the early 1980s. Used to the "swill" of American filter coffee, he fell in love with the real thing, and knew instantly he wanted to work for this offbeat and passionate company.

Pour Your Heart into It tells the story of Schultz's role in turning Starbucks into a major brand, which alone would have made it an interesting read, but it is also an autobiographical account of how the author's relationship with his father unexpectedly shaped the ethos of a global company. If you patronize Starbucks often you will find the history of the company fascinating, and if you have entrepreneurial aspirations this is a book to study.

Falling in love

Schultz grew up in subsidized high-rise housing blocks in a poor part of Brooklyn, New York. Even when newly built the homes carried a social stigma. His father had never finished school and throughout his life worked in unskilled jobs for exploitative employers. Particularly as a teenager, Schultz judged his father harshly for his underachievement.

With this background, when Howard was accepted into college—for his football rather than academic skills—it was a major event for the family. They had never left New York before, and drove a thousand miles to the campus of North Michigan University. Schultz majored in communications and also took classes in public speaking, interpersonal communications, and business.

After graduating, with no real idea of what he wanted to do, Schultz took a job selling wordprocessors for Xerox, making 50 cold calls a day. This he did for three years, paying off his college loans, before joining a Swedish company called Perstorp. In time he became the US manager of its stylish kitchen and housewares brand Hammarplast, a job paying $75,000 a year with a car and expense account, and managing 20 sales reps. He and his new wife Sheri, an interior designer, reveled in the Manhattan lifestyle and bought a loft apartment.

While working for Hammarplast, Schultz was intrigued by the large orders for a certain type of drip coffeemaker coming from a small company in Seattle. He went out to investigate and discovered Starbucks, a small chain of ground coffee retailers whose customers appreciated a good appliance for making their brews. He met the founders, Jerry Baldwin and Gordon Bowker, two cultured men who catered to a small niche market of educated coffee drinkers. Along with the coffee, Schultz was intrigued by the heritage and ethos of the company.

Baldwin and Bowker were literature lovers, and before they opened their first Seattle store in 1971 they had to think of a name for it. Starbuck was the first mate on the *Pequod*, the vessel in Herman Melville's *Moby-Dick*, a name they felt evoked the seafaring tradition of the early coffee traders. Their logo, a siren with flowing hair encircled by "Starbucks Coffee, Tea and Spice," was inspired by a Norse woodcut found in an old book. From the beginning, walking into a Starbucks store meant taking yourself out of the mundane world, the aroma of its dark roasted coffee combined with its wood furnishings evoking exotic, distant places.

Leaps of faith

Despite its benefits, Schultz had been growing restless in his job. "I sensed that something was missing. I wanted to be in charge of my own destiny." In 1982, to the dismay of his parents, he left his position and joined Starbucks, having persuaded the founders to hire him as their marketing director. Security had been replaced by passion.

In his first few months he was sent to a coffee trade fair in Milan. He loved Italy's crowded, atmospheric cafés, seemingly on every corner, and suddenly realized that the key to Starbucks' future was not just roasting and selling coffee but serving it. On this trip he had his first café latte, a mixture of espresso and warm, frothy milk that at the time was almost unheard of in America.

Returning home, Schultz's idea to open Starbucks cafés was dismissed as the whim of an overexcited marketing manager. He was eventually allowed to open a small café bar in the corner of a store, but despite brisk sales the founders still did not want to expand the idea. They were resolutely "not in the restaurant business"; cafés went against the whole idea of the company.

Torn between his love for Starbucks and a vision of opening Italian-style cafes across America, Schultz realized that his vision might only happen if he left to start his own company. This would be an even bigger leap of faith than joining Starbucks in the first place.

Selling a vision

Schultz tramped the streets of Seattle for a year giving presentations to investors. Out of 242 people he approached, 217 gave him an outright rejection. He was told many times that coffee was not a growth industry, that consumption in America had been declining since the mid-1960s, overtaken by soft drinks, and that the real money was to be made in technology start-ups.

Eventually, he rounded up enough money to open Il Giornale in the business district of Seattle. The café was a success and he began opening other branches. However, in 1987 came some interesting news: The Starbucks founders wanted to sell their business. Schultz's love for the company had not waned and he was desperate to buy it.

It had been difficult enough raising the $1.25 million for Il Giornale. How would he come up with $4 million for Starbucks? On a promise to investors of opening over 100 stores around America within a five-year timeframe (which seemed like an outlandish projection at the time), he got the money. Il Giornale and Starbucks were melded into one.

A people business serving coffee

In ten years, Starbucks became a company with over 1,300 stores and 25,000 employees. Though in the first three years it lost money, thereafter its growth of 50 percent a year turned it into a hyper-valuable business. On going public in 1992 it became a darling of the stock market, usually exceeding profit expectations thanks to the opening of a new store almost every business day.

Yet for Schultz, the Starbucks phenomenon was not simply about "growth" and "success" in a business sense. Above all, he wanted to create a company that nurtured its staff and treated them with respect. Though the customer was important, even more important for the long-term health of the business was to make sure the baristas and other staff were happy and loyal.

Starbucks became the first company to provide comprehensive healthcare for all employees, including part-timers working as little as 20 hours a week, and devised a stock option scheme to enrich the average employee, not just the executives. Starbucks became "a living legacy of my dad," Schultz notes, with an ethos and work practices that his father had never enjoyed. His view was:

If you treat your employees as interchangeable cogs in a wheel, they will view you with the same affection.

The company's largesse paid off not just in terms of high morale and dedication, but in staff turnover rates much lower than the industry norm. Clearly, long-term business prosperity rested on treating staff not just as "hires" but as *partners*, a term the company still uses.

Romance in the mundane

Schultz wonders about the key to Starbucks' success: Was it just the coffee, or something else?

If given a vital new twist, he notes, even mundane things can be turned into gold. In the same way that Nike took a commodity, running shoes, and made them into something special, so Starbucks changed the way people drank coffee: For a dollar or two more, they could have a real sensory experience. His aim was to "blend coffee with romance," creating a warm and enjoyable environment where along with a coffee you could listen to a bit of jazz or ponder life's questions.

A trip to Starbucks became an affordable luxury in an otherwise mundane day, providing a "third place" that was neither work nor home. Like all great innovations, Starbucks provided people with something they didn't know they had wanted. As the first in a new category, it became the industry leader and attracted many competitors. Schultz also talks at length about the company's research and development lab, which he believes will help it retain its edge in the future.

Final comments

At times, *Pour Your Heart into It* reads like a motivational book. Schultz never expected to achieve what he did, so part of his aim is to tell others what is possible when you dare to dream. When you see things others don't see but you believe strongly in them, he observes, you have to throw caution to the wind. There will be plenty of naysayers, but act anyway. His rule is: "If it captures your imagination, it will captivate others."

Unlike the brawny image created by CEOs like Jack Welch of General Electric, Schultz comes across as surprisingly sensitive, forever worrying about his company becoming too faceless and corporate. Though he is now personally worth over a billion dollars, money alone is clearly not what drove him. As a child of the 1960s, he was more interested in helping people to discover the delights of good coffee, creating a loved and respected brand, and being a responsible employer who really did value people. Incidentally, all earnings from *Pour Your Heart into It* have been donated to the Starbucks Foundation, which gives money to literacy programs and other causes.

At the time the book was written, Starbucks had only a handful of overseas stores. Now it is in 40 countries, and its total store count (self-operated and licensed) is over 13,000. When something becomes this ubiquitous it can fool us into thinking that its rise was inevitable. Many will say that gourmet coffee drinking was about to explode in America anyway, and Starbucks simply rode the wave. Yet ultimately, its success was built through attention to the customer and creating a good experience. Without a significant advertising budget, its reputation really did have to be built "one cup at a time."

1987

Do What You Love, the Money Will Follow

"The reason that this book's title contains the phrase, 'The Money Will Follow', is precisely because we must do the work first, invest of ourselves first, seed faithfully in the small, steady, incremental ways of our chosen work first, and then—as a harvest of abundant crops naturally follows the seeding, watering and constant caring process of seeds—the fruits of our efforts result."

"Biology points out the logic of Right Livelihood. Every species in the natural world has a place and function that is specifically suited to its capabilities. This is true for people too."

In a nutshell

Though we can't control when, the decision to do what we love sooner or later pays off.

In a similar vein

P. T. Barnum *The Art of Money Getting* (p 28)
Joe Dominguez & Vicki Robin *Your Money or Your Life* (p 74)
Anita Roddick *Business as Unusual* (p 238)
Sanaya Roman & Duane Packer *Creating Money* (p 242)

CHAPTER 44

Marsha Sinetar

Marsha Sinetar had a well-paid, secure job, a nice home, and a circle of family and friends nearby. Even though her work was not very fulfilling, promotions and material success stopped her from doing anything different; the job supported a nice lifestyle. There was a nagging feeling, though, that she should be doing something else, and although she believed in self-growth mantras like "What man can conceive, he can achieve," she also clung to the familiar.

However, one day she was driving along in Los Angeles when a thought, almost a strong voice, said to her: *Do what you love, the money will follow.* Not long after, she changed the direction of her career and moved to the countryside. In the years that followed, she worked only on the projects she loved, and her financial needs were always met.

Sinetar wrote *Do What You Love, the Money Will Follow* both as a manual for the "how" of doing what you love, and also as a guide to the spiritual aspects of work, sometimes called "right livelihood." With its jazzy cover and classic self-help title the book is easily dismissed, but it has acted as a private champion for thousands of people who needed a nudge to leave behind a job that left them hollow, for work that expresses who they really are.

First the love...

Part of the enjoyment of the book is the many examples of people who were in Sinetar's same predicament. She is careful to note that these were not people "who woke up one day to find themselves rolling in a 'fun job' and money," but individuals who went on journeys of the self in their desire for a "right livelihood."

Right livelihood is a Buddhist idea, Sinetar says, referring to "work consciously chosen, done with full awareness and care, and leading to enlightenment." Work that is consciously chosen naturally expresses the interests and abilities of the worker, and in doing it, he or she becomes a confident and satisfied individual.

From the title of the book, many readers expect to be able to quit their job one day and start earning big in their new profession within a month or two; but things rarely work out like that. The money will eventually follow the path you have taken, Sinetar observes, but you have to be prepared for a waiting period, to pay your dues.

Doing what you love does not always mean doing what you feel like doing. To pursue a new career you may first have to do hundreds of hours of training, or take on part-time jobs to pay the bills while you make your transition. Yet you will gladly do this if it allows you to do what you were meant to do.

...and then the money

People with low self-esteem often require a certain assurance of success before they do anything. Whatever they embark on must result in some kind of "flashy victory." The reality is that such victories may be years in coming, and you have to keep up a sense of self-worth even when there is limited success, trusting yourself and your abilities in the face of significant pressures to go back to what you were doing before. If your focus stays on how much money you can earn in your new career, you are not likely to be able to stick at it in the early days.

However, if your emphasis is on right livelihood, you will find you always have just enough money to pursue its development. You may be surprised to find that you feel wealthy, while others who work crazy hours to become rich will seem poor—a case of "Do what you love and money won't matter as much."

Sinetar employed a builder on her house who, unlike other workmen she had used, did slow, careful work. She sensed he was someone who had trusted "the money would follow" and got talking to him. He had a Master's degree in English and had begun an academic career, but did not fancy the treadmill of "publish or perish." He opted out and took his chances as a carpenter. At first he had earned a low wage as an assistant, but learned the ropes sufficiently that, a few years later, he could set himself up on his own. Now, he said, "I trust myself to be able to earn all the money I need."

Such a person is almost a rebel against a money-seeking culture in which high net worth is often equated with personal value. Yet this man was sure of his value, even if he had no expectation of getting rich. The paradox is that by pursuing what you love you tap into a source of energy that fires you on to do excellent, unique work. Your work inevitably gets recognized and people will be willing to pay good money for it.

Take the leap

In another example, a man wrote to Sinetar who had had a secure teaching career, but left it all behind to become a potter. He describes the step he took as "like walking off a cliff." He wasn't sure he would be successful, and didn't know how he would pay the bills, and yet he felt this was what he had to do.

The "universe" seemed to help him get established, and ten years later he could say how grateful he was for having taken the leap.

Leaving behind secure ways of working and living, most people have the same feeling of stepping into the abyss, Sinetar notes. Yet if there is a need to do the new thing, it will help overcome the fears. It also helps to look back on a history of success in other areas, remembering: "I took that step, even though I was afraid, and look how well it turned out."

Yet choosing to take the path you love is best seen as a choice rather than a risk, one taken after fully weighing all the factors (degree of talent, a possible market for what you do, and so on). You have to bank on your own resourcefulness, skill, and intelligence to solve problems, and draw on your reserves of self-confidence and self-esteem. But if you can weather the challenges and emerge in control of your work and your life, it will have been well worth it.

Don't be so hard on yourself

Work you don't like, Sinetar claims, is usually work you are not suited for. She once tried selling vacuum cleaners door to door in unfamiliar neighborhoods. For an introvert the task was horrible, and even though she was working her way through college and needed the money, she only lasted a day. She comments:

> *[We] are not born to struggle through life. We are meant to work in ways that suit us, drawing on our natural talents and abilities as a way to express ourselves and contribute to others.*

Humans are no different to animals in being designed and built for certain purposes.

People with high self-esteem believe they have a right to do work that is rewarding and enjoyable and that makes them happy. There is little difference between the work they do and recreation, and there is no need to go on exotic holidays when their job is this compelling. It is more fun to stay home.

Sinetar quotes novelist André Gide: "What seems different in yourself; that's the rare thing you possess. The one thing that gives each of us his worth, and that's just what we try to suppress. And we claim to love life."

Many people who try to climb up the greasy career pole long for a lower-key, less stressful occupation and a simpler life. They have taken the path they have thanks to parental or peer-group pressure, the media's idea of "success," or their own punishing expectations. Such people, Sinetar suggests, simply need to be kinder to themselves. The world will not fall apart if they earn less money; on the contrary, their lives will flower when they realize that life is about self-expression, not self-aggrandizement.

Work as enlightenment

In Sinetar's last chapter, "Work as love, work as devotion," she writes:

> *all major cultures have, somewhere within their instructive tradition, grasped this central truth: that work, done rightly, affords the individual an understanding of the key principles of life and the universe.*

Everyone who loves their work will recognize the truth of this statement. Though what you do produces a tangible result or product, what draws you back to it is the way greater knowledge in your specialty somehow illuminates other things. You love your work not just because it teaches you a lot about yourself, but because it becomes a key to understanding life, the universe, and everything.

Final comments

Some readers will feel that *Do What You Love, the Money Will Follow* contains too much psychobabble, with a fair amount of talk about self-esteem and the effects of your childhood. Yet given that the decision to do what you love is often reached after going through psychological contortions, Sinetar's focus is understandable. This is not a dry career manual; it is about the bigger questions of who you are and what really brings you happiness in life. These are not even psychological questions, they are metaphysical, and trying to sidestep them will inevitably result in misery. Sinetar's examples of people who followed their inner voice are fascinating, and yet they are not exceptional. Every reader is capable of doing the same. The key is to realize that doing what you love is not a luxury, but a necessity in living a truly prosperous life.

Marsha Sinetar

Sinetar spent five years as a public school teacher in California, then a further five years as a school principal. She was a school curriculum consultant and mediator for the California state board of education.

She has also taught management development programs at Loyola University's Industrial Relations Center in Los Angeles, and runs a private practice focusing on organizational psychology, mediation, and corporate leadership education.

Other books include Ordinary People as Monks and Mystics *(1986),* Work as a Spiritual Path *(1993),* To Build the Life You Want, Create the Work You Love *(1995), and* The Mentor's Spirit *(1998).*

1778

The Wealth of Nations

"It was not by gold or by silver, but by labour, that all the wealth of the world was originally purchased."

"It is not from the benevolence of the butcher, the brewer or the baker that we expect our dinner, but from their regard to their own interest. We address ourselves, not to their humanity, but to their self-love, and never talk to them of our own necessities, but of their advantages. Nobody but a beggar chooses to depend chiefly upon the benevolence of his fellow-citizens."

"To prohibit a great people... from making all that they can of every part of their own produce, or from employing their stock and industry in the way that they judge most advantageous to themselves, is a manifest violation of the most sacred rights of mankind."

In a nutshell

The wealth of a nation is that of its people, not its government.
Wealth is achieved through the division of their labor and the ever-greater specialization of their skills.
The foundation of all future prosperity is current savings.

In a similar vein

Milton Friedman *Capitalism and Freedom* (p 110)
Ayn Rand *Capitalism* (p 234)
Max Weber *The Protestant Ethic and the Spirit of Capitalism* (p 282)

CHAPTER 45

Adam Smith

Adam Smith was not the first political economist by any means (he was inspired, for instance, by the French physiocrats), but by identifying economics as a field of study in its own right, separate to politics, philosophy, law, and ethics, *An Inquiry into the Nature and Causes of the Wealth of Nations* established a new discipline. It was the first book on economics really to catch the public's attention, and is as much as anything else a great work of literature. Smith's informal style, and his fearlessness in criticizing the folly of rulers and the corrupting effects of vested interests, made him into a popular figure.

Not published until Smith was in his 50s, the book took fully ten years to write, covers two volumes, and weighs in at 380,000 words. Smith expounds at great length on details that are of academic interest only now, such as the production of wheat, ale, and barley in thirteenth-century England, the types of rents levied by lords and kings on agricultural land, how the price of silver dropped after the Spanish conquest of South America, and how a government might fairly tax salt, leather, soap, and candles.

Go beyond the historical details, though, and *The Wealth of Nations* is surprisingly engrossing and relevant. Written for the interested lay reader, it assumes zero knowledge of its subject, and over 200 years on still provides valuable lessons on basic economics. Most importantly, it provides a recipe for national prosperity that has not been bettered since, based on small government and the freedom of citizens to act in their best interests.

The effect of self-interest

Smith argues that it does not actually matter if societies are mainly driven by self-interest, since the overall effect is good. The "invisible hand" of the free market makes sure that individuals acting to their own highest benefit end up elevating the whole. This is not an excuse to act greedily or unjustly. It simply means that a person's honest labors to progress in life for the sake of himself or his family will lead to a good use of resources. A society allowed to act in this way will inevitably make the most of what it has, and over time grow prosperous. His famous remark about the butcher, brewer and baker (see opposite) was not just an insight into human nature, it underlined his philosophy of self-reliance: that we are more likely to help others, and be in a position to help them, when we have our own needs covered.

Wealth through specialization

It was no accident that Smith began his book with the subject of labor. He believed that how wealthy a country becomes depends more than anything on the organization of its labor force, specifically, as he put it, the "skill, dexterity, and judgment with which its labour is generally applied." It also rested on the proportion of the population engaged in useful work.

He comments that in rich countries, even though many people do not work, society as a whole abundantly supplies most people's needs. This is because rich countries characteristically have a much greater "division of labor" than poor ones. There is great efficiency in dividing up tasks according to the ability of people best able to do them, and time is saved in not changing from one task to another. Smith gives the now famous example of the manufacture of pins. In a workshop in which several stages in the making of the pins are divided up (i.e., one man performs the operation of drawing out the wire, another straightens it, another cuts it, and so on), many thousands more pins can be made in a week than in a workshop where one person has to perform all these tasks.

But it is not just in physical production that the principle of the division of labor applies. In advanced societies, Smith writes, philosophy or the creation of new ideas becomes the "trade" of a whole group of people, coexisting beside the more mundane jobs. With such specialization, "Each individual becomes more expert in his own peculiar branch, more work is done upon the whole, and the quantity of science is considerably increased by it." In a well-governed society, the division of labor leads to "universal opulence," allowing even the lowliest workers to cover all their needs.

What determines value

The real price of every thing, what every thing really costs to the man who wants to acquire it, is the toil and trouble of acquiring it.

According to Smith, it is the amount of labor that has gone into something's creation, saving the buyer having to go through the same labor, that sets its value. People become rich by providing something of extremely high utility that saves other people the labor of having to make it themselves. For instance, something that takes only an hour to create for a master, who has spent 20 years perfecting his task, may be worth more than something produced "in a month's industry, at an ordinary and obvious employment."

How nations grow rich

Smith provides a simple recipe for how countries can become wealthy, which begins with their citizens being good savers. He notes that prodigal people are a "public enemy," while every frugal person in society becomes a "public benefactor." These savings are then invested toward productive ends, which naturally increases the amount of people usefully employed.

This wealth formula of savings–investment–employment may seem obvious to us today, but in Smith's time it was not at all the prevailing view of how nations could grow rich. The mercantilist view held that the economic object of a nation was to build up its store of gold, silver, and other precious metals, either through trade or war. Smith's recipe, in contrast, seemed rather middle class and modest. It rested on the Protestant ethic of frugality, industry, and minding one's own business.

The other avenue by which countries could grow rich is trade. Smith notes that the most successful cultures of the past were all traders, usually maritime. Countries who trade will always be richer than those who do not, since the trading country is able to buy raw materials that it does not have itself and turn them into manufactured goods, which are much more valuable than raw commodities and which it can then sell at great profit to other countries. The essential point about national wealth is that it grows when things and money are circulated and exchanged. This was understood by the medieval European cities such as Florence, which amassed huge riches not by doing business simply with the countryside surrounding them, but with "the most remote corners of the globe." Cities and countries that myopically stayed within their own borders, in contrast, were destined to founder.

What not to do: Looting, wars, and luxuries

If a person spends their money on luxuries instead of building up capital, the day of financial reckoning will come. Likewise, Smith writes, a sovereign who spends huge sums on palaces, the pageantry of court, and unnecessary wars is looking for trouble.

Equally bad is the nation that believes it can get rich not by developing its land or industry, but by looting other countries for all they are worth. Smith notes that it was "the sacred thirst for gold" that brought the Spaniards to the New World, yet its end result was hardly beneficial to the long-term prosperity of Spain. Instead of plundering in search of fantastic gains, a country is better off slowly developing its own resources, and using trade to sell its surpluses and bring it what it needs to make high-value products.

Smith was skeptical of the monopoly trading companies (such as the East India Company) that used government mandates to make fortunes for their members, and he was not keen on the colonization of other lands. *The Wealth of Nations* was written a time when America was still a collection of British colonies, and Smith advocates Britain withdrawing itself. Britain's rulers, he writes, had always imagined America to be a gold mine, but it had, in fact, only ever been "the project of a gold mine." Colonization had cost the British taxpayer more than it was worth; it was time, he believed, to assume more modest ambitions.

Natural liberty

In Smith's time frustration with government red tape was at its zenith. Legions of officials ensured that every possible penny could be extracted by the state through various taxes, customs, excises, and arbitrary rules. *The Wealth of Nations* was a great success because it pointed instead to the principle of natural liberty, which assumed that people should be free to follow their economic interests with a minimum of government interference.

Smith insisted there were only three areas where government should have a role:

- Protecting a society from "the violence and invasion of other independent societies."
- Protecting citizens "from the injustice or oppression of every other member of it," and establishing a corresponding judicial system.
- Building and maintaining public works and institutions that are too expensive for a single individual to undertake, but that would benefit greatly society as a whole.

All these things should be paid for through taxes. However, when something benefits only a section of society rather than the whole, this should be paid for either privately, or by a tax on the users, for example tolls on tollroads. Though Smith advocated the creation of a basic schooling system to ensure everyone could read, write, and add up sums, he suggested that those who benefited the most from education should also be willing to pay for it.

Final comments

Though it may be a boring subject for some, the role of government is a vital matter when considering the creation of wealth and prosperity, since we all live in societies governed by laws and policies.

When *The Wealth of Nations* was published Europe was entering a new industrial era, and the nature of government needed to change quickly if there were not to be revolutions. People were fed up and wanted to be free to pursue their economic destinies. At first glance, rulers no doubt thought that the title of the book referred to the wealth of states, when in fact Smith used the term "nation" to mean the *people* of those countries. The smartest governments did not put faith in themselves to create prosperity, he believed, but rather in the ingenuity of their citizens.

The simplicity and common sense of Smith's delineation of government's role has largely stood the test of time. Today, governments have a tendency to grow large and bloated, moving into areas that are not really their business, but in time this inevitably makes the public poorer overall. Though they often believe in their ability to "pick winners" in terms of subsidizing particular industries to create jobs, Smith warns that such investment tends to corrupt the natural tendency of a society to allocate resources in the best way.

Smith's great work is now freely available on the internet. However, readers who do not feel inclined to tackle it but are still fascinated by the subject of how some countries do better than others are encouraged to read David Landes' modern classic *The Wealth and Poverty of Nations* (see the commentary in *50 Success Classics*).

Adam Smith

Smith was born in 1723 in Kirkcaldy, Scotland. His father had been the town's comptroller of customs but died six months before Adam was born. At 15 Smith went to Glasgow University to study moral philosophy, and then on to Oxford University. In 1748 he began giving public lectures in Edinburgh, and in 1751 was appointed to a chair of logic, later moral philosophy, at Glasgow University.

He resigned his post in 1763 to become the private tutor to a young Scottish nobleman, the Duke of Buccleuch. The pair traveled around Europe and met intellectuals including Turgot, Helvetius, and Quesnay. On returning to Scotland, Smith spent most of the following decade writing The Wealth of Nations. *Following in his father's footsteps, in 1778 he was appointed commissioner of customs in Edinburgh.*

On his death in 1890, he left most of his considerable estate to charity. He never married.

1996

The Millionaire Next Door

"Whatever your income, always live below your means."

"What we have discovered in all our research? Mainly, that building wealth takes discipline, sacrifice, and hard work."

"What can you give your children to enhance the probability that they will become economically productive adults? In addition to an education, create an environment that honors independent thoughts and deeds, cherishes individual achievements, and rewards responsibility and leadership."

In a nutshell

Most people become millionaires not by inheritance or winning the lottery, but earning a good income from work they enjoy, living well below their means, and investing their savings.

In a similar vein

David Bach *The Automatic Millionaire* (p 22)
T. Harv Eker *Secrets of the Millionaire Mind* (p 86)
Suze Orman *Women and Money* (p 208)
Dave Ramsey *Financial Peace Revisited* (p 228)

CHAPTER 46

Thomas J. Stanley & William D. Danko

When Stanley and Danko began their research into the lives and habits of America's wealthy in the 1970s, they were surprised to find very little existing information. They were business academics who happened to take an interest in the subject, and like most people assumed that millionaires are ostentatious people with a cultured taste for the finer things in life. Accordingly, their initial research method was to focus on upscale neighborhoods. But they got a surprise: Many inhabitants of these suburbs were not in fact wealthy, and moreover, many of the genuinely wealthy were living in more modest areas.

Stanley and Danko describe the research effort behind *The Millionaire Next Door* as "the most comprehensive ever conducted on who the wealthy are in America—and how they got that way," involving interviews with more than 500 millionaires, plus over 1,000 completed surveys made up of over 200 questions. The pair investigated not just your garden-variety millionaire, but "decamillionaires" whose net worth exceeds $10 million. In a revealing scene from their research, they had assembled a focus group of decamillionaires, making sure that they provided a buffet of gourmet appetizers and fine wines so they would feel at home. However, the visitors barely touched the goodies and instead nibbled on crackers. It turned out that the only gourmets on the scene were among the nonmillionaire research staff!

Such unexpected observations "changed the lives" of the authors. Stanley, for example, left academia, wrote several books on how to market to the affluent, and became an adviser to financial service firms on the needs of the wealthy. *The Millionaire Next Door* became the popular (very popular: 2.5 million copies sold) version of their research, and it makes for interesting reading.

Defining wealth

If you're fortunate enough to make a high income every year, does that make you wealthy? According to Stanley and Danko, definitely not. The proper measure of wealth is *net worth*. They note:

> *Most people have it all wrong about wealth... Wealth is not the same as income. If you make a good income each year and spend it all, you are not*

getting wealthier. You are just living high. Wealth is what you accumulate, not what you spend.

Based on this definition, in the research only about 3.5 percent of American households were found to surpass the million mark, yet nearly half of all American wealth was concentrated in these households. While most people live pay check to pay check, these people had enough accumulated wealth to live without working for at least 10 years, amounting to what the authors describe as a "go to hell fund."

The surveyed millionaires had a median net worth of $1.6 million, and an average of $3.7 million, with only 6 percent having a net worth of over $10 million. Clearly, these were not the super-rich, but average people who had done well during their lifetimes. In Stanley and Danko's minds this is all-important, since it suggests that this level of wealth is attainable for many people starting from scratch.

How are you doing?

To gauge your progress on the road to wealth, Stanley and Danko suggest that your wealth is best judged by comparing your net worth with your income and age. They provide a useful rule of thumb: Your baseline net worth (excluding inheritance) should at least equal your annual income times your age, all divided by ten.

If you are doing particularly well, having managed to accumulate at least twice this amount, you are a "Prodigious Accumulator of Wealth" or PAW, making you a top 25 percent wealth accumulator. With less than half the baseline net worth, you are an "Under Accumulator of Wealth" or UAW, putting you in the bottom 25 percent.

Profile of a millionaire

If typical millionaires aren't as glamorous as we might have supposed, what are they really like? The following profile gives an idea:

Usually the wealthy individual is a businessman who has lived in the same town for all of his adult life. This person owns a small factory, a chain of stores, or a service company. He has married once and remains married. He lives next door to people with a fraction of his wealth. He is a compulsive saver and investor. And he has made his money on his own. Eighty percent of America's millionaires are first-generation rich.

Stanley and Danko boil this profile down to seven common denominators of the wealthy:

1 They live well below their means.
2 They allocate their time, energy, and money efficiently, in ways conducive to building wealth.
3 They believe that financial independence is more important than displaying high social status.
4 Their parents did not provide money handouts.
5 Their adult children are economically self-sufficient.
6 They are proficient in targeting market opportunities.
7 They chose the right occupation.

The book has chapters elaborating on each of these traits, with some key points highlighted below.

Live well below your means

The three words that best characterize the affluent, Stanley and Danko write, are "Frugal, frugal, frugal." Frugality is the basis of all wealth building, and is the main trait that distinguishes PAWs from UAWs. The average millionaire manages to invest a full 20 percent of their annual household income, year after year, while nonmillionaires spend everything or almost everything that comes in.

Frugality also turns out to be a family trait. If your parents were frugal you're likely to be frugal also, and the spouses of most millionaires are often even more frugal than they are. Clearly, it is difficult to become wealthy if your spouse spends all your money—a bucket with a large hole in the bottom is difficult to fill.

Millionaires also buy inexpensive suits, and of course they wait to buy them until they're on sale. They do not typically drive flashy imported cars, but more often are to be found in American-made cars that are several years old, and many millionaires even prefer shopping for bargain used cars. Regarding housing, the typical millionaire bought their house many years ago and lives in a modest but pleasant neighborhood. Remember, they are the millionaire next door, not in Beverly Hills or the Hamptons. In short, millionaires are in firm control of their finances, and however much their wealth increases they stick with their old habits of budgeting and planning.

How millionaires were raised, and how they raise their kids

Most millionaires did not attend private schools, received limited financial assistance as working adults even if their parents were affluent, and received little or no inheritance.

Stanley and Danko offer sound advice, based on their research, into what has actually worked and not worked in terms of financially educating your children. They suggest:

- ❖ Don't give monetary gifts to your adult children. Gifts will make them financially dependent on you and will encourage them to be consumers. Instead, teach them your habits of frugality and discipline.
- ❖ Don't reveal your wealth to your children, at least not fully, until they are financially established adults. Otherwise, they may start spending more money than they should, in anticipation of receiving a large inheritance, and discussions about inheritance can undermine family relationships.
- ❖ Teach your children that what matters is achievement, not material symbols of success. Money can be a measure of achievement, but it certainly isn't the only one.

The central message is that the best gift you can give your children is to help them develop *character*. To do that, they have to face the challenges of life, learn from experience, and thereby develop courage, rather than being shielded by your wealth.

Choose the right career

The majority of nonretired millionaires are business owners, and in fact business owners are four times more likely to be millionaires than employees. However, before you rush out to start your own business, Stanley and Danko are quick to point out that the majority of business owners are not millionaires, and about 20 percent of millionaires are employees. Establishing and running a successful business is a tough challenge, so don't quit your day job if you're not confident that you'll be among those who make it.

The common thread among those who do succeed is tolerance for risk. This matters much more than picking the "right" type of business, and indeed many millionaires own relatively low-profile businesses such as dry cleaners and parts-supply companies. Not being burdened by pretense, millionaires are happy to capitalize on opportunity wherever they find it.

Regardless of whether they're business owners or employees, the majority of millionaires greatly enjoy their work, typically putting in 45 to 55 hours per week. This recalls Marsha Sinetar's maxim: "Do what you love, the money will follow." By contrast, "a large proportion of UAWs work because they need to support their conspicuous consumption habit."

Where do the wealthy spend their money?

Millionaires are frugal, but are they unrelenting misers? In fact, they do spend some money, and they generally do it wisely. Being savvy enough to have become wealthy, they naturally tend to spend their money in ways that maintain and increase their wealth, as well as the prospects for their children. This includes carefully procuring professional services from expert investment advisers, accountants, tax specialists, and lawyers. They also recognize that good education is a solid investment, and so many are willing to pay pricey private school tuitions for their children and grandchildren, although some consider such an expense to be frivolous. Last but not least, millionaires recognize that financial security has little value without your health, so they generally seek and pay for top-quality medical and dental care.

Final comments

The Millionaire Next Door may seem like a "how to get rich" manual, but this is not what the book actually aims to do. Stanley and Danko simply present their research findings about the type of people who have already become millionaires, and the reader is left to take on board the findings. Though some will find it slightly repetitious, the book is an enjoyable read that also contains character vignettes to help make the findings more memorable. Because it is essentially a research report for laypeople there is a certain amount of data and tables, but this objective grounding is very welcome compared to books written mainly from an author's personal experience.

Stanley and Danko's underlying message is that consumption and opulence aren't ultimately very important next to the peace that comes from doing fulfilling work and the discipline of slowly building up a nest egg over time. Aristotle noted that happiness was a direct result of such character development, and indeed the authors point out that next-door millionaires enjoy a higher level of life satisfaction than others. It seems that the discipline that makes them rich also delivers them a greater than average share of happiness.

Thomas J. Stanley & William D. Danko

Stanley *earned his PhD in business administration from Georgia State University. He was formerly professor of marketing there, and also served on the faculty of the State University of New York at Albany. Other books include* Marketing to the Affluent *(1997),* Networking with the Affluent *(1997),* Selling to the Affluent *(1997),* The Millionaire Mind *(2001), and* Millionaire Women Next Door *(2004). He lives in Atlanta, Georgia with his family.*

Danko *has a PhD from the Rensselaer Polytechnic Institute, and is associate professor and chair of marketing at the State University of New York at Albany.*

1987

The Art of the Deal

"I like thinking big. I always have. To me it's very simple: if you're going to be thinking anyway, you might as well think big. Most people think small, because most people are afraid of success, afraid of making decisions, afraid of winning. And that gives people like me a great advantage."

"I don't do it for the money. I've got enough, much more than I'll ever need. I do it to do it. Deals are my art form. Other people paint beautifully on canvas or write wonderful poetry. I like making deals, preferably big deals. That's how I get my kicks."

"I have an almost perverse attraction to complicated deals, partly because they tend to be more interesting, but also because it is more likely you can get a good price on a difficult deal."

In a nutshell

To succeed in business, balance boldness and promotion with patience, caution, and flexibility.

In a similar vein

P. T. Barnum *The Art of Money Getting* (p 28)
Felix Dennis *How to Get Rich* (p 68)
Conrad Hilton *Be My Guest* (p 164)
Andrew McLean & Gary W. Eldred *Investing in Real Estate* (p 190)
William Nickerson *How I Turned $1,000 into Three Million in Real Estate—in My Spare Time* (p 200)

CHAPTER 47

Donald Trump

Thanks to his self-promotion, extravagant lifestyle, and big deals, Donald Trump was already famous when *The Art of the Deal* was published, a symbol of capitalism, New York City, and the flash 1980s rolled into one.

Yet the book's timing was lucky, coming out just ahead of the troubles that beset Trump in the late 1980s and early 1990s and that brought him dangerously close to ruin. Much to his enemies' chagrin, he sorted himself out and came back bigger than ever. Whoever said there are no second chances in American life did not count on the power of a brand, and like the great showman P. T. Barnum a century before, a large part of Trump's fortune comes down to his name. When in 2003 producers approached him to be the focus of a new reality television series based on entrepreneurship, *The Apprentice*, he saw an opportunity to cement his fame with a new generation.

Yet despite the array of Trump books that have been published to capitalize on the success of that show, *The Art of the Deal* is still the best insight into the man. Though now 20 years old, it contains the essential philosophies and ways of working that have sustained his success for three decades. The only difference is that then he was a brash upstart willing to take on anything and anyone, and now he is a wise, if still very showy, business master. The scale of his operations may have grown, but the Trump of the 1980s is largely the same one as today. Here we look at some of the deals, beliefs, and strategies that have seen him thrive and prosper even in tough times.

Think big

Trump's father, Fred, was a developer of rent-controlled housing in the New York boroughs. Despite it being a low-margin and unglamorous form of developing, his tenacity ensured his success. Though the young Donald spent a lot of his boyhood following his dad around on sites, he always dreamed of Manhattan and of creating landmark projects that made a statement.

His first project in Manhattan was the Commodore, a huge, rundown hotel in a low-rent district. At the time, he notes, "I was only twenty-seven years old, and I'd hardly slept in a hotel," but he embarked on building a 1,400-room monster, which remained the biggest in New York for 25 years.

Promote, promote

It's a myth, Trump observes, that location is everything in real estate. It is important, but to make the most of any property (particularly apartments) what you need is to create a sense of worth or mystique that will make people want to buy. He remarks:

People may not always think big themselves, but they can still get very excited by those who do. That's why a little hyperbole never hurts. People want to believe that something is the biggest and the greatest and the most spectacular.

To get your project noticed you must be different, even outrageous, and being so increases your chances of becoming a story in the media. He does not court publicity for publicity's sake (in fact, he claims to be a very private person), however he notes that a small article in *The New York Times* will be worth many times more than a full-page advertisement costing $100,000—even if its slant is negative.

Have patience, then be ready to swoop

Despite his flashy image, a major element in Trump's success is being prepared to wait. For example, for years he prized the Bonwit Teller site that would eventually become Trump Tower, repeatedly writing to its owners to state his interest. He kept up his efforts, he notes, "because much more often than you'd think, sheer persistence is the difference between success and failure." When the site fell into the hands of new owners who were in a poor financial position, it was to Trump they turned to sell.

On another occasion, he read about a company in dire straits whose executives had been flying around in a corporate Boeing 727. At the time this plane cost $30 million new. Trump offered a measly $5 million for it, and in the end paid $8 million, still a hefty discount. If you can make seemingly outrageous demands while keeping a straight face, he claims, you will get bargains.

Many of his successes came from offering to buy assets before they were on the market. To many sellers, a bird in the hand is worth two in the bush. "The worst thing you can possibly do in a deal," he writes, "is seem desperate to make it." You need leverage: Find out what the seller needs or wants and give them this in addition to the purchase price.

Secrets of the deal maker

In New York City, big-time real-estate development is a complex matter. The city has strict and Byzantine planning and zoning laws, which means that most development proposals, particularly larger ones, are knocked back. The construction of the famous Trump Tower on 5th Avenue and 57th Street (with its marble waterfall lobby, luxury stores, and apartments owned by stars and billionaires) turned out to be a great success, but to get it built Trump had to wrangle with the city authorities about its height, its aesthetics (given its landmark position), and how much public amenity it would provide. Long and often fragile negotiations were required to buy the lease for the existing building, for the land the building sat on, for the air rights above the Tiffany store next door, and for a small pocket of land for a rear yard (another city requirement). He had to raise the money for the project, yet the banks were not willing to provide finance until everything was settled. It was only the success of his previous project, the Commodore/Hyatt hotel, that enabled him finally to get a mortgage.

A key to understanding Trump's success is that he actually likes handling complexity. What to others look like big problems, to him appear as massive opportunities that draw on his creative powers. All his deals are a case of juggling many balls in the air at once, and this is even before the first bricks are laid. The more complex the deal, he notes, the fewer developers will be interested in the first place—but this means greater potential rewards if it does come off. Most people do not have a stomach for such uncertainties, but Trump thrives on them.

Though one of his trademarks is hubristic confidence, in fact he always goes into any deal looking at what could possibly go wrong. "Protect the downside," he comments, "and upside will take care of itself." Every deal must have a fallback position. If he buys a site or a building, for instance, he has to be ready for his plans to be rejected. An intended tower block of apartments can be changed into office accommodation or a hotel if necessary. The dealmaker must be willing to let go of personal preferences to ensure a profitable outcome.

The way of The Donald

Other things we learn about Trump in the book include:

- In college, while his friends were reading comics and the sports pages, he was poring over listings of property foreclosures.
- His first abode in Manhattan was a rented studio apartment that looked onto a courtyard.
- He is not keen on parties or small talk, and he goes to bed early.
- He doesn't like to schedule too many meetings, preferring to see how the day unfolds. He routinely makes 50–100 phone calls a day.
- He's a stickler for cleanliness and makes sure that all his properties sparkle.
- He trusts his intuition, calling off deals that "don't feel right" even if they look great on paper. On the other hand, he has often gone ahead with deals against the opposition of his advisers (such as his purchase of the Hilton casino in Atlantic City, which was a great success).
- He got interested in the gambling business when he discovered that the Hilton corporation owned 150 hotels around the world, but its two casinos in Las Vegas provided 40 percent of its profits.

- He takes a lot of stands on principle: "I fight when I feel I'm getting screwed, even if it's costly and difficult and highly risky."
- His love of glamor, he says, was inherited from his mother, and his hard-work ethic from his father.
- He likes to hire women for many of his top jobs.
- His favorite place is Mar-a-Lago, a spectacular Florida property built in the 1920s by the heiress to the Post cereal fortune (now a private club), which he bought for a bargain price.
- He is proud of his reconstruction of Wollman Ice Rink in Central Park, completed in four months after years of delays by the city authorities.

Final comments

Who is the real Donald Trump? Though famously fond of exaggeration and self-promotion, underneath there is a true businessman who loves his work. In his biography of Trump, *No Such Thing as Over-Exposure*, Robert Slater writes that (despite the famous "You're fired" line from *The Apprentice*) few people are ever let go in the Trump organization, and generally The Donald is more forgiving and generous than his image suggests. He is also loyal, with trusted financial and legal people who have been with him for years. As Trump himself notes:

> *In my life, there are two things I've found I'm very good at: overcoming obstacles and motivating good people to do their best work.*

In its current renaissance, it is easy to forget that for much of the 1970s and 1980s New York City was in a mess, close to bankruptcy, and ridden with crime. But Trump clearly loved his city and thought it the center of the universe, and as a reward for that confidence was able to pick up valuable properties for low prices. He is often painted as vainglorious, but the other side of the coin is strong self-belief. Without it, he would have been no more than a small to medium-sized property developer.

Toward the end of *The Art of the Deal* Trump gets philosophical, wondering what, ultimately, is the meaning of all his empire building. His honest answer: He doesn't know, except that he loves doing the deals themselves, irrespective of how much money he now has. Life is fragile, he comments, so whatever you do you must have fun doing it.

Littered with interesting mentions of the great and the good of New York in the 1980s, including novelist Judith Krantz, television personality David Letterman, financiers Michael Milken and Ivan Boesky, Ian Schrager of Studio 54 fame, Mayor Ed Koch, fashion designer Calvin Klein, and the Cardinal of St Patrick's Cathedral, *The Art of the Deal* is a fun read along with its valuable lessons. It is also very well put together, thanks in part to the writing assistance of Tony Schwartz. Trump fans should also get the sequel, *The Art of the Comeback*, written ten years later.

Donald Trump

Born in Queens, New York, in 1946, Trump was the fourth of five children. His mother Mary was a Scottish immigrant from the Isle of Lewis, and his father the son of German immigrants (originally named Drumpf) who ran a hotel in British Columbia.

As a boy, Trump was assertive and aggressive. At 13 he went to New York Military Academy in upstate New York, where he stayed until his senior year. After graduating, he considered going to film school in California, but instead enrolled in Fordham University in the Bronx because he preferred to stay close to home. He attended the University of Pennsylvania's Wharton School of Finance (arguably America's best business school for entrepreneurs), graduating in 1968. In 1971 he began working for his father's company, the Trump Organization, before starting out on his own.

In 1977 Trump married Czech model and skier Ivana Zelnickova, who for several years worked as a manager in Trump hotels. It was Ivana who coined the nickname "The Donald." They had three children, Donald Jr., Ivanka, and Eric, but divorced in 1992 after Donald's affair with model Marla Maples, whom he married in 1993; they had a daughter, Tiffany. In 2004, Trump married Slovenian model Melania Knauss. With their son Barron (named after Barron Hilton) they live in Trump Tower in a penthouse valued at over $30 million.

The Forbes *Rich List of 2006 estimated Trump's fortune at $2.9 billion, making him America's 94th richest person.*

2003

The Soul of Money

"In each culture, geographic location, and personal interaction, I have seen the powerful grip that money has on our lives, the wounds and hardship that it can impose on us, and the immense healing power of even the smallest amount of money when we use it to express our humanity—our highest ideals and our most soulful commitments and values."

"Just as blood in the body must flow to all parts of the body for health to be maintained, money is useful when it is moving and flowing, contributed and shared, directed and invested in that which is life affirming."

In a nutshell

Generating, using, and spending money in a way that is consistent with your deepest values has a healing effect not only on you but on the world.

In a similar vein

Charles Fillmore *Prosperity* (p 98)
Joel T. Fleishman *The Foundation* (p 104)
Paul Hawken, Amory B. Lovins, & L. Hunter Lovins *Natural Capitalism* (p 146)
John Randolph Price *The Abundance Book* (p 218)
Sanaya Roman & Duane Packer *Creating Money* (p 242)
Muhammad Yunus *Banker to the Poor* (p 286)

CHAPTER 48

Lynne Twist

In the 1970s, when Lynne Twist's children were young, her husband was a well-paid executive and her family was living the high life. They had a nice house stocked with art and a wine cellar, expensive clothes, a sports car, a nanny, and exotic vacations. Nevertheless, Twist was struck by the contrast between the wealth of her social circle and the poverty of so many others.

Her cosy life broke open after attending some talks by human potential leader Werner Erhard, who had set a 20-year goal for ending world hunger. Twist and her husband decided to reorient their lives toward causes they believed in, and joined the work of the Hunger Project (established in 1977). Later she became involved in other initiatives such as rainforest protection, indigenous rights, and women's leadership.

Over four decades, Twist trained over 20,000 fundraisers in 47 countries and herself raised over $150 million, mostly from individuals. Her work has traversed the Sahel desert in Senegal, villages and slums in India, the Rift valley in Ethiopia, Mayan villages in Guatemala, and the Amazon rainforest in Ecuador, as well as affluent countries such Sweden, France, Japan, Canada, the UK, and the US. Along the way she met the likes of Mother Teresa and the Dalai Lama, and scientist and futurist Buckminster Fuller became a mentor.

This breadth of experience brought Twist a unique perspective on how people see money around the world. Her chief insight in *The Soul of Money* is that money isn't inherently bad or good, but that used wisely it has the power to transform both us and the world.

Money's hold

Twist lived for a time with the Achuar people, who for thousands of years have lived a rich life in the rainforest with no need for actual money. It was only when one of them stayed with her in America that she could see, through his eyes, how much of a money culture we live in. We incessantly worry about not having enough money, we define our value as people according to how much we have, we compete with each other for it, and we are addicted to consumption. Money controls us, rather than us controlling it. It thus affects our relationships, drives wars, and leads to environmental destruction. Twist's meeting with Mother Teresa shocked her, because she was told that part of her life's work should be to sympathize with the wealthy, many of whom suffer isolation, mistrust, damaged relationships, and "hardening of the heart."

The myth of scarcity

The root of our problem with money, Twist suggests, is a fallacious mindset of scarcity, the belief that everything is in limited supply—not just money, but material goods, time, rest, exercise, power, and love. This mindset afflicts both rich and poor, and leads to competition, mistrust, exploitation, envy, and a host of other symptoms, including the idea that ceaseless acquisition is the best way to live.

The tragedy of such thinking is that we can never step off the treadmill to appreciate what we have, and we come to value ourselves and others based on external factors rather than inner qualities. Yet Twist asserts that scarcity is a myth, a product of culture. She writes:

> *Scarcity is a lie. Independent of any actual amount of resources, it is an unexamined and false system of assumptions, opinions, and beliefs from which we view the world as a place where we are in constant danger of having our needs unmet.*

Twist's Hunger Project has been criticized for focusing on education and mindset above actually giving out food. However, she never says that physical aid is unnecessary, only that we should try to understand the nonphysical roots of poverty, a large component of which is the accepted belief in scarcity.

The truth of sufficiency

Twist moves on to the "surprising truth" of sufficiency. It is rarely the actual amount of what you have, but how you use it and appreciate it that makes the difference in your prosperity. She contrasts tribespeople who live in abundance from their natural environment with senior women managers whom she met working at Microsoft Corporation, who despite being millionaires had a sense of constant lack in relation to time for their families.

Whereas the mindset of scarcity drives competition, the mindset of sufficiency fosters collaboration, in which everyone's unique ability to contribute is recognized and valued, and where the outcome is win–win. Twist mentions the success of the Hunger Project in Bangladesh to demonstrate this power of collaboration. A series of workshops helped to steer many people from feeling hopeless to instead formulating a new vision of self-sufficient communities. This vision resulted in building of roads, farms, and fisheries, reduced crime by up to 70 percent in some areas, and in many areas doubled incomes.

Money's flow

Twist views money as a resource that flows like water, circulating around the world and leaving diverse consequences in its wake. Our task is to be conscious of this flow, both in our earning and spending choices. She counsels against accumulating money to too great an extent, as it becomes like a stagnant pool of water. It can no longer flow to good and useful purposes. We are naturally afraid to do this, but she gives the example of Mother Teresa, who reportedly never kept cash reserves, instead trusting that money would always come when needed, which it did.

In this context, fundraising is not simply about coaxing people to donate money, perhaps even against their will, but rather about helping them to "engage in their greatness" through the effective flow of their money. Twist once returned a check for $50,000 that she received from a corporation because she perceived it to be "guilt money," designed to take attention away from the company's moral failings. Real awareness of money's flow rules out blithely handing over money or food to people. At a practical level, this can actually worsen their long-term prospects by making them dependent on such "aid." The better way is to help them raise themselves to a level of self-sufficiency through a partnership based on mutual respect.

Final comments

Having spent decades traveling the world and seeing the best and the worst of money's power, Twist remains optimistic. Her book reinforces the distinction between wealth and money on one hand, and prosperity on the other. Whereas a hungry pursuit of the first can cause terrible damage to our souls, a focus on the second—which involves an appreciation that there is enough for everyone—can enrich us spiritually and emotionally.

There are now quite a few books on the meaning of money in our lives, but what sets *The Soul of Money* apart is Twist's experience of the extremes of wealth and poverty. With many personal stories and a compassionate voice, the book does not claim to be a scholarly work on the role of money. Some may find it too mystical, yet it is an engrossing read that will have you thinking more deeply about your unconscious attitudes, and how you can use money as a healing rather than a destructive power.

Lynne Twist

Twist was born in 1945. Apart from her role with the New York-based Hunger Project (which has Nobel Prize-winning economist Amartya Sen and Queen Noor of Jordan on its board), she has also been a vice chair of the Institute of Noetic Sciences, co-founder of the Pachamama Alliance to empower indigenous people to preserve the Amazon rainforest, and president of the Turning Tide Coalition.

Her Soul of Money Institute was established in 2003, and runs workshops and seminars. Twist is also a contributor to the book The Soul of Business. *She is married with three adult children and lives in San Francisco.*

1904–5

The Protestant Ethic and the Spirit of Capitalism

"He avoids ostentation and unnecessary expenditure, as well as conscious enjoyment of his power, and is embarrassed by the outward signs of the social recognition which he receives... He gets nothing out of his wealth for himself, except the irrational sense of having done his job well."

"Unlimited greed for gain is not in the least identical with capitalism, and is still less its spirit... But capitalism is identical with the pursuit of profit, and forever renewed profit, by means of continuous, rational, capitalistic enterprise."

In a nutshell

The spirit of capitalism is not greed and consumption, but the creation of order and the best use of resources.

In a similar vein

Andrew Carnegie *The Gospel of Wealth* (p 64)
Peter Drucker *Innovation and Entrepreneurship* (p 80)
Marsha Sinetar *Do What You Love, the Money Will Follow* (p 254)
Adam Smith *The Wealth of Nations* (p 260)

CHAPTER 49

Max Weber

Have you ever thought much about the economic system into which you were born? Would you say there was a "spirit" that moves it? Sociologist Max Weber was fascinated by the influence of thoughts and beliefs in history, and particularly why religion seemed to be a significant factor in determining levels of wealth.

Weber noticed that in the Germany of his time, the business leaders and owners of capital, not to mention the majority of higher-skilled workers and managers, were Protestant as opposed to Catholic. Protestants also had higher levels of educational achievement. The conventional explanation was that in the sixteenth and seventeenth centuries, particular towns and regions in Germany had thrown off the rule of the Catholic church, and in the sudden freedom from a repressive regime controlling every aspect of their lives they were able to pursue their economic interests and become prosperous.

In fact, Weber notes, it was the very laxness of the Church in terms of moral and societal rules that turned the bourgeois middle classes against it. These burghers actually *welcomed* the tyranny of Protestant control that would tightly regulate their attitudes and behavior. Weber's question was: Why did the richer classes in Germany, the Netherlands, Geneva, and Scotland, and also the groups that became the American Puritans, want to move in this direction? Surely freedom and prosperity come about when there is less, not more, religious control?

The capitalist spirit

At the outset of *The Protestant Ethic and the Spirit of Capitalism*, Weber admits that discussing the "spirit" of capitalism seems pretentious. Forms of capitalism had, after all, existed in China, India, Babylon, and the classical world, and they had had no special ethos driving them aside from trade and exchange.

It was only with the emergence of modern capitalism, he suggests, that a certain ethic grew linking moral righteousness with making money. It was not just that Protestants sought wealth more purposefully than Catholics, but that Protestants showed "a special tendency to develop economic rationalism"; that is, a particular approach to creating wealth that was less focused on the gain of comfort than on the pursuit of profit itself. The particular satisfaction was not in the money extracted to buy things (which had always driven money making in the past), but in wealth creation based on increased productivity and better use of resources.

Weber had studied non-Christian religions and their relationship to economics. He observed that Hinduism's caste system, for instance, would always be a big obstacle to the development of capitalism because people were not free to be professionally or socially mobile. The Hindu spiritual ethic was to attempt to *transcend* the world, an outlook not dissimilar to Catholicism's creation of monasteries and convents to remove holy people from the sins and temptations of the world outside. The Protestant ethic, in contrast, involved living with your eyes on God but fully in the world. Instead of being told that business was an inferior quest compared to the holy life, one could be holy *through* one's work. This gave believers a tremendous economic advantage.

The Protestant difference

Weber is careful not to say that there was anything intrinsically better about the theology of Protestantism. Rather, the general outlook on life and work that the early Protestant sects—Calvinists, Methodists, Pietists, Baptists, Quakers—drew from their beliefs made them singularly well adapted to modern capitalism. They brought to it:

- A desire for progress.
- A love of hard work for its own sake.
- Orderliness, punctuality, and honesty.
- Hatred of time wasting through socializing, idle talk, sleep, sex, or luxury (expressed in the sentiment "every hour lost is lost to labor for the glory of God").
- Attention to the most productive use of resources, represented by profit.
- Absolute control of self and aversion to spontaneous enjoyment.
- Belief in a calling, or "proving one's faith in worldly activity."

Many Calvinist writers had the same contempt for wealth that the Catholic ascetics did, but when you looked more closely at their writings, Weber noted, their contempt was for the *enjoyment* of wealth and the physical temptations that came with it. Constant activity could drive out such temptations, therefore work could be made holy. If it was where your spiritual energies could be expressed, then work could be your salvation. This combination of "intense piety with business acumen," as Weber describes it, became the cornerstone of many great fortunes.

Final comments

Today we criticize ourselves for being too much of a consumerist society, buying and using instead of saving and creating. Weber is worth reading to be reminded of the true spirit of capitalism: that it is not actually about a mad rush to spend and consume, but the creation of wealth through good use of resources, including our own talents.

There is always a gulf between people who are little concerned with the nature of the work they do as long as it brings in the money and gives them some social standing, and those who feel that their work must be fulfilling their potential. It is this group who continually breathe new life into economies and societies. If you have a "calling" or a sense of duty in the work you do, then your performance naturally gains an extra, powerful dimension. With a calling, Weber tells us, there is no problem at all in reconciling the economic and spiritual aspects of life.

The Protestant Ethic and the Spirit of Capitalism showed how character traits, strongly shaped by religion, could play a massive role in the creation of wealth. Yet these traits do not necessarily depend on a particular religion for their flowering, and can be witnessed the world over where economies have taken off. The Asian economies that have had such a spectacular rise over the last 20 years have only minor Protestant populations, but their industrious, conscientious citizens have much in common with the dutiful and self-denying burghers of seventeenth-century Germany.

Max Weber

Weber was born in 1864 in Erfurt (then Prussia), the oldest of seven children. His father was a liberal politician and bureaucrat whose family was wealthy from linen weaving. His mother was a devout Calvinist.

In 1882 Weber enrolled at the University of Heidelberg to study law, and two years later he transferred to the University of Berlin, where in 1889 he obtained a doctorate with a thesis on Roman agrarian history. His wide-ranging interests in history, economics, and philosophy, plus a willingness to comment on German politics, made him a leading intellectual. In 1896 his father died and he entered a long period of depression. The Protestant Ethic and the Spirit of Capitalism *was one of his first writings to emerge from this time.*

After the First World War, Weber helped draft Germany's new constitution and played a role in the founding of the German Democratic Party. He died in 1920, and in 1926 his wife Marianne Weber, a feminist and sociologist in her own right, published a celebrated biography of her husband.

Weber's other writings include The Theory of Social and Economic Organization, The Religion of China: Confucianism and Taoism, The Three Types of Legitimate Rule, On Charisma and Institution Building, *and* Economy and Society.

1999

Banker to the Poor

"When she receives that $15 loan, she is literally trembling, shaking. The money is burning in her fingers. Tears roll down her eyes because she has never seen so much money in all her life. She never imagined it in her hand. She carries it as she would carry a delicate bird or a rabbit, until someone tells her to put it away in a safe place lest anyone steal it... This is generally the beginning for a Grameen borrower."

"The Grameen loan is not simply cash, it becomes a kind of ticket to self-discovery and self-exploration. The borrower begins to explore her potential, to discover the creativity she has inside her.
I would say that with Grameen's two million borrowers, you get two million thrilling stories of self-discovery."

"We should judge the quality of life in a society not by looking at the way the rich in that society live, but by the way the lowest percentile of the people live their lives."

In a nutshell

If given the opportunity, the poorest will do what it takes to become prosperous.

In a similar vein

Andrew Carnegie *The Gospel of Wealth* (p 64)
Joel T. Fleishman *The Foundation* (p 104)
Anita Roddick *Business as Unusual* (p 238)
Lynne Twist *The Soul of Money* (p 278)

CHAPTER 50

Muhammad Yunus

In 1974, Bangladesh was enduring one of its worst famines. As an economics professor, Muhammad Yunus was in a comfortable position and did not need to pay much attention to what was happening outside the walls of his university. However, when "skeleton-like people started showing up in the railway stations and bus stations of Dhaka" (the capital) he began to wonder about his economic theories. What was their worth when babies could die from a simple lack of food?

He decided to go to the nearby town, Jobra, and learn about poverty first hand. What he discovered amazed him.

A cycle of economic slavery

One of the first women Yunus spoke to, Sufia Begum, was making bamboo stools to sell, but had to continually borrow money from traders at high interest in order to buy her raw materials. She then had to sell the stools back to the trader. Earning a profit of only 2 US cents a day, she was never able to accumulate enough money to buy her own bamboo. So dependent was she on the traders, she had barely enough to feed herself. In *Banker to the Poor* Yunus writes:

> *In my university courses, I dealt in millions and billions of dollars, but here before my eyes, the problems of life and death were posed in terms of pennies. Something was wrong.*

The system ensured that this woman could never save a penny or invest in herself or her little business, yet people like her were poor not because they were lazy or stupid—they worked long hours doing complex tasks. In the absence of any financial institutions to serve the poor, a situation of "financial apartheid" had arisen, with the credit market for the poor being left to money lenders, who charged shocking rates of interest. All these people really lacked was some credit to get in control of their own destinies. Capital, even tiny amounts, could be the difference between self-esteem and desperation, even between life and death.

Yunus realized that if he lent small amounts of money to people such as Sufia at low interest, they could instantly begin to move out of the cycle of poverty. His first loans, to 44 families in Jobra, amounted to $27 in total. These were people no bank would ever consider lending to, since they had no collateral and were mostly illiterate, not able to fill in an application form. Yunus did not consider himself a banker, yet here was a clear need that could be satisfied with tiny resources.

The poor are bankable

Yunus's experiment in Jobra was the beginning of an institution, the Grameen Bank, which by 2007 had lent a combined total of over $6 billion to the world's poorest families, lifting most of them out of poverty for good. The word Grameen means "village," since in the beginning it considered itself a rural or village bank.

In his efforts to establish Grameen, Yunus's biggest obstacles seemed to be attitudes and beliefs about the poor. These included:

- ❖ They need lots of training before they can do anything.
- ❖ They are not able to save.
- ❖ They will just run off with any money they receive.
- ❖ Thanks to their poverty they have lost all ambition.
- ❖ Credit will destroy families, because men won't like their wives being in charge of finances.

Contrary to these prejudices, Yunus's bank follows the principle that "the poor are bankable." Not only is it morally right to lend to them, but you can make a profit doing so.

In the early days, every banker he spoke to dismissed his idea of lending to the very poor because it ran up against banking's holy cow—the need for collateral. Yet to his surprise, Yunus found that the very poor are actually much less risky to lend to than richer people, with loan payback rates of over 98 percent. This, he believes, is because their very lives are at stake. They are desperate to get out of poverty, so a small loan seems like a tremendous blessing and a vote of confidence. Paying the money back is what they must do to become prosperous and respectable people.

Why women?

Grameen's best customers were destitute women. Desperate to improve the lives of their children, they wanted sanitation, three meals a day, and a roof that did not leak. While men tend to have their own spending priorities, any money a woman has will tend to go toward her children or the upkeep of the home.

Husbands and the village mullahs were naturally antagonistic to Grameen lending mainly to women, but most came round to the idea when they saw how it could transform the family's fortunes. Among many other benefits, women who took out loans were much less likely to be beaten by their husbands. Their increased financial clout also led to a reduction in practices such as child marriage and dowry payments.

Yunus frequently makes the point that Grameen loans are more than just money: They are a key to self-growth and fulfillment. He observes of the typical lender:

All her life she has been told she was no good, that, being a woman, she only brought misery to her family, because now they had to pay for a dowry, which they could not afford... But today, for the first time in her life, an institution has trusted her with all this money. She is stunned. She promises herself she will never let down the institution which has trusted her so much. She will struggle to make sure every penny is paid back. And she does it.

A loan can mean dignity, often for the first time in a woman's life. Charity, on the other hand, only keeps people in the position they are in, robbing them of the chance for self-development on their own terms.

Billions of entrepreneurs

Grameen has often had a difficult relationship with the World Bank. Yunus notes that most World Bank money, and the money dispersed by large aid organizations, does not end up with the people who really need it. It tends to be spent on big projects or infrastructure such as roads and bridges. While these may be useful, they do not actually make a poor person wealthier.

While very much in favor of free-market capitalism, Yunus notes its tendency to make already well-off people richer without necessarily lifting up the poor. The "trickle-down" effect is a myth, as there are often two or three economies operating in parallel. In addition, while jobs are always seen by governments and aid agencies as the key to becoming a rich economy, self-employment is actually more sustainable. Instead of trying to increase the gross national product of a whole country, Yunus argues, the focus should be on increasing the real income of the lowest 25 percent of its population. With self-employment the profit and benefits stay in the country, rather going overseas. In addition, these micro-businesses are usually too small to have negative effects on the environment.

As a "private-sector self-help bank," Grameen takes advantage of natural market forces to bring the poorest into the river of prosperity. "All human beings are potential entrepreneurs," Yunus comments, but to have the opportunity to express their talents they often require seed funding. The wealthy do not understand that what are comparatively tiny amounts of money to them can make the difference between poverty and prosperity to others.

Rise of an institution

In 1983, Grameen became a proper, separate banking institution with the help of the Bangladeshi government. Over the years its services have grown to include housing loans and finance for flush toilets and water pumps, health insurance and education loans, and even the establishment of mobile phone networks in villages. Today, over 60 countries have Grameen clones, providing micro-credit to their poorest in addition to the bank's own operations.

Yet perhaps the most fascinating aspect of the bank's rise is its involvement in well-off countries. Bill and Hillary Clinton became interested early on, and assisted Grameen with programs to lend to the poor in the state of Arkansas. The bank has also helped Native Americans and poor city blacks get off welfare and start businesses. Micro-loans in rich countries, Yunus notes, often mean that what are currently "hustles" can be turned into proper businesses.

What has been the secret to the bank's phenomenal growth? Surprisingly, whenever it enters a new community or region, its officers are instructed to take a "go slow" approach, with no more than 100 borrowers in the first year. By starting low-key and small, rather than foisting its ways and ideas onto a community, the bank engenders trust. This is a form of capital that can't be bought.

Final comments

At the world micro-credit summit in Washington, DC in 1997, Yunus told the audience:

> *We believe that poverty does not belong in a civilized human society. It belongs in museums.*

He commented that if it took only 65 years between the first flight of the Wright brothers and humans going into space, it was quite possible to eradicate poverty in our lifetime.

In 20 or 30 years' time, we may be amazed how many people were lifted out of poverty for good, not through aid handouts but via ingenuity and resourcefulness. Real prosperity is not something that can be awarded or donated, but is founded on hard work plus the vital intangibles of confidence, dignity, and a sense of control. These are worth many times the cost of any loan, and by daring to change the way things are done in the banking industry, Grameen has unleashed the wealth-creating power of individuals who may otherwise have been trapped by penury.

Banker to the Poor is an inspirational, colorful read that weaves Yunus's personal life with the story of Grameen bank. It is also a window into the fascinating history of Bangladesh, a country whose name is synonymous in many minds with poverty, yet which in the future might be seen as the cradle of a prosperity revolution.

Muhammad Yunus

Born in 1940, Yunus was the third oldest of nine, and grew up in Chittagong, Bangladesh. His father was a jeweler. At school Yunus was routinely top of his class, and won a scholarship to the prestigious Chittagong Collegiate School.

In 1957 he began studying economics at Dhaka University, and was awarded a Master's degree in 1961. He worked as a teacher at his old college, and in his spare time set up a packaging and printing plant that employed 100 people.

Yunus won a Fulbright Scholarship to America, studying at the University of Colorado, Boulder, then at Vanderbilt University in Tennessee, where he obtained his PhD. While in America he met his first wife, Vera Forostenko, and returned to Bangladesh after the country won its independence in 1971. He took up a position as head of Chittagong University's economics department, and began his work in poverty reduction after the 1974 famine in Bangladesh.

Yunus and the Grameen Bank were jointly awarded the 2006 Nobel Peace Prize. In 2007 he was made a founding member of the Global Elders, a leadership group chaired by Desmond Tutu focusing on world peace and human rights. He is now married to Afrozi Yunus, a physics professor.

Prosperity Principles

Despite the diversity of views, from the literature it is possible to identify a range of "prosperity principles." Organized into the four categories of wealth attraction, creation, management, and sharing, this section aims to provide a useful further concentration of wisdom distilled from the ideas, strategies, and philosophies in *50 Prosperity Classics*.

Principles for attracting wealth

- Paradoxically, wealth (and happiness) comes most easily to those who forget themselves in the service of others. The law of giving infallibly returns more to the giver than they contribute.
- When you focus on other people and circumstances as the source of your prosperity, you tend to lose it. But when you recognize God, a higher power, or the universe as the source of your supply, money begins to flow. Actual money does not make you secure; what does is a thorough knowledge of the universe's power to provide.
- To receive good things you must first cleanse your mind of clutter and negative emotions. In forming a vacuum, you allow good things to rush in. When you are resentful, you are bound to the person or situation you resent. In forgiving, you free yourself and allow the floodgates of prosperity to open.
- The universe is perfectly ordered, therefore the person who makes their own affairs more orderly is attuned to universal riches. To receive more money, you must first demonstrate that you can manage what you already have well, however little it is.
- The basic law of the universe is that things come into being that did not exist before. When you create mental pictures of health, wealth, and happiness, you are not trying to change the laws of nature, but instead fulfilling your unique promise to bring these things into being.
- According to the law of attraction, whatever you put your attention on through thought or desire becomes reality. You attract to yourself things or people that are the equivalent of your current state of being, or "vibration."
- The "creative process" is the specific way in which you can use the law of attraction to obtain what you want. It involves: Asking the universe, and being very clear about what you want; Believing, acting, and speaking as though you have already received what you have asked for; and Receiving—feeling great that it is coming to you, which sets up the necessary vibration to manifest the desire. This process is summed up in the Bible: "All things whatsoever ye pray and ask for, believe that ye have received them and ye shall have them."

- Deciding to elevate your mood or feeling in each moment is vital for increasing your vibration, which in turn attracts things, people, and feelings of a like vibration. To be both rich and happy, you must make a positive mental attitude a basic habit of living.
- If you are low on funds, praise and bless whatever you have, and imagine it growing larger. Blessing both what you have and what others have puts the law of increase into motion.
- Gratitude is the key to an abundant life, because it puts you in a state of mind that attracts even more of what you are grateful for. Love, appreciation, and thanks are the essence of prosperity. It is right to become a giver, but you must also learn to be a good receiver.

Principles for creating wealth

- The foundation of a prosperous life (combining material wealth, health, and mental wellbeing) is personal character, formed from self-control and cultivation of virtue. A person of integrity, trust, and good character is "bankable"; their riches evolve out of who they are as much as what they do.
- Definiteness of purpose is essential to the success of the wealth creator. A clear purpose enables you to see setbacks as temporary, banishes fear and doubt, and inspires the help of others.
- Do more than is asked or expected of you, "go the extra mile." Putting in an extraordinary effort with no guarantee of gain is the basis of most great fortunes.
- Whatever you do, provide, or create, make sure you do it in an outstanding way. Remember the Latin dictum *In excellentia lucrum*—in excellence is profit.
- The fear of failure or embarrassment is the greatest obstacle to achieving wealth. Fear puts a brake on action, yet if you are not willing to fail you will forever be bound in circumstances that involve little risk. With little risk there are only small rewards.
- Learn, don't blame. It is easy to blame people or events when things are not going smoothly, but the enlightened wealth creator seeks only to learn in every situation. Don't complain, look for opportunities.
- Thinking big is the basis of all great enterprises and fortunes. You are constantly thinking, therefore it takes no more effort to think big instead of small.
- Wealth flows to the person who has a high tolerance for uncertainty or disappointment. Handle disappointment well, and you will make more attempts to achieve your goals. By the law of averages, where others have given up you will succeed.
- Wealth-minded people do not try to avoid risk or complexity. They even embrace large problems because they know that solving them can produce significant value.

- It is not enough to want to be rich, you must *commit* to it. Providence moves all for the person who determines to stick it out, doing what they can to make a venture work. The half-hearted achieve half-success.
- Choose your vocation wisely. Love of your work sets up a "circle of excellence" that cannot fail to deliver great gains over time. But along with love and talent, you must work hard.
- If you think you see the future, act on it. Hunches based on in-depth knowledge are usually right. If something captures your imagination, chances are it will capture that of others too.
- Everything that you see around you, someone has made a fortune from. All you need is one idea that can make you your fortune, and it is probably to be found in your own backyard.
- Don't be afraid to be different. On entering any new field or an industry, aim to really shake it up and provide new value.
- The surest way to wealth is to create a product or service that increases the ease and speed of results.
- Above all, it is customers that create wealth. Have customers before you even start your business.
- The seed of entrepreneurship is a wish to be in control of your own destiny.
- The purpose of entrepreneurship is to deliver new satisfaction and value. It is built on unexpected successes that are quickly capitalized on.
- Riches follow ownership. Own something, or at least a part of something.
- Have many sources of income. Do not depend on a single wage for your financial security.
- Wealthy people create money-producing systems. Middle-class people work within and for these systems, and so never get rich.
- All wealth is created first in the mind. Therefore, a political-economic system that fosters and protects the freedom to think, innovate, create, and prosper, with free and open markets in which to trade the product, is a moral system.

Principles for managing wealth

- Live within your means. If you are not wealthy, do not have a wealthy lifestyle. You will get rich by imitating the mindset of the wealthy, not by imitating their spending.
- Poor people are focused on spending money; the wealthy are focused on creating it, saving it, and investing it.
- Most people see money as cash in their hands to be used and spent. Wealthy people understand money primarily as seeds to be planted that will grow into money trees.
- Plan your spending. Never shop on impulse. The longer you plan a purchase for, generally the more money you will save.
- Document your spending. It is the first step to getting control of your finances.

- Become a habitual saver. Pay yourself the first 10 percent of what you earn, before tax, and invest it. The discipline of saving (given a certain amount of time) can make you rich. Do not risk your peace of mind or relationships by chasing a quick dollar.
- Use the magic of compound interest by reinvesting all interest or dividends you earn.
- Savings allow you to pick up bargains and take advantage of opportunities.
- Earning more will not solve your debt problem (debts increase to match earnings). Learning how to manage money responsibly will.
- The frugal enjoy what they have more, get more use out of what they own, and delight in the ability to make gifts when they wish.
- Have an emergency fund that covers your living expenses for three to six months. If something happens and you need money, you will not have to go into debt or depend on the charity of others.
- Resist invitations to own a credit card. Debit cards now perform all the functions that credit cards were once useful for, and will not lead you into a debt spiral.
- Pay for most things with cash. You will spend less.
- When you do borrow money, make sure it is for a productive asset or one that is likely to appreciate, and pay off the loan as soon as you can.
- Don't be someone who "knows the price of everything and the value of nothing." In stock investing, consider yourself part owner of a company you are investing in, not a trader.
- Don't try to beat the market or speculate. Trust the long-term ability of stock markets to deliver good returns overall.
- With the power of leverage and modest price appreciation, plus a normal degree of patience, in two or three decades you can build a real-estate fortune.
- Too little or too much money magnifies personal deficiencies, or reveals the good character that was already there. Therefore, in relation to your financial life, work you do on your personal qualities is never wasted.

Principles for sharing wealth

- Money is a kind of energy and it is always active. To bring the greatest benefit to the greatest number, it must flow and circulate.
- Generating, using, and spending money in a way that is consistent with your deepest values has a healing effect not only on yourself but on the world.
- You never really possess wealth, but are a steward of it until you die. When a fortune is made, the creator has a duty to apply at least some of it to causes and projects that will assist and elevate others.

- With clear goals and a focus on results, private wealth in the form of foundations can change the world.
- Prosperity's basis is a healthy natural environment. Without clean air, water, and a fertile earth humanity has nothing. Invest, spend, or make money in a way that causes no harm and is good for the planet.
- If given access to finance, the world's poorest people will strive for, and achieve, self-reliance and prosperity.

50 More Classics

1 **William Bernstein** ***The Four Pillars of Investing*** **(2002)**
Acclaimed as the best modern guide to stock investing. Pillars include knowing something about market history, and appreciating that investing is about psychology.

2 **Victor Boc** ***How To Solve All Your Money Problems Forever*** **(1997)**
Mail-order volume in the tradition of Joe Karbo that nevertheless provides a powerful wealth recipe based on affirmations and "glad giving."

3 **Eric Butterworth** ***Spiritual Economics*** **(1998)**
Clear explanation of New Thought prosperity principles, used in many church reading groups.

4 **Ron Chernow** ***Titan: The Life of John D. Rockefeller Snr*** **(2004)**
Unsurpassed biography of the man who amassed more wealth than any American prior to Bill Gates, and how he gave it away.

5 **David Chilton** ***The Wealthy Barber*** **(1998)**
Popular fable explaining the basics of personal finance. Asserts that readers can become well-off even on a normal wage. Similar ideas to Bach's *The Automatic Millionaire*.

6 **Deepak Chopra** ***Creating Affluence*** **(1998)**
A–Z guide to manifesting wealth through awareness of quantum physics and spiritual principles.

7 **Yvon Chouinard** ***Let My People Go Surfing*** **(2006)**
The founder of the Patagonia outdoor products company shows how being green and good to your workers can be pillars in building a great company.

8 **Paul Collier** ***The Bottom Billion*** **(2007)**
The world has never been richer, so why are there still a billion desperately poor people? An Oxford professor's look at why civil war, dependence on natural resources, and corruption continue to hold back prosperity in the poorest countries—and what to do about it.

9 **Robert Collier** ***Riches Within Your Reach*** **(1947)**
Originally titled *The Law of the Higher Potential*, former advertising man's application of metaphysical ideas to the process of wealth creation.

10 **Christine Comaford-Lynch** ***Rules for Renegades*** **(2007)**
Entrepreneur, software engineer, and former Buddhist monk provides powerful tips for business and life success revolving around confidence in yourself to make a difference.

11 **Nicholas Darvas** ***How I Made $2,000,000 in the Stock Market*** **(1960)**
Amusing and still popular account of the development of a successful stock-picking system, written while the author traveled the world in a ballroom dancing troupe.

12 **Lee Eisenberg** ***The Number: A Completely Different Way to Think About the Rest of Your Life*** **(2006)**
Addresses the question of working out how much you need to have a comfortable retirement. Lacks practical advice, more a philosophical journey about your goals and priorities.

13 **Tim Ferris** ***The 4-Hour Workweek*** **(2007)**
Manifesto for getting out of the 9–5 trap, creating self-managing businesses that allow you to travel and work from anywhere. Has attracted plenty of criticism, but provides many practical tips.

14 **Marc Fisher** ***The Instant Millionaire*** **(1993)**
Enjoyable, powerful fable on the power of goals and self-belief in realizing abundance.

15 **Philip A. Fisher** ***Common Stocks and Uncommon Profits*** **(1996)**
A strong influence on Warren Buffett, Fisher shows why it is better to pay more for a great, growing company than seek to find undervalued companies that may never be great.

16 **Edwene Gaines** ***The Four Spiritual Laws of Prosperity*** **(2005)**
In the spirit of Catherine Ponder and Charles Fillmore, Gaines points to tithing, setting goals, forgiveness, and finding your life purpose as the ways to prosperity.

17 **Shakti Gawain** ***Creating True Prosperity*** **(1997)**
The author of *Creative Visualization* dissects the connection between money and happiness, urging readers to identify their deepest longings rather than simply trying to earn more.

18 **Charles J. Givens** ***More Wealth Without Risk*** **(1995)**
The "Dale Carnegie of investing" died in 1997 but his work is still popular. Readers who followed his contrarian approach would have emerged unscathed from the crash of 2000.

19 **Joel Greenblatt** ***The Little Book that Beats the Market*** **(2005)**
Successful hedge fund manager and professor's "magic formula" for investing based on the view that stocks are worth only what they consistently return to the investor.

20 **Rita Gunther McGrath & Ian McMillan** ***The Entrepreneurial Mindset*** **(2000)**
Best book on creating new value in companies by focusing on the customer, in the style of Peter Drucker.

21 **Charles F. Haanel** ***The Master Key System*** **(1917)**
Businessman's metaphysical foray into the relationship between thoughts and reality. Rumor has it that the book inspired Bill Gates to leave Harvard to start Microsoft.

22 **Friedrich von Hayek *The Road to Serfdom* (1944)**
Written while the Second World War was still raging, far-sighted analysis of the evils of central planning and totalitarianism. A big influence on promoters of political liberty and free markets, including Milton Friedman.

23 **James Hughes *Family Wealth* (2004)**
Self-published title that became a bestseller thanks to insightful advice to families who have made money and want to avoid the syndrome of "shirtsleeves to shirtsleeves in three generations."

24 **George Kinder *Seven Stages of Money Maturity* (2000)**
Profound but practical insights into the psychology of money by a top financial planner. Has helped many reconsider their financial attitudes and become prosperous.

25 **Ray Kroc *Grinding It Out: The Making of McDonald's* (1977)**
Entrepreneurial classic telling how a 52-year-old milkshake salesman created one of the iconic companies of our times.

26 **Edwin Lefevre *Reminiscences of a Stock Operator* (1935)**
Fictionalized biography of Jesse Livermore, one of the greatest stock-market traders, focusing on crowd psychology and timing.

27 **Rieva Lesonsky *Start Your Own Business* (2007)**
Now in its fourth edition, bestselling start-up title covering 800 pages, from the editor of *Entrepreneur* magazine.

28 **Michael Losier *Law of Attraction* (2003)**
Outlines principles found in *Ask and It Is Given* and *The Secret*, but goes into detail on the mechanics of manifesting desires.

29 **Burton G. Malkiel *A Random Walk Down Wall Street: A Time-Tested Strategy for Successful Investing* (2007, 9th edn)**
Princeton economics professor's million-selling title on where to invest, read by novices and professionals alike.

30 **Kevin Maney *The Maverick and his Machine: Thomas Watson Snr and the Making of IBM* (2004)**
Riveting biography of Watson and his creation of the first real information-age corporation.

31 **David McClelland *The Achieving Society* (1961)**
Harvard psychologist's intriguing insights into the "achievement motive" that drives entrepreneurs.

32 **Joseph Murphy *Your Infinite Power to Be Rich* (1966)**
The author of *The Power of Your Subconscious Mind* turns his mind to prosperity. Many great insights.

33 **John Nathan *Sony: The Private Life* (2001)**
Fascinating account of the founders of the Sony Corporation, who saw only opportunity amid the ashes of Japan's Second World War defeat, and their ethos of being different to succeed.

34 **Jacob Needleman** ***Money and the Meaning of Life*** **(1991)**
Philosopher's learned exploration of the idea that money is not just a means of exchange but that its pursuit allows for the fulfillment of human potential.

35 **Maria Nemeth** ***The Energy of Money*** **(2000)**
Psychologist's exploration of our deep beliefs and habits about financial matters, and how seeing money as a form of energy can set us free.

36 **Michael Phillips** ***The Seven Laws of Money*** **(1974)**
A "hippie capitalist" shows how money flows to those who "do the right thing" and respect its objective rules and laws.

37 **Daniel Pink** ***Free Agent Nation*** **(2002)**
Explores the rise of millions of "free agents" who wish to take control of their work destiny and become prosperous without a corporate crutch.

38 **C. K. Prahalad** ***The Fortune at the Bottom of the Pyramid: Eradicating Poverty through Profits*** **(2004)**
Using practical free-market techniques, not government, to raise living standards worldwide.

39 **Joseph Schumpeter** ***Capitalism, Socialism and Democracy*** **(1942)**
Introduced the concept of "creative destruction," in which innovation shakes up established economies. The entrepreneur is the driving force in this process.

40 **Steven S. Scott** ***The Richest Man Who Ever Lived*** **(2006)**
Drawn from the example of King Solomon's life and the wisdom contained in the book of *Proverbs*, provides a storehouse of guidance for achieving wealth and happiness.

41 **George Soros** ***Soros on Soros: Staying Ahead of the Curve*** **(1995)**
Philosophy and trading strategies from one of the great investors of our time.

42 **John P. Speller** ***Seed Money in Action: Working the Law of Tenfold Return*** **(1964)**
Presents the idea that any money given away always comes back to the giver tenfold, and that giving is itself is a reliable path to wealth.

43 **Barbara Stanny** ***Secrets of Six-Figure Women*** **(2004)**
Based on interviews with 150 women who earn over $100,000 per year; inspiring tips for how to break out of the pattern of "underearning."

44 **Richard Templar** ***The Rules of Wealth*** **(2006)**
British businessman's 100 rules for prosperity. Not a recipe for overnight riches, it instead advocates hard work, self-knowledge, and copying the mindset of the wealthy.

45 **Andrew Tobias** ***The Only Investing Guide You'll Ever Need*** **(2005, updated edn)**
A perennial that provides solid advice on all aspects of personal finance and investing.

46 **Elizabeth Towne** ***How to Grow Success*** **(1904)**
Money is not success, but success includes the ability to command money.

47 **Joe Vitale *The Attractor Factor* (2005)**
Marketing guru's popular interpretation of the law of attraction, combining metaphysics with many practical tips.

48 **William Walker *Thought Vibration, or The Law of Attraction in the Thought World* (1906)**
New Thought classic comparing the law of attraction to the law of gravity. Influenced later prosperity writers.

49 **Stuart Wilde *The Trick to Money Is Having Some* (1995)**
In a lighthearted style, Wilde provides many spiritual and practical tips for bringing more money into your life, such as being thankful for even the smallest amounts you receive or find.

50 **Bruce Wilkinson *The Prayer of Jabez* (2000)**
American pastor's mega-selling revelation of an obscure passage from the Bible. If uttered daily, the "Jabez prayer" promises prosperity, "enlarged territories," and divine protection.

Credits

The editions below were those used in researching the book. Original publication dates are stated in each of the 50 commentaries.

Works freely available on the internet are preceded by an asterisk. Before downloading or using them you should check if they are legally in the public domain in the country where you live.

*Allen, J. (1905) *The Path of Prosperity*, SpiritSite.com, www.spiritsite.com/writing/jamall/index.shtml.

Allen, R. G. (2005) *Multiple Streams of Income: How to Generate a Lifetime of Unlimited Wealth*, Hoboken, NJ: John Wiley.

Bach, D. (2005) *The Automatic Millionaire: A Powerful One-Step Plan to Live and Finish Rich*, London: Penguin.

*Barnum, P. T. (1880) *The Art of Money Getting or Golden Rules for Making Money*, Project Gutenberg, www.gutenberg.org/etext/8581.

*Behrend, G. (1921) *Your Invisible Power: A Presentation of the Mental Science of Judge Thomas Troward*, New Thought Library, http://newthoughtlibrary.com/behrendGenevieve/yip_01.htm.

Bogle, J. C. (2007) *The Little Book of Common Sense Investing: The Only Way to Guarantee Your Fair Share of Stock Market Returns*, Hoboken, NJ: John Wiley.

Branson, R. (2005) *Losing My Virginity: The Autobiography*, London: Virgin Books.

Byrne, R. (2006) *The Secret*, New York: Atria Books.

Carnegie, A. (2006) *The "Gospel of Wealth" Essays and Other Writings*, ed. and intr. David Nasaw, New York: Penguin.

Cunningham, L. (ed.) (2002) *The Essays of Warren Buffett: Lessons for Investors and Managers*, revd edn, Singapore: John Wiley.

Dennis, F. (2006) *How to Get Rich*, London: Random House.

Dominguez, J. & Robin, V. (1992) *Your Money or Your Life: Transforming Your Relationship with Money and Achieving Financial Independence*, New York: Penguin.

Drucker, P. F. (1985) *Innovation and Entrepreneurship: Practice and Principles*, New York: Harper & Row.

Eker, T. H. (2005) *Secrets of the Millionaire Mind: Mastering the Inner Game of Wealth*, London: Piatkus.

*Fillmore, C. (1936) *Prosperity*, Unity on the Web, http://websyte.com/unity/pro.htm.

Fleishman, J. T. (2007) *The Foundation: A Great American Secret—How Private Wealth Is Changing the World*, New York: PublicAffairs.

Friedman, M. (1962) *Capitalism and Freedom*, Chicago: University of Chicago Press.

Friedman, T. (2006) *The World Is Flat: A Brief History of the Twenty-First Century*, London: Penguin.

Gerber, M. E. (1995) *The E-Myth Revisited: Why Most Small Businesses Don't Work and What to Do About It*, New York: HarperBusiness.

Graham, B. (1965) *The Intelligent Investor: A Book of Practical Counsel*, 3rd edn, New York: Harper & Row.

Hansen, M. V. & Allen, R. G. (2002) *The One Minute Millionaire: The Enlightened Way to Wealth*, London: Vermilion.

Hawken, P., Lovins, A., & Lovins, L. H. (1999) *Natural Capitalism: Creating the Next Industrial Revolution*, London: Earthscan.

Hicks, E. & Hicks, J. (2004) *Ask and It Is Given: Learning to Manifest Your Desires*, London & Carlsbad, CA: Hay House.

Hill, N. (1965) *The Master-Key to Riches*, New York: Fawcett Crest.

Hilton, C. (1957) *Be My Guest*, New York: Fireside.

Karbo, J. (1973) *The Lazy Man's Way to Riches*, Chippenham: Success Classics Library.

Kawasaki, G. (2004) *The Art of the Start: The Time-Tested, Battle-Hardened Guide for Anyone Starting Anything*, London: Portfolio.

Kiyosaki, R. T. with Lechter, S. L. (1998) *Cashflow Quadrant: Rich Dad's Guide to Financial Freedom*, New York: Warner.

Lynch, P. with Rothchild, J. (1989) *One Up on Wall Street: How to Use What You Already Know to Make Money in the Market*, Harmondsworth: Penguin.

McLean, Andrew J. & Eldred, Gary W. (2005) *Investing in Real Estate* (5th edn), Hoboken, NJ: John Wiley.

Mundis, J. (1990) *How to Get Out of Debt, Stay Out of Debt and Live Prosperously (Based on the Proven Principles and Techniques of Debtors Anonymous)*, New York: Bantam.

Nickerson, W. (1969) *How I Turned $1,000 into Three Million in Real Estate—in My Spare Time*, New York: Simon & Schuster.

O'Clery, C. (2007) *The Billionaire Who Wasn't: How Chuck Feeney Made and Gave Away a Fortune Without Anyone Knowing*, New York: Public Affairs.

Orman, S. (2007) *Women and Money: Owning the Power to Control Your Destiny*, New York: Spiegel & Grau.

Pilzer, P. Z. (1995) *God Wants You to Be Rich: The Theology of Economics*, New York: Simon & Schuster.

Ponder, C. (1971) *Open Your Mind to Prosperity*, Marina del Ray, CA: De Vorss.

Price, J. R. (1996) *The Abundance Book*, London: Hay House.

Ramsey, D. (2003) *Financial Peace Revisited*, New York: Putnam.

Rand, A. (1967) *Capitalism: The Unknown Ideal*, New York: Signet.

Roddick, A. (2005) *Business as Unusual: My Entrepreneurial Journey, Profits with Principles*, Chichester: Anita Roddick Books.

Roman, S. & Packer, D. (1988) *Creating Money: Keys to Abundance*, Tiburon, CA: H. J. Kramer.

Schultz, H. with Yang, D. J. (1997) *Pour Your Heart into It: How Starbucks Built a Company One Cup at a Time*, New York: Hyperion.

Sinetar, M. (1987) *Do What You Love, the Money Will Follow: Discovering Your Right Livelihood*, New York: Dell.

*Smith, A. (1910) *An Inquiry Into the Nature and Causes of the Wealth of Nations, Vol. I*, London: J. M. Dent.

Stanley, T. J. & Danko, W. D. (1996) *The Millionaire Next Door: The Surprising Secrets of America's Wealthy*, New York: Pocket Books.

Trump, D. with Schwartz, T. (1987) *The Art of the Deal*, New York: Ballantine.

Twist, L. & Barker, T. (2003) *The Soul of Money: Reclaiming the Wealth of Our Inner Resources*, New York: W. W. Norton.

Wallace, J. & Erickson, J. (1992) *Hard Drive: Bill Gates and the Making of the Microsoft Empire*, New York: HarperBusiness.

*Weber, M. (1930) *The Protestant Ethic and the Spirit of Capitalism*, trans. T. Parsons, intr. A. Giddens, London: Routledge.

Yunus, M. with Jolis, A. (1999) *Banker to the Poor: The Autobiography of Muhammad Yunus, Founder of the Grameen Bank*, London: Aurum Press.

Acknowledgments

This book was largely written in Oxford University's Bodleian Library, a beautiful place that surrounds the reader with the collected thought and writings of thousands of scholars going back centuries. Thomas Bodley funded the library with the stipulation that it be open to all. In the same vein, I hope that the secrets of prosperity, often locked away in books, are brought into the light of everyday life for more people.

Thanks to everyone at Nicholas Brealey Publishing: Nick Brealey, who as usual helped to refine the concept; Sally Lansdell, who edited the manuscript and provided valued suggestions; Angie Tainsh for your marketing efforts in the UK; Trish O'Hare and Chuck Dresner for your hard work at promoting the 50 Classics series in North America; and Ken Leeder for another great cover.

Many thanks to Irfan Alvi, without whose valuable editorial assistance it would have been difficult to get the book written on schedule. Thank you also Irfan for your many great suggestions that have made this a better book.

Thanks to the living authors of works covered, with particular gratitude to Catherine Ponder, whose five decades as a prosperity teacher laid the foundation for many later writers; and to two great theorists of wealth creation who died recently: Milton Friedman, whose ideas about the freedom to create and produce will inspire generations to come; and Peter Drucker, who made the fields of innovation and entrepreneurship into a science that could be studied by anyone.

And to my late father Anthony, whose discipline as a saver and investor and strong belief in economic freedom exemplified many of the principles in these pages.

50 Spiritual Classics

Timeless Wisdom from 50 Key Books of Inner Discovery, Enlightenment and Purpose

"What an uplifting journey I had reading *50 Spiritual Classics*! If you only ever read one spiritual book, let it be this one. The insightful and inspirational commentaries cover an amazing range of ideas and writings. I predict that *50 Spiritual Classics* will become a classic in itself."
Susan Jeffers PhD, author of Feel the Fear and Do It Anyway, Embracing Uncertainty *and* Life Is Huge!

"*50 Spiritual Classics* is a kaleidoscope of inspiration that lets the reader delve into the ideas of many of our great spiritual thinkers."
The Watkins Review

50 Spiritual Classics captures the diversity of life journeys that span centuries, continents, spiritual traditions and secular beliefs: from the historical *The Book of Chuang Tzu* to modern insight from the Kabbalah, from Kahlil Gibran's *The Prophet* to Eckhart Tolle's *The Power of Now*, from Don Miguel Ruiz's *The Four Agreements* to Rick Warren's phenomenon *The Purpose-Driven Life*.

The first and only bite-sized guide to the very best in spiritual writing, this one-of-a-kind collection includes personal memoirs and compelling biographies of such diverse figures as Gandhi, Malcolm X and Black Elk; Eastern philosophers and gurus including Krishnamurti, Yogananda, Chögyam Trungpa and Shunryu Suzuki; and Western saints and mystics such as St Francis of Assisi, Hermann Hesse and Simone Weil.

50 Spiritual Classics makes universal the human spiritual experience and will inspire spiritual seekers everywhere to begin their own adventure.

50 Success Classics

Winning Wisdom for Work and Life from 50 Landmark Books

"A highly readable collection! *50 Success Classics* presents a smorgasbord of some of the best thinking on what success really means."
Ken Blanchard, co-author of The One Minute Manager®

"I can't imagine anyone needing any other success book after reading 50 Success Classics. It has every piece of wisdom you'll ever need to make your life extraordinary."
Cheryl Richardson, author of Take Time for Your Life

"This incredible book gives you the very best of success literature ever written—in one easy book that you can read and reread for years. I hope it sells a million!"
Brian Tracy, author of Million Dollar Habits

Pursuing a new direction? Seeking a path to authentic achievement? Inside *50 Success Classics*, discover the all-time classic books that have helped millions of people achieve success in their work and personal lives.

Practical yet philosophical, sensible yet stimulating, the 50 all-time classics span biography and business, psychology and ancient philosophy, exploring the rich and fertile ground of books that will capture your imagination and inspire you to chart a course to personal and professional fulfilment.

Mapping the road to prosperity, motivation, leadership and life success, *50 Success Classics* summarizes each work's key ideas to make clear how these timeless insights can inform, inspire and illuminate. Find out how to *Think and Grow Rich*, acquire *The 7 Habits of Highly Effective People*, become *The One-Minute Manager*, solve the challenging puzzle of *Who Moved My Cheese?* and discover *The Art of Worldly Wisdom*.

50 Self-Help Classics

50 Inspirational Books to Transform Your Life

From Timeless Sages to Contemporary Gurus

"A tremendous resource for anyone seeking a 'bite-sized' look at the philosophies of many self-help legends, including sacred scriptures of different traditions. Because the range and depth of the sources are so huge, the cumulative reading effect is amazing. Alternatively, it educates and edifies, affirms and inspires. Often both."

Stephen R. Covey, author of The 7 Habits of Highly Effective People

"This is an exceptional and diverse collection for anyone interested in understanding the possibilities of the self."

Ellen Langer, Professor of Psychology, Harvard University

"Butler-Bowdon has summarized some of the most remarkable thoughts—thoughts with wisdom, I might add—that will enlighten and lead the reader to understand the very nature of human nature. It will soon become the 51st classic!"

Warren Bennis, author of On Becoming a Leader

Thousands of books have been written offering the 'secrets' to personal potential, fulfilment and happiness. But which are the all-time classics? Which can really change your life?

Tom Butler-Bowdon has cut through a vast field of writing to bring you the essential ideas, insights and techniques from the 'literature of possibility'. From 50 legendary works that span the world's religions, cultures, philosophies and centuries, he summarizes each classic's key ideas and assesses its merits for the time-strapped reader.

A unique guide that acknowledges everyone's yearning for a more meaningful and successful life, yet appreciates that each of us is inspired by different philosophies and ideas.

£12.99 UK/$19.95 US PB Original 312pp ISBN 978-1-85788-323-7

www.nicholasbrealey.com